Scenes and Monologues from Steinberg/ATCA New Play Award Finalists, 2008–2012

Scenes and Monologues from Steinberg/ATCA New Play Award Finalists, 2008–2012

Edited by
Bruce Burgun

Assisted by
Mark Kamie

Introduction by
**Jay Handelman, Bill Hirschman,
and Jeffrey Eric Jenkins**

APPLAUSE THEATRE & CINEMA BOOKS
An Imprint of Hal Leonard Corporation

Published in 2013 by Applause Theatre & Cinema Books
An Imprint of Hal Leonard Corporation
7777 West Bluemound Road
Milwaukee, WI 53213

Trade Book Division Editorial Offices
33 Plymouth St., Montclair, NJ 07042

Printed in the United States of America

Book design by UB Communications

Library of Congress Cataloging-in-Publication Data

Scenes and monologues from Steinberg/ATCA new play award finalists, 2008-2012 / edited by Bruce Burgun ; introduction by Jay Handelman, Bill Hirschman, and Jeffrey Eric Jenkins.
       pages cm
    Includes bibliographical references and index.
1. Acting. 2. Monologues. 3. American drama—21st century. I. Burgun, Bruce, editor of compilation.
    PN2080.S2395 2013
    792.02'8—dc23
                            2013013328

ISBN 978-1-4768-6878-3

www.applausebooks.com

*This collection is dedicated to all the
talented playwrights bravely working to
give the American theater community
more to see, feel, realize, and understand.
Thanks, thanks, and ever thanks.*

Contents

Introduction

The American Theatre Critics Association

The American Theatre Critics Association, Inc., is proud to be involved in the publication of this collection of scenes and monologues drawn from scripts recognized as among each year's best in the annual Harold and Mimi Steinberg/American Theatre Critics Association New Play Award and Citations.

The association, commonly known as ATCA, is the only national organization of professional theater critics, and our members work for newspapers, magazines, radio and television stations, and online outlets across the United States. Since its founding in 1974 by a group of leading theater critics who had been gathering at the O'Neill Theater Center in Waterford, Connecticut, the association has worked to foster greater communication among theater critics in the United States and abroad, to improve the training and development of critics at different stages of their careers, to advocate absolute freedom of expression in theater and theater criticism, and to increase public awareness of the theater as an important national resource.

Three years after its founding, the new play prizes now known as the Steinberg/ATCA Awards were established. Since 2000, they have been funded by the Harold and Mimi Steinberg Charitable Trust.

From its early years, ATCA has organized semiannual conferences in different cities or theater centers around the country and the globe to give its members greater opportunities to explore the remarkable artistic resources that abound outside their own home cities. The association sponsors training seminars for young critics, administers other playwriting awards, creates programs that encourage enthusiastic debate about important issues to the theater and the media business, and invites prominent critics to speak in our annual Perspectives in Criticism program. ATCA also continues to support the National Critics Institute at the O'Neill Theater Center, where young and experienced critics have a chance to further their own craft and broaden their experiences.

We hope that this volume provides plenty of inspiration for your own love and appreciation of the theater.

—Jay Handelman
Chair, American Theatre Critics Association
Sarasota, Florida
September 2012

For more information: www.americantheatrecritics.org

The Harold and Mimi Steinberg/ATCA New Play Award

The Harold and Mimi Steinberg/ATCA New Play Award obliterates the notion that theater is a moribund elitist medium abandoned by anyone under retirement age.

The procession of vibrant and groundbreaking new works that ATCA has culled from regional productions every year since 1977 is proof that theater prevails over the economy, a splintered society, and countless media options; the scripts are indicative of a growing, evolving, and relevant art form.

They confirm that America's regional theaters have persevered as this country's preeminent crucible for new works despite vanishing government support and faltering donations. The recommended plays encompass a dizzying range of styles and themes, produced by experienced and novice playwrights who are inarguable evidence that theater remains vital and relevant.

The prize recognizes excellence in playwriting, not production. While nascent scripts are refined in the rehearsal room with directors, actors, and designers, the quality has to be evident on the page of the final production script.

This has evolved into the largest competition recognizing work specifically developed in regional theaters because of the generosity of the Steinberg Charitable Trust, which has funded these prizes since 2000. The top award recipient receives $25,000 and the two citation recipients receive $7,500 each.

Honorees have included Lanford Wilson, Marsha Norman, August Wilson, Jane Martin, Arthur Miller, Mac Wellman, Adrienne Kennedy, Donald Margulies, Lynn Nottage, Horton Foote, Craig Lucas, and Bill Cain. Each year's recipients are chronicled in *The Best Plays Theater Yearbook* alongside the ten best plays produced that year in New York City. The complete list can be found at www.americantheatrecritics.org.

In concert with our M. Elizabeth Osborn Award and Francesca Primus Prize, the program is the American Theatre Critics Association's commitment to helping playwriting flourish into the twenty-first century by providing reaffirming encouragement, often occurring at difficult times in a writer's career.

An eligible work must be recommended by an ATCA member. It must receive its first full professional production in a regional theater during the calendar year. It can be remounted elsewhere, but it cannot have a production within the five boroughs of New York City during that year. A committee of ten to fourteen ATCA members read as many as thirty scripts. In recent years, the honorees have been announced at the Humana Festival of New American Plays at Actors' Theatre of Louisville. Many selections have gone on to New York productions and subsequently received other recognitions, including the Pulitzer Prize. More importantly, many of them have received numerous regional theater productions.

For theater artists seeking scenes to work on, these plays reflect the ongoing sea changes in playwriting that challenge actors and directors—an increasing reliance on shorthand in storytelling for savvier and younger audiences, stylistic and elliptical approaches, cinematically visual tableaux, the incorporation of digital technology to re-create seemingly impossible visions. Pundits variously quip that there are only seven or eight or twelve themes in art. But these scripts show not simply new milieus for those themes, but increasingly sophisticated social and psychological approaches that performers need to master.

We hope that this volume will help in that never-ending development of the thespian's craft.

—Bill Hirschman
Chairman, ATCA New Plays Committee

BILL HIRSCHMAN *is an award-winning newspaper theater critic and arts reporter who is currently founder of the professional arts journalism website Florida Theater On Stage (www.floridatheateronstage.com). His work has appeared in* Variety, American Theatre *magazine,* Playbill.com, A&E *magazine, the* South Florida Sun-Sentinel, *and the* Miami Herald, *among other outlets.*

In the Beginning: The Harold and Mimi Steinberg Charitable Trust[1]

It was in early 1993 that the Harold and Mimi Steinberg Charitable Trust first made a powerful impact on the nature of new-play production in the United States. But few—except, perhaps, the trustees themselves—could have imagined how the focus of the Trust might reshape the artistic landscape

---

1. Portions of this introduction first appeared in Jeffrey Eric Jenkins, "Funding the Theatrical Future: The Harold and Mimi Steinberg Charitable Trust," in Robert A. Schanke (ed.), *Angels in American Theatre: Patrons, Patronage, and Philanthropy* (Carbondale, Ill.: Southern Illinois UP, 2007) 242–58.

into the twenty-first century. A small news item buried on page twenty-six of the *New York Times*'s Friday Arts section made nonprofit theater in the United States take notice immediately. The Steinberg Trust had given $1 million to the American Repertory Theatre in Cambridge, Massachusetts, "for the production of new American plays." According to Robert Brustein, ART's artistic director at the time, it was believed to be the largest single grant to support the production of new American work.[2]

Even if the "paper of record" took little notice of the Trust's largesse, the impact on the New York theater community was immediate. Barry Grove, executive producer of Manhattan Theatre Club, said,

> I thought I had known all of the funders of the arts and our antennae went up when we heard there was this new organization out there—and we approached them. . . . What was wonderfully exciting and refreshing about this group is that we were actually in a room talking to the principals.[3]

That presentation must have gone well, because the Trust announced in late September 1993 that Manhattan Theatre Club would receive $1 million in a five-year grant similar to the one for American Repertory Theatre. This time the Trust's generosity was treated prominently in Bruce Weber's Friday *Times* theater column, along with the news that the New York Shakespeare Festival—then under the direction of George C. Wolfe—had received its own $1 million grant from the Trust.[4]

The relationship between the Trust and the American Theatre Critics Association began in 1999, when the two groups entered discussions aimed at providing better funding for the critics' group's prestigious new-play prizes. The national critics' association had begun its play awards in 1977, with citations honoring at least one play that premiered somewhere in the growing network of regional theaters beyond New York City. By 1986, the organization began to obtain funding from major newspaper publishers that underwrote a $1,000 cash prize for a top honoree and two citations for honorable mention. When the Trust and the theater critics came to terms, it led to the creation of the American Theatre Critics/Steinberg New Play Award and Citations, first

---

2. "Boston-Area Theater Wins $1 Million Grant," *The New York Times*, January 15, 1993, C25. In a *Boston Globe* article on the same date, reporter John Koch stated that the grant had been committed by the Trust in spring 1992 (John Koch, "Grant Means Power, Plays for ART," *Boston Globe*, January 15, 1993, 45).

3. Quoted in Jenkins, "Funding," 243.

4. Bruce Weber, "On Stage, and Off," *The New York Times*, October 1, 1993, C2.

given in 2000.[5] For the theater critics' association, the new funding meant that its prestigious prizes now had greater immediate financial impact—$15,000 for the award and $5,000 for each of two citations—than even the Pulitzer Prize. In 2006, the Trust increased its funding so that the award is now worth $25,000 and the two citations earn $7,500 each. The prizes are now referred to as the Harold and Mimi Steinberg/ATCA New Play Award and Citations.[6]

At the first ceremony honoring the Steinberg New Play Award and Citation recipients in 2000, Trust director James D. Steinberg said, "In the beginning was the word, and that is what we are here to honor tonight. My father and mother loved the theater and were especially passionate about new works, which is why the Trust is so pleased to be a part of this great tradition."[7] That tradition continues as the American Theatre Critics Association and Harold and Mimi Steinberg Charitable Trust annually honor the best contemporary theater writing. This volume of scenes from honorees breaks new ground and extends the tradition.

—Jeffrey Eric Jenkins
President, Foundation of the American Theatre Critics Association

JEFFREY ERIC JENKINS *is Professor of Theatre and Head of the Department of Theatre at the University of Illinois. President of the Foundation of the American Theatre Critics Association, he has also edited the* Best Plays Theater Yearbook *since 2001.*

---

5. Jenkins, ed., *The Best Plays Theater Yearbook 2003–2004*, (Pompton Plains, NJ: Limelight Editions, 2005), 396–97.

6. In the interest of full disclosure, it is worth noting that the author was chairman of the American Theatre Critics Association when the awards program with the Trust was presented and approved. He is also series editor of *The Best Plays Theater Yearbook*, to which the Trust has displayed consistent generosity.

7. James D. Steinberg, remarks at American Theatre Critics Association awards ceremony, April 1, 2000, Actors Theatre of Louisville, Louisville, Kentucky.

Editor's Note

For the members of the New Plays Committee the excitement begins in December. Scripts come pouring in from all over the country. Electronically or on hard copy, they come from prestigious regional theaters and fledgling storefront companies, from A-list playwrights or first-heard-of names.

For the past several years, I have been a proud member of that committee. I have also been a teacher of acting for over thirty years. Scene study instructors are consistently looking for material where the circumstances are fresh and immediate, with which the actors may more readily identify. Almost immediately, I was bowled over by the wealth of sharp, insightful, and exciting scene work contained in these Steinberg/ATCA nominations.

The individual scenes were chosen for their balance of conflict, arch of transition, and the ferocity of the circumstances. The primary search for all artists of the theater is to find plays that address a concern with which we all feel an immediate and passionate connection—presented in the most exciting and contemporary of forms.

Explanation of circumstances was deliberately kept to a minimum. In my experience, comprehension of the drama is rarely abetted by editorial explanation and often misleading. I wholeheartedly advocate for a reading of the full play. However, insightful students and perceptive teachers will discover details within the action sufficient to bring the scene to life.

Variety of length was also a conscious choice. Should length be a concern, scenes can be started later or end sooner. Some inclusions, such as the Sheri-Gamila scene from *Pilgrims Musa and Sheri in the New World* or the multiple-character scene from *Water by the Spoonful*, can be divided into two scenes. Some scenes, such as the Mary-Sharon scene from *Detroit*, can be reduced to a monologue. We leave this to the discretion of the teacher and/or student.

The initial intention for this book was to provide actors, directors, and theater educators with the most immediate and outstanding material. Scene books tend to have a short shelf life. However, taken together, even the non-practitioner will be struck by the composite portrait of America with all its complexity and current relevance, absurdity and irony. Comfort comes from knowing we are not alone. Insight revolves from experience revealed with uncensored honesty. Enjoy the ride. I believe this collection contains work from our finest American playwrights working today.

My sincere thanks to Mark Kamie for his immeasurable contribution to this book. My gratitude to John Cerullo and Carol Flannery at Applause for their patience and guidance for a first-time editor. As always, I am indebted to my wife, Kate, for her unbounded inspiration. Above all, much appreciation to the Harold and Mimi Steinberg Charitable Trust for their unprecedented generosity and to the American Theatre Critics Association for their dedication to the growth of the American theater.

—Bruce Burgun

Scenes and Monologues from Steinberg/ATCA New Play Award Finalists, 2008–2012

Part 1

Male-Female Scenes

9 Circles
by Bill Cain

CHARACTERS: Reeves (19/20), an American army private in Iraq; Young Female Lawyer (YFL), a public defender

PLACE: A holding cell in the USA

CIRCUMSTANCE: After being honorably discharged, Reeves has been arrested for acts that he may have committed during the war. He had been on a three-day drinking bender.

(*YFL enters the cell and looks for* Reeves. Reeves *is out cold on the floor of the cell.*)

YFL: Mr. Reeves. (*Nothing.*) Mr. Reeves. (*Losing patience.*) Mr. *REEVES*.

(Reeves *starts awake. Looks around.*)

REEVES: Where am I? . . . Man, I hate waking up and not knowing where . . .

(*Completely hung over, he looks around at his surroundings. Sees the* Young Female Lawyer.)

Oh. (*Then back to sleep.*) I want a lawyer.

YFL: Mr. Reeves, I am a lawyer.

REEVES: I mean a *real* lawyer.

YFL: I am a real lawyer.

REEVES: Really? You *look* like a public defender.

YFL: Well, I am a public defender.

REEVES: Great. Just great. Nothing personal. It's just—tell you the truth—I've been through this before.

YFL: Well. To tell you the truth—I haven't.

REEVES: Great. Fucking great.

(Reeves *farts satisfyingly. Shrugs. Goes back to sleep.*)

YFL: I am fully competent to get you through the arraignment. Then you're done with me and you can hire whatever lawyer you want.

REEVES: I got no money and a beat-up car. How can I hire any lawyer I want? You. You're my lawyer. You're my—defender.

YFL: Tomorrow, Mr. Reeves—Mr. Reeves? Mr. Reeves, all you have to do tomorrow is watch for me to nod my head and, when I do, say in a loud clear voice—not guilty.

(*She starts out.*)

Reeves: Hey, defender. Defender! I can't lose my license.

(*He's embarrassed about needing the car. Not giving a shit entirely would be real freedom. However—the truth is—*)

I *need* the car.

YFL: Mr. Reeves. In all probability—you will never drive a car again.

Reeves: That's a mean thing—just—what a *mean* thing to say. (*Then getting it.*) OK. I'm sorry for what I said about public defenders. OK? Now—worst case. *Worst* case. What kind of time am I looking at?

YFL: You are looking at the death penalty, Mr. Reeves.

Reeves: The death penalty? For a DUI? (*Then—*) Even a public defender—even a lame public defender—ought to be able to get less than the *death penalty* for a DUI.

(*She does not respond.*)

This isn't a DUI, is it? (*Then—*) What did I do? Did I get in a fight? Did I black out? I didn't hit somebody with the car, did I? (*No.*) Whatever. I was drunk. I had the right to be. I don't know why *everybody* isn't drunk. You know why I was here?

YFL: You were here for—for the funeral. (*Impressed.*) I understand you served with him?

Reeves: (*Bragging.*) Him? *Them.* I "served" with all *three* of them. Funerals in Texas, Oregon, and Arlington. (*Shaking off the hangover.*) Can't go to them all. I thought—Arlington ought to know how to do a funeral. Don't get me wrong, it was nice, but—

YFL: (*With some awe.*) Texas.

Reeves: You saw it?

YFL: On the news.

Reeves: People every twenty feet. Everybody holding flags. For miles. Not bad for a dropout who pumped gas. He just got married. You know that? He didn't tell his folks. Just us.

YFL: Eighteen. She was—

REEVES: Eighteen. Hell, he was—. (*Bizarrely bragging.*) It's *my fault* he's dead. Hell, it's my fault *all three of them* are dead. If I had been there . . .

YFL: You think you could have protected them?

REEVES: (*Not exactly.*) I make people nervous. People get careful when they're around me. (*Then*—) You feel a little careful around me? Don't you? (*Silence, then*—) Well, they *needed* to be *careful*. If they'd let me stay over there, those soldiers would still be—. (*Twitch-wince, then*—) What the hell. GUILTY. I was drunk. I was driving. Whatever happened, it's my fault. Plead me guilty.

(*The professional emerges in our lawyer.*)

YFL: Mr. Reeves, there are only two words that I want to hear from you and "my fault?' are not those words. Say "my fault" to the judge tomorrow and you will make me look like I didn't do my job—like I didn't defend you— for a public defender, that's *bad.* Two words. (*Cuing.*) Not—???

(*Reeves is getting to like her.*)

REEVES: Not guilty. OK? (*Yes.*) Hey, what did I do? What am I "not guilty" of?

(*She takes out paperwork.*)

No. Just—your own words—that's all.

YFL: You should hear the charges again.

REEVES: Again?

YFL: *Listen* this time. (*Then*—) 1. *On or about March 12, 2006, outside the United States, to wit, in Iraq*—while a member of the United States Army—

REEVES: Wait. . . . Iraq? (*Yes.*) Iraq? (*Very puzzled.*) I didn't have my car in Iraq.

YFL: Would you like me to start over? (*No.*) *While a member of the United States Army subject to Chapter 47 of Title 10 of the Uniform Code of Military Justice—the defendant, Daniel E. Reeves, did, with malice aforethought, unlawfully kill a person, an Iraqi man by shooting, an offense punishable by more than one year, if committed, in the special territorial jurisdiction of the United States, all in violation of Title 18, Section 7 and 3261(a)(2). . . .*

(*Silence. Then*—)

REEVES: (*Completely unconcerned.*) Hell—they're not going to take my car away for that.

(*Then—with a building edge*—)

YFL: 2. *On or about March 12, 2006, outside the United States, to wit, in Iraq—*

REEVES: *Iraq*—did I kill people over there?

YFL: —*while a member of the United States Army—*

REEVES: You bet I did.

YFL: *Subject to Chapter 47 of Title 10—*

REEVES: How many?

YFL: —*of the Uniform Code of Military Justice—*

REEVES: Nowhere near enough.

YFL: *The defendant—*

REEVES: You want to know what I plea?

YFL: *Daniel E. Reeves, did—*

REEVES: Guilty.

YFL: —*with malice aforethought—*

REEVES: Kill people?

YFL: —*unlawfully kill another person. An Iraqi—*

REEVES: *That's what I was supposed to do.*

YFL: An Iraqi woman. (*Then—from memory.*) *An offense punishable by more than one year, if committed, in the territorial jurisdiction of the United States in violation of Title 18 , Section 7 and 3261(a)(2).*

(*Silence. Then, sizing up the situation—*)

REEVES: You're not a *regular* public defender, are you?

YFL: Federal.

(*Silence. Then, deeply puzzled—*)

REEVES: How can what happened *over there* be a crime *over here*?

YFL: (*No clue.*) Like I said—I've never been through this before. (*Then—*) 3. *On or about March 12, 2006—*

REEVES: Cut to the—

YFL: *Daniel E. Reeves did unlawfully kill—an Iraqi child.*

(*A moment. Then—sobering up—*)

REEVES: I made a mistake over there. Fisher. Fisher did it right. I should have done what Fisher did.

YFL: Fisher?

REEVES: Oregon.

YFL: What did he do?

REEVES: He *died* over there. You know what they did to him? You see the video?

YFL: Yes, I saw the video.

REEVES: They cut off his head.

YFL: (*Enough.*) I saw the video.

REEVES: *That's* why people are lining the streets. That's what makes him a hero. He got his head cut off. The mistake I made was coming home alive.

YFL: Well, you may get your wish yet, Mr. Reeves. People are most definitely out for your head.

REEVES: (*Realizing—*) Fuck. *Everything* we did over there is a crime over here.

YFL: (*Becoming personal.*) Mr. Reeves? We're at war. Terrible things happen in a war. I know that.

REEVES: You know that?

YFL: (*Even more personal.*) Terrible things happen. Yes, I know that. I believe—under the right circumstances, anyone—*anyone*—is capable of terrible things. I think that's why I became a public defender.

REEVES: No, that we're at war. You know *that*?

YFL: Yes.

REEVES: How? How do you know that?

YFL: How do I—

REEVES: I mean, it could be like the moon landing. Couldn't it? Do you think we landed on the moon? Really. Do you?

YFL: Mr. Reeves. Daniel—

REEVES: Do you?

YFL: Yes, we landed on the moon.

REEVES: We landed on the moon? We did?

YFL: Yes.

REEVES: You think *you*—any *part* of you—landed on the moon?

YFL: Well . . . no.

REEVES: So *we* didn't land on the moon. You're pretty sure of that? You pretty sure you didn't land on the moon.

(*Yes, then violently.*)

Then how can you be *so fucking sure* we're *at war*? *You're* about as much at war as you are on the *fucking moon.*

YFL: I mean, the country is at—

REEVES: The *Marines* are at war. The *Army* is at war. The country? You know what this country is fighting? (*She doesn't.*) *An obesity epidemic!* (**With vast contempt.**) Now what fucking Iraqi accused us of—

(**REEVES** *grabs the papers from her.*)

Who wrote that? Who—(*Reading.*) *SOI1 was interviewed and explained that*—(*Then*—)—SOI1? Who the hell is—

YFL: SOI. Source of Information. It was in a stress debriefing.

REEVES: A stress debriefing? Iraqis don't get—

YFL: It was an American soldier. Talking to a counselor.

REEVES: An American? Soldier? Said?

(*YFL takes the papers.*)

YFL: *SOI1 explained that SOI2, SOI3, PFC Daniel E. Reeves, and KP1*—

REEVES: KP1?

YFL: Known Participant 1 . . . *were conducting duties at TCP2*—

REEVES: Traffic Control Point 2—

YFL: *—200 meters from the residence where the crime occurred.*

(**YFL** *creates the event*—)

Prior to departing, TCP2, SOI1—

REEVES: *In your own words.*

YFL: (*This is hard.*) Well—it says Private Daniel Reeves and several of his squadmates—currently in the brig in Iraq—went to a house. There Private Reeves herded an Iraqi man, woman, and child into the bedroom where he shot and killed them. Then he went into the living room where two of the soldiers were holding a woman down and he raped, then killed her. Afterwards, they set her body on fire. (*Then*—) I don't know why they call her a woman. She was fourteen.

(*Silence. Then*—)

REEVES: Do you think we did this? Is that what you think?

YFL: Terrible things happen.

REEVES: (*Astounded.*) YOU THINK WE—? WE don't DO things LIKE THIS. *In-sur-gents* did this. We *investigated* it. That report—it's *nothing* but *lies.*

YFL: Perhaps. Still, there is something to be learned from it. (*A moment, then*—) There is only one name in this report. In this whole report, there is only *one* name.

REEVES: Daniel E. Reeves.

YFL: Exactly. (*With some sympathy.*) Daniel, you are going to need a lawyer—not only a real lawyer, an extraordinary lawyer—to get you through this—but for tomorrow, you are innocent until proven guilty.

(*As she goes*—)

REEVES: You're going to help me, aren't you? I'll get you through tomorrow. Tomorrow? Tomor—?

YFL: A lawyer will be appointed for you, Mr. Reeves.

REEVES: By who?

YFL: The government.

REEVES: Wait a minute. Who wants me dead?

YFL: The government.

REEVES: Well, that's not good. Is it?

(**REEVES** *laughs out loud. Inappropriately.*)

YFL: Be careful what you say tomorrow. Two words. "Not guilty," Mr. Reeves. "Not—"

REEVES: (*Fuck you.*) Two words, "HONORABLE DISCHARGE."

Annapurna
by Sharr White

CHARACTERS: EMMA, Ulysses's ex-wife; ULYSSES, has terminal lung cancer and relies on an oxygen tank to breath (both mid-50s)

PLACE: Ulysses's mobile home in the remote Rockies; spring

CIRCUMSTANCE: Emma left with their child one night. Twenty-plus years have passed since they saw each other.

EMMA: Ulysses . . .

ULYSSES: —What do you want.

EMMA: —Ulysses.

ULYSSES: I said, what do you want, Emma, you plant yourself right there and tell me what the hell you can want.

ULYSSES: Look. . . . I got married.

ULYSSES: —So?

EMMA: And I've, I've . . . left. Him.

ULYSSES: —Congratulations.

EMMA: —Three days ago—Peter, his name is Peter. I just got in the car, and . . . drove. Here.

ULYSSES: Meanin' . . . what, exactly.

(EMMA *is perhaps too proud to say what this means, but she allows herself to give a slight gesture: a combination nod, shrug, shake of the head.*)

You told me you were just passin' through.

EMMA: Right! I am!—Well, I mean . . . eventually.

(*Slight beat.*)

ULYSSES: OK. Get out.

EMMA: Now, now, wait a second, I just got here.

ULYSSES: I said, get out, I don't got time for this shit.

EMMA: —Really!—

ULYSSES: —Yeah, I got things to do.—

EMMA: —Like what?

ULYSSES: Like watchin' the dog lie around in the shade!

EMMA: Looks like you've been doing that for too long already!

ULYSSES: Well, maybe *I* know when to let a sleepin' dog lie!

EMMA: Ha! Ha!

ULYSSES: JUST WHAT DO YOU NOT UNDERSTAND ABOUT THE WORDS GET THE FUCK OUT?

(*Ugly silence.* **ULYSSES** *holds his tube to his nose so he can suck oxygen more strongly.*)

EMMA: (*Quietly.*) Well. . . . I can see this was a bad idea.

(*Silence.* **ULYSSES** *waits for* **EMMA** *to go. She doesn't move.*)

ULYSSES: What're you waitin' for?

EMMA: You're not going to help with the bags?

ULYSSES: WILL YOU JUST . . . ? (*She turns for the bags.*)—I mean, what do you expect me to say, Emma? It's been . . . !

(*Beat.*)

EMMA: (*Quietly.*) Right. Twenty years.

(*Long beat.*)

ULYSSES: (*Sullen; perhaps actually a little protective.*) And what's the matter, didn't get a goddamn movin' truck?

(**EMMA** *shakes her head.*)

So you're tellin' me that's all you took?

(**EMMA** *nods.*)

But I guess this is pretty much how you do it, huh?

EMMA: Do what?

ULYSSES: Leave people. In the middle of the night with just a little bit of stuff. It's how you left *me*.

EMMA: I never said I left Peter in the middle of the night.

ULYSSES: But you did, didn't ya'? (*Slight beat. This is an affirmative.*) All this time, I still know who you are.

EMMA: Like you knew who I was before.

ULYSSES: Yeah. Nothin' like wakin' up one day with a mean headache and your family missin' to illustrate just how wrong you can be about someone.

(**Ulysses** *examines his fingers.*)

Emma: You OK?

Ulysses: Burnt my fingers.

Emma: Well, why'd you do that?

Ulysses: It was bad meat.

Emma: I mean, why'd you reach right down into the pan like that, you knew it was hot.

Ulysses: I don't know! I don't know why I did it! I don't know why I do anything I do!

Emma: Let me see.

Ulysses: No.

Emma: Give them here.

Ulysses: No, I said. (*Examines himself mournfully. A beat.*) Five minutes. No funny stuff.

Emma: Like what?

Ulysses: Don't pretend you've never been given a finger without takin' the whole hand.

Emma: That's bullshit.

Ulysses: That's the truth. Getting some clothes on.

(**Ulysses** *exits into the small bedroom, where we see him root through a pile of laundry.*)

Emma: (*Calling to him.*) Thank. God.

Ulysses: —You know what?

(*Slight beat.* **Emma** *glances around. For the following conversation* **Ulysses** *will be in his room, carefully pulling on cutoffs.*)

Emma: (*Speaking through the walls.*) If it was bad meat, why were you cooking it?

Ulysses: I like the smell of it.

Emma: Of bad sausage?

Ulysses: Can't tell it's bad in the pan. Smells good as good, then. Optimistic. No mornin' so optimistic as one with the smell of sausage fryin'.

Emma: You did used to say that.

Ulysses: Still do, apparently.

(**Emma** *looks around. Tension.*)

EMMA: (*Probing.*) Guess you're not writing?

ULYSSES: . . . No.

EMMA: Nothing?

ULYSSES: Why?

EMMA: Because Sam . . .

(ULYSSES *stops and gives a loaded chuckle.*)

. . . imagines. You sitting on some . . . treasure trove.

(*Beat.*)

ULYSSES: Where'd he get that idea?

EMMA: Oh, well . . . *you* know. How kids . . . come up with things.

ULYSSES: Actually I *don't*. I don't know what kids do. Think you know that.

EMMA: —I mean, he's not a kid anymore, he's . . .

ULYSSES: —Twenty-five. 17 July.

EMMA: . . . That's right.

ULYSSES: What, think I'd forget?

EMMA: . . . No. (*Tense beat.* ULYSSES *steps into the kitchen/living area only in cutoffs and his ever-present backpack.*) . . . He . . .

ULYSSES: —Sammy—

EMMA: —Sam, he goes by Sam now. Uh. Apparently hired a . . . private detective.

ULYSSES: —Why the hell'd he do that?

EMMA: To find you.

ULYSSES: Number's listed, coulda' hired *me*, I woulda' told him where I was.

EMMA: Right, except you don't have a phone—

ULYSSES: (*Back into his room again to root through laundry.*)—Details.

EMMA: —and you've had a gazillion addresses and your publisher won't reveal anything and apparently Sam's been obsessing, and . . . thinks time is . . . of the essence.

ULYSSES: For what?

EMMA: To uh . . . well, for him to, to, uh . . . meet you. (ULYSSES, *in his room, is silent. Tension.*) Did . . . did you hear me?

(ULYSSES *has picked up a short-sleeved shirt from the pile of laundry in the bedroom and now moves back into the kitchen/living area.*)

ULYSSES: Only better smell than sausage is a nice yeasty bread dough rising on the counter, would do that if this place had an oven, but it don't.

EMMA: (*Quickly, quietly.*) You heard me, I know you heard me.

ULYSSES: Fresh, crusty baguette slathered in butter?—Holy crap, just made my mouth water, you see that?

EMMA: I didn't.

ULYSSES: Water almost came *right* out of my mouth. Anyway, got five pounds of bad sausage in there.

EMMA: Five . . . *pounds*? In, in . . . ?

ULYSSES . . . the mini-fridge—*don't* open it, you'll throw up. Still got that weak stomach, I'll bet.

EMMA: . . . I . . . I do, yes.

ULYSSES: Bought it last week at the dollar store.

EMMA: You bought *meat*? At the *dollar store*?

ULYSSES: Good bargain, was only a dollar. Got it home, package started swelling, got the botulism or something, thought, Oh hell, nothing does go right, does it? You know? Think you caught a break and it's not a break at all? Just a, a . . . trap. Like a hope trap. Get your hopes up for something and then just quick as can be—bam!—it's yanked away. Well, thought to myself, Screw this, this ain't gonna trap me, I'm gonna show this damned meat a thing or two, I'm gonna turn this . . . badness. Into a little optimism. Plus I can feed the dog.

(*She stares at him.*)

EMMA: You make me nuts, you know that?

ULYSSES: —Pretty sure my son already met me. Pretty sure he met me every fuckin' day for the first five years of his life.

EMMA: Well, he says he doesn't remember you.

ULYSSES: Well, he should!

EMMA: (*Firm, not mad.*) Don't. You. Shout. At. Me. (*Nice.*) OK?

(*Small beat. He hands her the shirt.*)

ULYSSES: (*Quiet.*) Think you're gonna appreciate this. Got the cowboy pockets.

Emma: (*Quiet.*) Why would I appreciate it?

Ulysses: You always did like the cowboy pockets.

Emma: I thought they were silly.

Ulysses: (*A little sharp.*) Thought you'd appreciate it.

Emma: (*Examining the shirt.*)—Well, really what's not to admire about a stained, plaid, short-sleeved, cowboy-pocket shirt with . . . half a collar and—oh—a hole in the right shoulder, that someone is actually going to wear instead of using to change their oil.

(*Beat.*)

Ulysses: What've you told 'em? About me.

Emma: He's . . . read all your books.

Ulysses: Know how many poems I've written in the last ten years?

Emma: How many.

Ulysses: One.

Emma: That's all?

Ulysses: And what about all my letters, sent 'im all the letters. He read the letters?

Emma: (*Nodding vigorously.*)—Oh . . . !

Ulysses: Never wrote back, though. Wished you'd sent me somethin'. Drawin'. Report card. Somethin'.

Emma: He . . . has a vision of you being some . . . noble . . . superman. Banished to your castle in the wilderness or something by your evil ex-wife.

Ulysses: Well, I'll tell ya', we're all in trouble if I'm *Der Ubermensch.* (**Ulysses** *assumes a position that will allow* **Emma** *to pull the shirt over him. She helps.*)— Funny how some things I can't do. Can throw sausage at a dog, but can't get a shirt on.

Emma: Snap it all the way?

Ulysses: Saw, just in the center, I got to ventilate. Come one PM with the sun on the roof, you're gonna want to ventilate too.

Emma: —He thinks I . . . ruined his life.

Ulysses: Well, didn't ya'?

Emma: No! I didn't!

Ulysses: I mean, you pretty much kidnapped him, right?

Emma: *Really!* That's your side of the story!

Ulysses: Yeah! It is!

Emma: And honestly what about that would have ruined his life! I mean . . . (*Looking around the devastated trailer, incredulous.*) My . . . *Godddddddddd*, Ulysseeeeeees.

Ulysses: You don't got to say it like *that.*

Emma: Why not? Honestly, are there any other words for it? What on earth . . . *happened* to you.

Ulysses: (*Small beat.*) One thing leads to another.

Emma: That's . . . *all?*

Ulysses: That's the *Reader's Digest* version.

(*Small beat.*)

Emma: Apparently he found out from this private investigator that you've been in a hospital? In Denver?

Ulysses: (*Little laugh.*) Was that or Salt Lake City, but I never did trust a Mormon with a knife. Jackass Marty McNeely guy in the double-wide—actually drove me all the way over the pass and back.

Emma: And he apparently found out . . .

(**Emma** *suddenly, surprisingly—especially to herself—begins weeping.*)

Emma: (*Mad with herself.*)—s . . . s . . . sorry. I . . . s . . . swore I wasn't going to . . . do this!— . . . found out . . . um . . . that you're dying . . .

Ulysses: Oh, that. . . . Yeah.

Emma: (*Sitting, weeping.*) I . . . just didn't know what to *do* . . . I . . . I've . . . I've . . . *hated* you . . . for so long! Or I . . . I . . . I *told myself* I did, every . . . every day some weeks—*still!*—I wake up and thank heaven that I'm not with you anymore, but when I heard everything I just packed my bags and, and, and, and . . . (*Wiping her eyes.*) Why would I do that?

Ulysses: You're . . . askin' me?

Emma: I'm sorry, I'm, I'm very . . . confused. About some things. Right now.

Ulysses: You ain't the only one. (*A beat.* **Emma** *unzips her duffle bag and takes out, improbably, a vase with a silk flower. She sets it on* **Ulysses***'s counter.*) Whoa, whoa, now . . . now hold on now, what do you think you're doin'?

EMMA: It's funny when you walk out after so long. What do you take? It was in my hallway bathroom. Complete with fake flower. And this, too. (*She lifts out a wooden bowl.*) Snuck out the back door, grabbed it on the way.

ULYSSES: OK now, you put that back. (*She sets it down. Pulls out a paper bag of apples, upends it into the bowl.*) Whoa! What do you think you're doin, I said you got just five minutes!

EMMA: (*Exuberant relief.*) You know what?—I don't know what I'm doing! I actually have . . . no idea! (**EMMA** *begins unpacking her belongings.*)

ULYSSES: Whoa, whoa, whoa . . .

EMMA: (*Stacking clothes.*)—Look! Sorry! I know this is crazy! But the second I heard about everything, I, I, I . . . *knew*. That you were in trouble! (*With optimistic purpose.*) And just look at this shithole!

(*Outside, the dog begins barking.*)

ULYSSES: Now see what you done, you got her all riled up again. (*Pulling tube out, calling out front door.*) Jenny! Hey, girl, you don't got to get all upset now . . .

EMMA: Put that tube back in your nose.

ULYSSES: (*Panting.*) Put that shit back in your bag.

EMMA: No.

ULYSSES: Then NO! (**ULYSSES** *steps out the trailer door.*) Jennifer! Hey there, sweetie, you stop that barkin' now . . .

EMMA: (*To the empty doorway.*) You're . . . *infuriating*, you know that?

ULYSSES: (*Calling from offstage.*) And I suppose you're easy as pie! (**EMMA** *pulls a large bottle of water out of her duffle.*)

EMMA: (*Calling out the door.*) I mean, I, I, I thought you'd at least be relieved! To see me!

ULYSSES: (*Calling from offstage.*) Maybe it's complicated!

EMMA: Or . . . grateful! Or thankful!

ULYSSES: Thankful! For what!?

EMMA: Because someone still cares! About . . . someone!—God knows why. I thought you'd . . . you'd . . .

(**EMMA** *looks around, holding her water. She sees the mini-fridge. Moves toward it.*)

ULYSSES: (*Offstage.*) Waaaaaait! *Don't* open that mini-friiiiidge!

(*Too late.* EMMA *opens the fridge and is confronted by the bad meat.*)

EMMA: (*Scrambling back in revulsion.*) Oh! Mmmm! Mmmm!

(EMMA *stumbles downstage with her hands over her mouth. Drops to her knees. Holds her stomach. Bends over.*)

Becky's New Car
by Steven Dietz

CHARACTERS: WALTER, wealthy businessman and widowed (60s); BECKY, middle-class woman (late 40s)

PLACE: An auto dealership

CIRCUMSTANCE: Becky is married to Joe, a roofer.

WALTER: Good evening—

BECKY: We're closed.

WALTER: Yes, I know, but I wondered if—

BECKY: You'll need to come by tomorrow.

WALTER: —Yes, but you see, this is kind of an emergency, I need to—

BECKY: The dealership closed three hours ago, so if you'd—

WALTER: I won't take up much of your time. I can write you a check, give you a credit card, have my accountant wire the full amount to you—whatever you prefer.

BECKY: The full amount for what?

WALTER: I need to buy some cars. As a gift for my employees. We have our company breakfast at 7 a.m. tomorrow morning and we've had a pretty good year, so I want to get them all a little something. But I'm just terrible at gifts. My wife, Sheila, she was so good at it. She had a *knack*. Knew just the perfect thing to buy for people—no matter what the occasion. But ever since she passed, I'm a total wreck. I'm told I should hire a gift consultant, put a sort of swag master on my payroll, but I really wouldn't know where to begin—

BECKY: Look, now is not a—

WALTER: —so, I had my driver take me to some *stores*—I had no idea there were so many stores, they're *everywhere*—and I walked around those stores, not a clue, no idea what to get, and so I told my driver to take me home and right away, there we were, *stuck in traffic* . . . and I looked out the window and I said to myself: *cars*. People like cars. I'll get them some *cars*. So I know it's late, but may I please buy some of your cars?

(*Pause.*)

BECKY: How many do you need?

WALTER: Nine. Just nine of them will do.

BECKY: *Nine* cars . . .

WALTER: I could arrange payment for them tonight—and maybe you could just put the keys in little gift boxes—Sheila always kept a shelf filled with these neat little gift boxes, fitted with ribbons, just perfect—anyway, I thought I'd just hand out these boxes at the company breakfast and shake their hands and be done with it.

(*Pause. She stares at him.*)

BECKY: What . . . um . . . what kind of cars would you like?

WALTER: Oh, whatever you think. Nine of 'em.

(**BECKY** *hands him a brochure—still not really believing all this.*)

BECKY: Maybe you should look at this—these are the current models.

WALTER: (*Paging through brochure, agitated.*) Oh, see—this is where it gets tricky—maybe just one of each style—

BECKY: And what colors?

WALTER: See what I mean?! This is impossible! God, I miss Sheila.

BECKY: (*Re: the brochure.*) Towards the back, there are color and fabric swatches—interior and exterior. Plus we offer—

WALTER: No, no, no, I can't do *this*. My driver is waiting. I'm supposed to be at a birthday party for my daughter and I don't have a gift for *her* either—unless you count my *entire net worth*, which she'll inherit the moment I drop dead from trying to *buy some gifts for all these people!*—so please, I know how this must sound and how foolish I must look, but . . . can you help me?

(*She stares at him. A beat. Then: she takes the brochure from* **WALTER**'s *hands, saying—*)

BECKY: (*All business.*) I recommend our all-wheel-drive sport coupe. Very popular. My husband . . . he always wanted one of these.

WALTER: Oh, *did* he?

BECKY: And the thing is: you don't need to pick colors or interiors in advance—the new owners can do that when they come in. Also, I suggest you buy each of them the same car—to avoid the appearance of playing favorites.

WALTER: That's very smart.

(*She's quickly punching numbers into a calculator as she talks.*)

BECKY: They could take delivery almost right away. And if you choose the "Top Flight" package on each car, they can add any extras they might want.

WALTER: Good. Let's do that.

BECKY: Okay—

(*The calculator spits out a very long piece of paper—*BECKY *rips it off—and hands it to* WALTER.)

—your cost for nine of these cars, taxes, title, and fees comes to this number right *here*.

(**WALTER** *looks at the number for a long moment. Then: he looks up into* BECKY'S *eyes.*)

WALTER: You still wear your ring. I do, too. I thought about leaving it with Sheila—having it buried with her . . . (*Touching his ring.*) It was my daughter who told me to hold on to it. That it would be a nice reminder. (*Beat.*) I see you've done the same.

BECKY: Pardon?

WALTER: Kept your wedding ring.

BECKY: Well—yes.

WALTER: It's lovely.

BECKY: Thank you—yes, I wear it because, I mean—

WALTER: Was he a good man? Was he kind to you?

BECKY: Yes—he was—*is*—I mean, he still *is*.

WALTER: Oh, I know the feeling—

BECKY: He's still with me—we're still together—

WALTER: Exactly—that's what I tell people, too—

BECKY: No, you—

WALTER: —it's like she's still with me, right by my side, guiding me through my days—

BECKY: Yes, but my husband is still—

WALTER: —and leading me here tonight. Leading me to you. I'm Walter. And you are . . .

(*She says nothing. He lifts one of her business cards from the desk. Reads.*)

. . . It's spelled "uh-huhRebecca.

(*He extends his hand.*)

I'm sorry for your loss, Rebecca.

BECKY: You don't understand—

WALTER: I like that name: Rebecca. It has substance. Ballast. I hope you don't let people call you "Becky."

BECKY: Well—

WALTER: "Becky" is the name of a dull housewife in a sad movie about a poor family struggling to hold on to their vanishing hopes and dreams. In the movies, a "Becky" always gets the shaft.

BECKY: Walter, I need to tell you about my husband—

WALTER: And I need to tell you more about Sheila—I think that's *healthy*, to do that kind of sharing—but let's not do that here. Let me pay you for these cars and then maybe we can go somewhere—get a bite to eat.

BECKY: You have a party to attend—your daughter's birthday.

WALTER: And of course you'd remember that! Of course you place family above everything. Sheila was like that too. You're right, I should go—and I still don't have a gift for my daughter.

BECKY: Does she need a car?

WALTER: She has plenty of cars. Maybe I'll get her a loft downtown. Kids like lofts, don't they?

BECKY: I bet they do.

WALTER: Here is my card—with my accountant's name on back.

BECKY: (*Re: his card.*) Walter Flood—I've seen that name.

WALTER: Maybe on billboards.

BECKY: Do you advertise there?

WALTER: I *am* the billboards. I own the billboards.

BECKY: Which ones?

WALTER: Pretty much all of them. Go ahead—you can say it: they're an eyesore—visual pollution—

BECKY: Well—

WALTER: —and all of that is true. Believe me, if I could have made *hundreds of millions of dollars* by doing something *good and noble* for the world, I by God would have done it. But my father handed me this business and said, "Walter, don't screw it up." You play the hand you're dealt.

BECKY: You must have played it well.

WALTER: Who knows. Life is chaos and holidays. Who can say why things turn out the way they do. All I know is that my life has become the story of a handful of people I met by chance and the things we did together.

(*Pause. She is staring at him.*)

BECKY: We have these gift keys . . . they don't belong to any actual vehicles, but they look real, and people use them when they're giving a car as a gift.

WALTER: I'll need nine of them.

BECKY: And some gift boxes.

WALTER: Perfect.

(*Pause.*)

May I keep your card, Rebecca?

BECKY: Sure.

WALTER: And may I call you?

(*Pause. She stares at him, then turns to the audience.*)

BECKY: (*To audience.*) I made a sound that was sort of a cross between "Mm-hmm" and "Hmm-mm"—

(**WALTER** *turns and leaves.*)

—and I thought, "Well, okay, *THAT happened*"—no big deal, except for the fact that I failed to explain to this kind gentleman that my husband is not currently *dead*.

End Days
by Deborah Zoe Laufer

CHARACTERS: RACHEL, a nihilistic Goth; NELSON, Rachel's new neighbor, dresses like Elvis (both 16 years old)

PLACE: School cafeteria, late September 2003

CIRCUMSTANCE: Rachel and her family fled NYC to suburbia after 9/11. Nelson has a huge crush on Rachel.

(RACHEL *sits at a long, empty table, reading a textbook.* NELSON *heads toward her, struggling to hold his tray while maneuvering around the sling and the guitar. There is now a large bandage across the bridge of his nose.*)

NELSON: Rachel! Hi! Rachel. Mind if I join you?

RACHEL: (*Refusing to look up.*) Yes.

NELSON: Oh.

(*He looks around blankly.*)

RACHEL: There's an empty table over there.

NELSON: Okay.

(*But he just stands there, silent for a moment. Then:*)

You were so amazing this morning. At the blackboard. Had you worked out that equation before? Because you wrote it out so fast. It's like you were channeling it or . . . something . . .

(*RACHEL* finally looks up at him.*)

RACHEL: What happened to your nose?

NELSON: This? Oh, I was just horsing around with some of the guys.

RACHEL: If you'd stop dressing like that, they might stop beating you up.

NELSON: No, no. We were just roughhousing. It was all in fun.

A VOICE FROM OFFSTAGE: Hey, freak!

(*An empty milk carton comes flying through the air and clocks* NELSON *in the head. Laughter.*)

NELSON: (*Laughingly, to them.*) You guys! Anyway, Nurse Liz is real nice. Stopped the bleeding in about two seconds. Patched me right up.

RACHEL: Whatever.

(*She goes back to her book.*)

NELSON: I was saying to your dad, it's too bad you're not taking physics. With your calculus, you'd be a natural.

RACHEL: Yeah. Look, don't come by my house anymore, okay? And don't tell anybody about . . . anything at my house. Okay?

NELSON: You can count on me, Rachel. What happens between us, stays between us.

RACHEL: Great.

(*She goes back to her book. Barely acknowledges him through the following.*)

NELSON: (*Trying to consult some notes, while balancing his tray.*) I can't believe how alike our houses are.

RACHEL: Uh-huh.

NELSON: Have you lived there long?

RACHEL: No.

NELSON: Where are you from?

RACHEL: New York.

NELSON: New York City? Wow. You're from New York City. How great is that?

RACHEL: Great.

NELSON: Why did you move?

RACHEL: My dad lost his job.

NELSON: Oh. How did he . . .

RACHEL: It blew up when a plane flew into it.

NELSON: A plane . . . Wow. Was he okay?

RACHEL: Oh yeah. He's great.

(*Another milk carton beans* **NELSON** *in the head. Laughter offstage.*)

NELSON: (*To offstage boys.*) Hey! You've got quite an arm!

(*Another carton comes flying in.*)

RACHEL: (*Shouting offstage.*) Stop it, you freakin' goons!

(*More laughter offstage.*)

(*To* **NELSON.**) Sit. Would you just sit for Christ's sakes.

Nelson: Gee. Thanks.

(*He eagerly sits down and starts eating his macaroni and cheese.*)

They've got very good macaroni and cheese here. Much better than my last school. Less gooey.

Rachel: I'd really like to just read, okay?

Nelson: Yeah? Me too. I love to read. Did you ever read this?

(*He holds up his book.* A Brief History of Time.)

Rachel: What is it?

Nelson: It's only the greatest book ever written.

Rachel: What *is* it?

Nelson: Stephen Hawking explains pretty much everything in the universe.

Rachel: Does he explain why you're dressed like that?

Nelson: No, you know, like all the great scientific theories from Aristotle and Ptolemy pretty much up until now.

Rachel: Oh.

Nelson: You would love it.

Rachel: I don't think so.

Nelson: No, you would—I mean, it all comes down to math. Unification. To have a mathematical equation that integrates Einstein's general relativity with quantum mechanics. An equation that encompasses everything.

Rachel: And then what?

Nelson: And then we know how it all works.

Rachel: And then what?

Nelson: And then we can figure out how it all started.

Rachel: And then what?

Nelson: Ummm. And then we know.

(**Rachel** *goes back to her book.*)

He's so amazing. Stephen Hawking. He's got A.L.S.—they told him he'd die when he was like twenty, and he's lived more than forty years past that and he rides around in a motorized wheelchair and he talks through a computer. It's like the greatest brain on the planet riding around on this chair. You want to borrow it?

Rachel: No thanks.

Nelson: It's okay. I've got my name in the cover.

Rachel: No.

Nelson: It's really easy. I mean, it's written in a way that anyone can understand.

(*Pause.*)

Come on. Take it. And then you can tell me what you think.

(*She takes the book.*)

Great! Wow! This is so great!

Rachel: I probably won't read it.

Nelson: But you might.

Rachel: I might.

Nelson: And then we could talk about it. Oh my God. That would be just about the greatest thing ever.

(**Rachel** *looks at him for a long moment.*)

Rachel: You should stop wearing that outfit.

Nelson: That's okay.

Rachel: They won't stop beating on you till you stop.

Nelson: I'm used to it.

Rachel: But why get used to it? Why not just be normal?

Nelson: Why do you wear that outfit?

Rachel: So people will leave me alone.

Nelson: Oh.

Rachel: Clearly it's not working.

Nelson: Some people think he's like a savior or something. Elvis. That he didn't really die, or that he'll rise again.

Rachel: They're nuts.

Nelson: Maybe. My mom loved him. She got me an Elvis outfit for Halloween when I was five and I would never take it off.

Rachel: That was probably cute. When you were five.

Nelson: Yeah. So I just kept on wearing it. Everywhere. Even to my mom's funeral I wore it. My dad finally threw it away and I wouldn't get dressed. Went to kindergarten in my underwear.

Rachel: You're kidding.

Nelson: Nope. So eventually he got me a new one. I find it really comforting. We've got the same birthday. Elvis and I. January 8th. And guess who else has it?

Rachel: Who?

Nelson: Guess.

Rachel: No.

Nelson: Come on. Somebody amazing.

Rachel: Just tell me for Christ sakes.

Nelson: Stephen Hawking! The guy I was just telling you about! The book guy.

Rachel: So?

Nelson: Isn't that cool?

Rachel: Maybe you should dress like him.

Nelson: It's okay. They always beat me up the first month or so. But it gets old after a while. I expect it'll stop soon.

(*A barrage of milk containers starts hammering at them. Laughter offstage.*)

Rachel: (*Snapping from 1 to 10 in about a second. Picks up the milk containers and starts pummeling them back.*) Leave us alone, you freakin' assholes!

Nelson: Wow. You've got great aim!

Rachel: Friggin' Neanderthals!

(**Nelson** *picks up a container with his good arm and hurls it back, weakly.*)

Nelson: Friggin' Neanderthals! (*He grins, delighted.*)

Great Falls
by Lee Blessing

CHARACTERS: MONKEY MAN, a prizewinning writer and Bitch's ex-stepdad; BITCH (17 years old), a victim of rape

PLACE: A roadside picnic table

CIRCUMSTANCE: Monkey Man has taken Bitch on a road trip.

MONKEY MAN: So. Lots to decide at this point. Have you been thinking?

BITCH: Yeah.

MONKEY MAN: Totally up to you. Completely your decision.

BITCH: I think—

MONKEY MAN: But before you say, I think it's important to mark a moment like this. Here we are, astride the continental divide so to speak—on our own, free to explore. We're talking, we're exploring, the Pacific Northwest is only a couple mountain ranges away—

BITCH: No.

MONKEY MAN: And— (*After a beat.*) And just like Lewis and Clark we could—

BITCH: No.

MONKEY MAN: We *could* see the Columbia River Gorge, and Astoria and Cannon Beach and—

BITCH: No.

MONKEY MAN: And the wide and endless . . . unswimmably cold . . . Pacific. It's west, it's the way of the future. Why not?

BITCH: I don't have time.

MONKEY MAN: We have months of time. It's summer. I'm a writer, for God's sake; no one needs me. You're going to college this fall. This is a great—

BITCH: It's where *you* went, when you were a little kid. It's where your parents took you, and you love it 'cause you *had* two parents. But I don't. So I'm not going there, 'cause I can't go there, 'cause I don't have two parents—*get* it? I've only got Mom, and she *hates* trips. We tried that a couple times and we were *all* miserable. And I don't want to see the ocean with you any more than I wanted to see Old Faithful with Old Faithless.

So I didn't do that, and I'm not doing this—and I'm not going one more foot unless *I—drive*!

Monkey Man: (*After a beat.*) I had so much more to show you.

Bitch: Maybe we need a new tour guide.

Monkey Man: Do you think your brother's ever going to speak to me again?

Bitch: No.

Monkey Man: I know he's not speaking now, but he's only fourteen. He's got so much more growing up to—

Bitch: He cut up every picture of you in the house. They were all in this box, and Mom went to throw them away, and when she opened it, it was all just confetti. (*After a beat.*) Once he bought a book of yours.

Monkey Man: He did?

Bitch: And peed on it. When it dried out, he burned it.

Monkey Man: I should've adopted you guys; then I'd have some rights. Visitation.

Bitch: And you call me insane.

Monkey Man: That's not insane, that's . . . That's not insane.

Bitch: What were you thinking?

Monkey Man: What?

Bitch: When you were with . . . When you were with other women.

Monkey Man: I was not with that many other women. I was with three.

Bitch: All at once?

Monkey Man: Three women in eight years. Not exactly Don Juan material.

Bitch: Model of restraint. So? What were you thinking?

Monkey Man: It was complicated.

Bitch: Right.

Monkey Man: I'm not even sure I could— Why do you want to know?

Bitch: Thought as long as you took the trouble to bring me to Dickville, you must want to talk about it.

Monkey Man: There's a lot I need you to understand.

Bitch: Mom gave me the names, dates, places. We just have no idea what you were thinking.

MONKEY MAN: There was an interviewer on a book tour. Tulsa. I didn't know they had bookstores. They had a radio station, though, and she interviewed me and was . . . taken with my work. A lot of women are taken with it. The styles, the themes, whatever. They seem to think I capture something about them—

BITCH: Right.

MONKEY MAN: They proposition me. They do. Lonely, untouched . . . *under*touched . . . Glad to read a serious voice writing about other lonely untouched—

BITCH: You are such a sleaze—

MONKEY MAN: It's serious literature. I win prizes. (*A beat.*) I always said no. Even before I was with your mother. They were too vulnerable. My writing brought out these . . . I don't know, spiritual expectations in them. I didn't feel sufficient. It was like—

BITCH: (*Indicating the smokestack.*) Like your spiritual schlong would have to be as big as that?

MONKEY MAN: You really are a poet.

BITCH: So why'd you suddenly say yes?

MONKEY MAN: I don't know.

BITCH: Yes, you do.

MONKEY MAN: It was a few years into the marriage. Things with your mother had calmed down, so to speak, in the sex department—on their way to what ultimately would be a dead calm. It just made her uncomfortable. She'd never say why, she wouldn't discuss it. . . . We were both too polite, or terrified or—You really want to hear about this? (*As she stares at him.*) It got so she didn't want anything . . . unusual in our relations. There was less foreplay, less—

BITCH: Oral sex?

MONKEY MAN: Among other things.

BITCH: So the woman in Tulsa blew you?

MONKEY MAN: Among other things. Do we really have to—?

BITCH: And what was Mom? Missionary? Lights out?

MONKEY MAN: Aren't you supposed to be saying "too much information" about now?

Bitch: Knowledge is power.

Monkey Man: I think the real reason—what I was thinking, as you say—
was that I was becoming very afraid your mother would be the last
woman I'd ever make love to. So I slept with this other woman—once, to
take the pressure off. It wasn't because I loved your mother any less. (*As*
Bitch *laughs at him.*) I loved her. I did.

Bitch: So you slept with two more women?

Monkey Man: Much later. You'd been doing all that therapy, bouncing off
walls at five-hundred-dollar-a-day clinics, and she was utterly distracted
by what was going on—

Bitch: So you thought you'd help out by looking up an old girlfriend—

Monkey Man: To talk. Just to talk. And she was an old colleague, not a
girlfriend. We never actually dated. (*Going on, with a sigh.*) I was in L.A. for
a conference. I looked her up. That was all. I just looked her up and—

Bitch: Did her.

Monkey Man: We were at funny places in our lives.

Bitch: You didn't leave her bedroom for a week. Mom was very grateful for
the details, by the way.

Monkey Man: That wasn't my idea. She demanded specifics. She said she
couldn't heal otherwise, or some shit.

Bitch: God, you're gullible.

Monkey Man: It's my special brand of charm, okay?

Bitch: And the last one?

Monkey Man: That was to get out of the marriage. I didn't know it then,
but . . . It was so I could tell her and . . . make her ask for a divorce.

Bitch: Why?

Monkey Man: 'Cause I couldn't ask for one. I felt too guilty, too
debilitated—

Bitch: Too chickenshit. (*After a beat.*) Receptionist. Nice going.

Monkey Man: They call them associates at the publishing house. She had a
variety of duties.

Bitch: Did you love her?

Monkey Man: 'Course not.

BITCH: Did you even like her?

MONKEY MAN: Not much.

BITCH: If you and Mom were having problems, why didn't you talk about it?

MONKEY MAN: I don't know. We told ourselves we weren't.

BITCH: You ever fight?

MONKEY MAN: No.

BITCH: Not even once? Didn't you want your marriage to get better?

MONKEY MAN: I didn't think it could. I didn't think . . . it deserved to.

BITCH: I got better. You never gave up on me.

MONKEY MAN: You're a writer. You always had that, no matter how crazy you got. It made me believe in you.

BITCH: And Mom?

MONKEY MAN: I remember when I told her about my affairs. I had the irrational idea that somehow she could hear about them and understand that I wasn't in love with these women. I was just so happy that two people could be in bed enjoying themselves, and there didn't have to be these enormous steamer trunks of baggage. That's what I wanted for us. I wanted that to be us. But I could never get it, because—

BITCH: She was abused.

MONKEY MAN: Yes. When she was little, by a relative—she *thinks*.

BITCH: Just like I was, by—

MONKEY MAN: (*With sudden violence.*) I know! You think I don't know!? Jesus Christ, it's all I *hear*! You, your mom—for all I know, *her* mom. Maybe it goes back ten generations; what the hell's the *difference*?! Your mother had a responsibility at *some point* to grow the fuck up and learn how to be a wife to me! I have a life, too—and I will not let *anyone* dictate that I get no sex, no real intimacy with a partner 'til the day I fucking die! So I had affairs. I didn't have a million of 'em, but I had my share, and I am grateful for every one! Women deserve to be cheated on, 'cause they cheat men every day—every *fucking day*! (*After a silence.*) I didn't mean that.

BITCH: Yes, you did.

MONKEY MAN: Bottom line is, I couldn't handle it. Life as a never-ending tragedy controlled by some . . . *event* . . . that occurred years before I ever showed up. I don't know who could face that. I couldn't; I cheated.

BITCH: You were a coward.

MONKEY MAN: I was *not* a coward, I was— (*Stopping, under her intense gaze.*) I was— (*Hesitating again.*) No one could expect me to . . . (*Another beat, as she stares at him.*) I was a coward.

BITCH: That's why you're divorced.

MONKEY MAN: Yes.

BITCH: That's why Mom doesn't ever want to speak to you.

MONKEY MAN: Yes.

BITCH: That's why this is your last trip with me. Ever.

(*He looks at her. She stares steadily back at him.*)

We're going back now. My way. (*Holding out her hand.*) Give me the keys.

Inana
by Michele Lowe

CHARACTERS: **YASIN**, an Iraqi, chief of the Mosul Museum; **SHALI**, his Iraqi wife by arrangement

PLACE: A hotel room in London

CIRCUMSTANCE: Yasin flees Iraq with suitcases full of antiquities in order to protect them from Western invaders.

(**YASIN** *enters the hotel room.* **SHALI** *is waiting for him.*)

YASIN: Did anyone ring?

SHALI: No, no one.

YASIN: Were you here the whole time?

SHALI: Yes, Yasin, I was alone for twelve minutes.

YASIN: And nobody rang?

SHALI: Did you hear that, Yasin? I was alone!

YASIN: I'm sorry to have left you so long.

SHALI: I'm sorry your friend died.

YASIN: He was creating a library in Tehran. He'd been able to get sixteen thousand books out before the fire. They said he knew his time was coming, so he'd doubled and tripled his efforts.

SHALI: There were books in the suitcase?

YASIN: The first Arabic translation of Isaiah with illuminated pages, six books of drawings that date before the Ottoman Empire, twelve books by Wamidh Mohammed, an alphabet illustrated by the painter Omar Kirtani—all one of a kind books found nowhere else. Not even in the British Museum.

(*Pause.*)

What if the British have changed their minds? What if they don't want to meet with me?

SHALI: Why wouldn't they?

YASIN: I am nothing compared to the people who work there. I have neither the experience nor the degrees.

SHALI: You have worked in Babylon and Nineveh. You're the chief of the second largest museum—

YASIN: These people have traveled all over the world.

SHALI: But you've lived and worked in the cradle of civilization. Can they say that?

YASIN: There's another department of Near East studies at the Victoria and Albert Museum. Perhaps tomorrow I could call over there.

SHALI: Why do you need to see another?

YASIN: There are probably teaching posts where I could be useful.

SHALI: You mean work? Here?

YASIN: The meeting tomorrow was about—

SHALI: But if you really don't believe the British Museum will call, there's no reason to stay. You don't need to find another—

YASIN: Shali.

SHALI: We can leave tomorrow.

YASIN: Shali, you must know.

SHALI: I don't know anything except that I'm looking forward to going home.

YASIN: We are home.

(*Silence.*)

SHALI: I'll go without you. I'll leave tomorrow.

YASIN: Don't go.

SHALI: Where's my ticket? My return ticket.

(*He doesn't respond.*)

Please tell me where it is. I beg you.

YASIN: I can't.

SHALI: I just want to see it. I won't touch it.

YASIN: I'm sorry.

SHALI: I beg you, please.

YASIN: There is no return ticket.

(*Silence.*)

SHALI: No one knows where I am.

Yasin: Your father knows.

(*Silence.*)

Shali: I'm sure he didn't want me to go.

Yasin: He understood that you're my wife now.

(*She suddenly panics.*)

Shali: I have to go home.

Yasin: Shali—

Shali: I need to go home now.

(*She wildly throws clothes in suitcases.*)

Yasin: We are staying here.

Shali: I'm not staying in this dirty hotel room with filthy plates and disgusting tea and people in the airport that stare at me. I demand to go home. I demand that you take me there. NOW!

Yasin: I can't help you, I'm sorry.

Shali: My sister Mena—I didn't finish—I promised her I wouldn't leave until she'd learned everything. She doesn't know it all. She has to learn. She has to LEARN. SHE HAS TO LEARN!

(*He embraces her and then steps back to look at her.*)

Why did you—?

Yasin: What is that in your—?

Shali: You can't run at me like that.

Yasin: I'm sorry.

Shali: Certain things still need to be explained.

Yasin: What is that?

Shali: What is it I have there? Something hard, where it should be soft? Something empty where it should be full? You're asking about my left arm or what should be my left arm. Would you like to see it?

Yasin: I don't—

Shali: Shall I take off the coat now?

Yasin: Did I—?

Shali: You haven't done anything. Do you want me to remove my coat, yes or no?

YASIN: Yes.

(*She takes off her coat. Her left arm is missing below the shoulder. She wears a prosthetic device inside her white satin glove.*)

SHALI: So you understand why we have to go back. The rest of me is still there in the hospital outside of Samarra. In the refrigerators. We have to go.

YASIN: They said that to protect you.

SHALI: No, it's true. My father told me—

YASIN: Your father created the lie.

SHALI: His friend worked there. He showed me pictures.

YASIN: He lied to comfort you.

SHALI: I think you're the liar.

YASIN: I swear to you, there is no hospital.

SHALI: Liar!

YASIN: Shali my love—

SHALI: LIAR! You just want to keep me here! For what?

YASIN: To be my wife!

SHALI: How can I be your wife if I only have one arm?

YASIN: You could have no arms and be my wife!

(*Silence.*)

SHALI: I saw it in my father's workroom. It was for you, wasn't it? We hadn't seen my father for weeks. My brother said it would be his greatest achievement. I peeked inside once in the middle of the night. The light was out and I had my . . . I had my flashlight with me. I saw her by the light of the little flashlight I brought. I would look inside his work room late at night. It was the only way I could see what he was doing and feel some connection to him still. There was a statue of a woman without an arm. Was it Inana?

YASIN: It was.

SHALI: So you bought two statues. You were better off keeping the stone one. She's worth more.

YASIN: Not to me.

SHALI: You don't seem like the kind of man who would traffic in forgeries.

YASIN: You don't seem like the kind of woman who'd believe in imaginary hospitals.

SHALI: What ten-year-old girl calls her father a liar? I wanted to believe it as much for him as for me. I wanted to be such a good girl. Shali. There were two of me. The one before and the one after. I always wanted to be the other Shali. We all yearn for the other self, the one that is connected somehow to our childhood and then it's pried from our memory by time until finally we are forced to let it go. I didn't realize it was so until I stood here with you. I don't want her back now. Really, I don't. You are the first person in my life to tell me the truth.

(*Pause.*)

I'm hungry.

(*He rummages through his suitcase and pulls out a bag of dates. She finds another orange in her bag.*)

YASIN: I can never return to Mosul. There are things I've done.

SHALI: (*Teasing him.*) Evil things?

YASIN: Yes, very evil.

SHALI: Oooh hooo.

YASIN: But very necessary.

SHALI: Will you tell me what you did?

YASIN: I've sworn an oath not to tell.

SHALI: I will swear the same. Who else knows the secret?

YASIN: No one.

SHALI: (*Delighted.*) No one! Then it would just be us who knew?

YASIN: No one else.

SHALI: I swear if you tell me, I'll never tell another soul the evil thing you did, no matter what.

YASIN: (*Teasing her.*) Even if you are captured?

SHALI: Yes.

YASIN: And even if you are—

(*He stops short.*)

SHALI: And tortured, yes.

YASIN: I'm sorry.

SHALI: I wasn't tortured. They just cut it off. I don't remember everything
that happened. Someone told me a man held me down. I had been
walking on the street with my father. We had gone to visit his cousin who
lived in Basra. I remember there was an old garden set back from the
street next to a house, and inside the garden was a date tree. I was hungry
and I wanted something to eat. I took the date and suddenly there was a
man standing next to me screaming at me. He demanded I give it to him
and I ate it instead. It was the most sweetly wonderful thing I had ever
tasted. I remember my father was laughing, so I reached for another one.
The man grabbed me by the arm and dragged me into the house, this
honey-colored palace. There were women looking at me from one of the
balconies. I don't remember the room. Even my father couldn't protect
me. Even my father, who was such a big man, a large man, could not stop
them. I was—

(*The phone rings.*)

Yasin?

YASIN: Finish your thought.

SHALI: *The phone.*

(*The phone rings again.*)

YASIN: You were going to say that even at the age of ten, you were too beautiful.

SHALI: Yasin, answer the phone.

YASIN: Shali, there's something I need to tell you.

SHALI: But it could be them.

(*The phone rings again.*)

YASIN: Listen to me—

SHALI: Yasin—

(*The phone is silent.*)

YASIN: I did not send the original statue to Baghdad.

SHALI: No, I didn't think so.

(**YASIN** *picks up one of the suitcases as the hotel room transforms.* **YASIN** *and* **SHALI**
are in the desert near Nineveh, Iraq. There is a moon in the night sky.)

YASIN: I am a very bad liar.

SHALI: It's a quality to be admired in a man.

YASIN: I sent them your father's Inana, the copy.

Shali: But they will think it's the original.

Yasin: Yes.

Shali: My husband is a clever man.

(*Lights fade up on two statues of Inana, the copy and the original.*)

Yasin: The Temple of Ishtar is in Nineveh, in the middle of the widest plain. In 1853, Hamza Rassam found Inana there. Since then it's been excavated and studied many times for many years. Hundreds of antiquities have been found and spread throughout Iraq. And some black market thieves have taken them beyond. There's an underground vault in the temple twenty feet below ground. I discovered it years ago.

Shali: You took her home.

Yasin: Yes.

Shali: Where Ralwa could watch over her.

Yasin: Ralwa and Hama and Abdel-Hakim and Yusuf and the rest of the ghosts, there are hundreds of thousands of them. Let the living find her there in calmer generations.

Shali: There will never be calmer generations. But she will be found again.

Yasin: God willing.

(*Lights down on the two statues.* **Shali** *regards the heavens.*)

Shali: "A moon in a light blue sky."

Yasin: We are inside the poem.

Shali: Or the poem is inside us. (*Off the suitcase.*) What did you bring?

Yasin: The museum.

Shali: In your suitcase?

Yasin: When objects go missing during war, many are found, but there's no evidence where they rightfully belong. Databases get destroyed. Computers go missing. If something ends up on a desk in Japan and we try to claim it belongs to us, we need proof. Inside is the proof.

(*He opens the suitcase and shows her thousands of index cards stacked inside. He shuffles through a stack and hands her three.*)

Shali: (*Reading.*) "Small winged lion from the palace of Sargon the Second." "Large clay pottery oven dated 4000 BC." "Three cuneiform tablets from Khorsabad."

YASIN: There's also a copy of each on Mohammed's desk.

SHALI: "This marriage, this silence full mixed with spirit."

(*He closes the suitcase. They are bathed in the light of the moon.*)

YASIN: You are standing here and I still don't know who you are, yet I feel closer to you than to anyone or anything I have ever known.

SHALI: I am ninety-two reds, thirty yellows, fifty-two oranges, and forty blues. Yasin, my love, I am yours.

On the Spectrum
by Ken LaZebnik

CHARACTERS: MAC, has Asperger's syndrome—passing as "typical" after years of mainstreaming and therapy; IRIS, is autistic (both early 20s)

PLACE: Iris' apartment

CIRCUMSTANCE: Mac and Iris are meeting in person for the first time after negotiating a business deal online. Iris converses by typing on an iPad with specialized VOCA software.

(*A beat.* MAC *looks around the room.*)

MAC: Do you have a fear of laundry?

IRIS: (*Heather.*) Yeah. Big time.

MAC: Me too. There are so many choices of detergents, it really bothers me. Liquid or powder, and then there's Cheer or Gain or Tide and there's all the different kinds of Tide, like Tide Free and Tide Total Care, and then there's the whole issue of fabric softeners.

IRIS: (*Heather.*) I'm very disturbed by fabric softeners.

MAC: Yeah. Me too.

IRIS: (*Heather.*) Laundry is like . . . paralyzing.

MAC: We get paralyzed with fear. (*He looks at* IRIS. *She looks at him for a moment, then averts her gaze.*) Fear about possibilities.

IRIS: (*Heather.*) Yes.

MAC: All those possibilities. (*She looks up at him. Now he looks away. A long silence.* MAC *gestures to a stack of newspapers and books.*) You read a lot.

IRIS: (*Heather.*) Yes. Mostly online.

MAC: I like books. I go to the library—the Jefferson Market Branch on Sixth Avenue and Christopher—

IRIS: (*Heather.*) I love that branch!

MAC: You've been there?

IRIS: (*Heather.*) I look at it online. We have to have this building in the Otherworld! It was modeled after Mad King Ludwig II of Bavaria's castle called Neuschwanstein.

Mac: You know more about it than I do, and I've actually been there.

Iris: (*Heather.*) That's the beauty of the Internet. I don't have to get outside this room to know the world. I have friends online all over the world. I always have someone to chat with. When it's the middle of the night here, it's morning in Europe, or when it's early morning here, it's nighttime in Australia. There's always someone online.

Mac: Sounds like you chat a lot.

Iris: (*Heather.*) It's not just chat. I'm an online activist. When celebrities pop up online saying how important it is to cure autism, I start blogging and sending out messages. You know, it's like these people want to take part of my brain—the part that makes me what I am—and cut it out. Cure autism. It's like saying, "Cure your ability to focus deeply," or "Cure your high IQ."

Mac: You have a high IQ?

Iris: (*Heather.*) I'm sure I do. I don't know.

Mac: Don't you?

Iris: (*Heather.*) What really gets to me is they present themselves as suffering so deeply—the things we go through with our children, these children who are tragically maimed. Then they get into all the cures: Chelation, no vaccines, gluten-free diets—

Mac: I was gluten-free for a while. It didn't really seem to do anything.

Iris: (*Heather.*) My mom could never get it together to do gluten-free. She'd read about it and she'd throw out all the bread, but then she'd discover gluten in some weird place she hadn't realized, like Payday bars, and she'd say the hell with it.

Mac: Do you like Payday bars?

Iris: (*Heather.*) I love Paydays! They're the best.

Mac: Me too!

(*A beat.*)

Iris: (*Heather.*) It's a difference, not a disability. The Internet proved that. All of a sudden these people that everyone thought couldn't talk or were retarded were communicating online and their brains were suddenly revealed. It's like someone in the sixteenth century who had horrible eyesight was given a pair of glasses.

Mac: What if that person were completely blind?

Iris: (*Heather.*) Then I wouldn't give them glasses.

Mac: So a blind person has a disability.

Iris: (*Heather.*) I'd say that's the definition of a disability: a physical condition that can't be changed.

Mac: Therefore a blind person cannot do everything that a sighted person can—for instance, drive a car.

Iris: (*Heather.*) What are you, a lawyer?

Mac: I'm studying—

Iris: (*Heather.*) That was a joke.

Mac: But the point is there are autistic kids who should not drive cars. They are so heavily affected that they can't respond to changes in traffic and it would be unsafe for them to drive a car, and it's because of a physical condition, neural impulses in their brain. I would call that a disability.

Iris: (*Heather.*) That's such an extreme example—

Mac: But it exists.

Iris: (*Heather.*) My point is that all this money raised to "find a cure" could be better spent teaching heavily affected kids how to cope in society. A society that for the most part sucks.

Mac: The glass is always full.

Iris: (*Heather.*) What does that mean?

Mac: My mother has this theory. You know how they say some people see the glass as half full and some people see it as half empty? The optimists see it as half full—

Iris: (*Heather.*) And the realists see it as half empty.

Mac: My mother's theory is that it's always full. She'll draw this picture of a glass with a line in the middle and say: Fifty percent water, fifty percent oxygen, equals always full.

(*A pause.*)

Iris: (*Heather.*) She sounds nice.

Mac: Yeah. She is. She really is.

Iris: (*Heather.*) My mother . . . I think she's sort of autistic, too. I mean, she was never diagnosed, but she gets obsessed with things. Like me.

Mac: A lot of moms do that. Get obsessed. About all sorts of stuff.

(*A beat.*)

Iris: (*Heather.*) Do you like M&M's?

Mac: Yes.

Iris: (*Heather.*) I love M&M's. (***Pulling out two packages of M&M's from the clutter.***) How do you eat them?

Mac: I eat the brown ones first. That's my only M&M rule.

Iris: (*Heather.*) I sort them by color to start with— (***Sorting out the M&M's.***) Here's my yellows, my greens, my reds—then I eat each color in alphabetical sequence. Beginning with green. When they introduced blue M&M's it really threw me.

Mac: Yeah. I hate it when they experiment like that. (***A beat as they sort and eat their M&M's.***) Do you have my check?

Iris: (*Heather.*) Oh. Yes. Well.

Mac: Is there a problem?

Iris: (*Heather.*) My mother actually has the checkbook because I guess technically the money is in her name, in her account, and she hasn't been around this week, so I don't have it.

Mac: That sucks.

Iris: (*Heather.*) Yeah. Sorry.

Mac: (*Agitated.*) I mean, wow.

Iris: (*Heather.*) I'm really sorry.

Mac: If you knew that, why didn't you tell me?

Iris: (*Heather.*) If I told you, you wouldn't have come here.

Mac: Exactly. I would have saved myself a trip on the subway.

Iris: (*Heather.*) But then you wouldn't be here. (*A pause.*) Mac, Mac, Cormac the King . . . When I was a little girl I sat in my room and lined my dolls up in a straight row: Barbie, then Cassy, then Debbie, then Emily, then Flora—I lined them up alphabetically, and my mother tried play dates but they never quite worked out because other girls would move Flora in front of Debbie and I would get very mad. Then the other girl would get upset and never come back. (*A beat.*) So I grew up. In high school I was in special ed, and I guess they were nice but none of the boys were what I'd call desirable, and then I graduated and I had a transition coordinator who sucked and so I've taken online classes, and my father died and left me this apartment and I was happy to have a tower that was my own. That's what I call it—my stained-glass tower. A tower that is full of dark and colored light and it is all my own. And I have spent many hours in my lonely tower. I love my tower, but then the night falls and the dark comes and I am alone . . . very alone . . . and I think . . . Mac, Mac, I think . . . I have been waiting for someone to come. Someone who will . . . Mac, Mac . . . who will . . . hold me.

(*A pause.*)

(**MAC** *moves close to her. He closes the lid of her iPad.* **IRIS** *shudders and starts to rock.* **MAC** *sets down the iPad.* **IRIS** *rocks back and forth.* **MAC** *reaches his arms around her. She stops rocking. He holds her for a moment. Then she fiercely hugs him. They stand embraced.* **MAC** *pulls his head back.* **IRIS** *doesn't look at him.* **MAC** *lifts her chin with his hand. He leans in slowly and kisses her.* **MAC** *pulls out of the kiss and looks at her.* **IRIS**—*slowly, carefully—speaks. Her own speaking voice, in contrast to the voice we've previously heard in her online blog, is pressured.*)

You're finally here.

MAC: Here I am.

(*She places her head on his chest.*)

IRIS: I don't know how to kiss.

MAC: You were okay.

IRIS: I . . . have never kissed anyone.

MAC: Oh.

IRIS: You are my first kiss.

(**MAC** *lifts her face up toward him. He kisses her again.*)

MAC: Can you be softer?

IRIS: Okay.

(*They kiss again.*)

MAC: That's nice.

IRIS: Good. That felt very good.

(*She puts her head on his chest again. Then she leans up and kisses* **MAC.**)

IRIS: I have kissed you now.

MAC: I like your voice.

IRIS: It's not pretty.

MAC: That's okay.

IRIS: My lips . . . are not used to talking. Or kissing.

MAC: I like them.

(*They kiss again.* **IRIS** *pulls her head back.*)

IRIS: Do we have sex now?

MAC: No. I think we're supposed to make out some more first.

IRIS: Okay. And then we have sex?

MAC: I don't have a condom.

IRIS: That's a problem.

MAC: Yeah. I didn't think this would happen.

IRIS: Me neither. (*A pause.*) It was too much to hope.

MAC: If you had told me this was a possibility, I would have stopped at CVS and bought a condom. Although I'm not sure which kind to buy. There's a lot of choices in condoms. It's sort of like laundry detergent.

IRIS: Yeah. (*A pause.*) Have you ever bought a condom?

MAC: No.

IRIS: Next time . . . can you buy one?

MAC: I could go out and do that now.

IRIS: No. Don't leave me.

MAC: Okay.

IRIS: Never leave me. Could you just stay here?

MAC: Like—forever?

IRIS: Yes. We can live in our crystal palace forever.

(*She hugs* **MAC** *to her, fiercely. She kisses him.* **MAC** *slowly breaks from the kiss.*)

MAC: At some point I have to go home. (*A pause.*) My pajamas are there. And my LSAT books. And my inhaler, and a lot of things. My mother. (*Pause.*) My mother is making dinner.

IRIS: Tell her you're staying in the Otherworld forever.

(*She hugs him again.*)

So this is happy.

(**MAC** *looks down and then slowly smiles.*)

Our Enemies:
Lively Scenes of Love and Combat
by Yussef El Guindi

CHARACTERS: **MOHSEN**, a former school teacher turned writer, Arabic; **NOOR**, a writer and an Egyptian American

PLACE: A publisher's apartment

CIRCUMSTANCE: Both writers have been courted by the publisher to write stories from an Arab's perspective.

MOHSEN: The grown-ups have gone. (*In Arabic.*) Would you like that drink now?

(*Holds out tray to her.*)

NOOR: (*Shaking her head; in Arabic.*) No thanks.

MOHSEN: How's your Arabic?

NOOR: Passable—I don't have much chance to practice it. I mostly remember the curse words of course.

MOHSEN: Ah, well; I will have to test you on those. (*He smiles.*) You sure you don't want that drink?

NOOR: I'll stick to this.

MOHSEN: I make a great martini.

NOOR: Really?

MOHSEN: I do. . . . You laugh.

NOOR: No—I smiled.

MOHSEN: Why?

NOOR: No reason. . . . I'm in a gathering of people I don't know. One smiles—isn't that like the default expression?

MOHSEN: Why don't I make a martini for two, and then if you change your mind, you can try it. It isn't a religious thing for you, is it?

(**MOHSEN** *goes to the drink cart, where he puts down the tray, if he hasn't already, and proceeds to make a martini.*)

Don't be embarrassed if it is.

Noor: Why would I be embarrassed? Because I'm, what—in the company of—sophisticates?

Mohsen: I can usually tell who can and can't hold their drink. I imagine it tends to tip you.

Noor: No; I just tend to get brutally honest.

Mohsen: Oh, well; then I will insist you try this.

Noor: I'm honest enough as it is. Drink just turns all that honesty into weaponry.

(*Quiet laugh from* **Mohsen.**)

You're the one laughing now.

Mohsen: In the company of strong, attractive women—especially Arab women—laughter tends to be my default reaction. (*Slight beat.*) I'm sorry Olivia never told you I would be here.

Noor: Why would that be a problem?

Mohsen: She thinks my presence will grease the wheels, so to speak.

Noor: For what?

Mohsen: To turn your talents to the subject they'd like you to write about.

Noor: Which is—?

Mohsen: You. Charming you.

Noor: Why they think I'd make an interesting subject, I don't know. They barely know me.

Mohsen: It's what you represent to them.

Noor: What they choose to project on me.

Mohsen: It comes down to the same thing, doesn't it?

Noor: Which is bogus. Either way.

Mohsen: That depends on your perspective. If you see it from your own limited biography, then yes, it might feel like the putting on of a false . . . a falsehood. Then again, if you step out of your own—one's own obsessive navel gazing and see your place in the larger picture, you might see how your voice carries the weight of a lot more people than your own little world. And might even feel obliged, and privileged, if you have talent, to be in that position. And to honor it.

Noor: How did Olivia figure your presence would grease the wheels? Not that—I'm having a pleasant enough time.

MOHSEN: Olivia was hoping we'd find common ground. You know how people are paired up at parties. I think she was hoping I could be a mentor of sorts.

(*Inadvertent, quiet laugh from* **NOOR**.)

We really must stop laughing at each other. One of us might take offense.

NOOR: I mean none.

MOHSEN: Are you sure?

NOOR: Trust me: I become quite expressive when I want to be offensive. You'll know.

MOHSEN: Again, I am tempted to see that. . . . I'll bet you light up when you are. And seeing how attractive you are already, being offensive must make you a real knockout.

(**NOOR** *laughs.*)

You like that one?

NOOR: (*She shrugs.*) I—

MOHSEN: I can't wait to see your book-jacket photo. I hope they'll capture this: sardonic, intelligent, and a little arrogant. Do you have a boyfriend?

NOOR: Er . . .

MOHSEN: Because I would love to sleep with you.

(**NOOR** *isn't sure she heard him correctly.*)

I hope you don't mind my honesty, but I sense you can handle it. Yes?

(**NOOR** *seems to teeter between laughing and wanting to say something unpleasant.*)

I'm sorry—I take it back. I thought you were . . . sophisticated enough to take the comment at arm's length and see it as a compliment. Please, let's rewind. I'm a . . . I'm a little nervous myself. And when I am, I—tend to put the cart before the horse and then wonder why I—(*A laugh.*)—I have to choose such poor analogies to excuse my bad behavior. Not that I have a particular cart or horse in mind.

NOOR: I do have a boyfriend.

MOHSEN: Oh; well, thank God. The pressure is off. Isn't that silly? I hope we can speak frankly—from one artist to another, in the pursuit of—being frank, always. Because you know, I do feel kind of obliged to make a move. Isn't that strange? As if my sense of being a man is somehow attached to doing that. And not doing so would bring it into doubt because you were expecting it? We are so peculiar as people, no?

Noor: Maybe you're just struggling with your masculinity.

Mohsen: You think so?

Noor: And not acknowledging certain urges you should. Which makes you say dumb things to compensate.

Mohsen: Ah. Well, that is certainly a theory.

Noor: I think I'll go help Olivia and Russel.

Mohsen: Poor Olivia doesn't realize that you hate my guts. And that I might actually put you off writing for them.

(**Noor** *stops, looks at him. If he hasn't gotten to shaking the martini mix he's made, perhaps he does so now.*)

Noor: That's quite the assumption. But if you assume that, then your coming on to me was—what?

Mohsen: You're very attractive, and I am drawn to you. But that is more from a sense of feeling you dislike me intensely, which makes me want to say contrary things to—be contrary. Which is very childish, I admit.

Noor: Just so you don't waste any more energy: you're not on my radar either as an author, or as a man, for me to feel anything.

Mohsen: I take it you fall in the camp of those who think what I've written has been deeply harmful to some Arab or Muslim cause.

Noor: I haven't even read your book.

Mohsen: Oh come on. You've been gnashing your teeth since you walked in and saw me.

Noor: Your vanity is amazing.

Mohsen: You know, I can actually picture you throwing my book across the room; followed by curses for my traitorous ways, for airing all that dirty laundry about us. Why couldn't he have kept his big mouth shut, yes?

Noor: You even draw strength from your critics. It's all publicity for you, none of it lands.

Mohsen: All of it lands. I've just realized there's no point in being big about it and letting it go. Otherwise people will walk all over you.

Noor: Look: (*A laugh.*) I really want to save you time here. I have no idea what being a bestseller must do to your ego, how it must warp it till it becomes a three-ring circus—(*Another laugh.*) with you as your own audience, but, er, maybe a reality check might be helpful? Because—who are you again?—if it wasn't for some news outlets who use your book for their twisted editorials, you'd be—who? An elementary school teacher with a few anecdotes. Which I have no problem with; I don't get as worked up as others do by what you say, I don't really care; you're nobody in my world.

MOHSEN: Right, you're more interested in fluff, from what I hear. Bodice rippers and sweaty torsos. That way you can stay at a safe distance and not risk anything, and lob rocks at those who actually care and try to do something good for us, here and abroad.

NOOR: Confirming their worst beliefs about Muslims and Arabs, that's doing something good?

MOHSEN: I haven't done that at all.

NOOR: Oh, really, is that what you think?

MOHSEN: (*Overlapping last couple of words.*) But in general, yes, if the bones have been set wrong, you break them and reset. But it seems you are familiar with my book after all.

NOOR: I read the book jacket. So you're the bone breaker now? Gee, our community is in really good hands.

MOHSEN: But really, secretly, you've read it, yes? You couldn't resist.

(**NOOR** *heads for the kitchen but is again stopped by the next comment.*)

You must really resent my success. The "mukwagee's" son who makes it big in America. And you with all your advantages still struggling. If we were still in Cairo, you'd be handing your clothes for my mother to iron. A job she had to take up when my Iraqi father died. And I, I would be invisible to you. A nobody carrying your clothes, and here I am in America beating you at your game. Does that irritate you? Make you resent everything that comes out of my mouth because I have a platform to speak? And here you are, someone who will forever be on the verge of success because you will never have the guts to get your hands dirty and expose those things that need to be dealt with.

NOOR: Mohsen: If that's the story you need to run in your head to make you feel better for exaggerating and outright lying, that's okay; but just don't drag the rest of us into your delusions.

MOHSEN: And what's yours? That everything's okay? And those who've been privileged with the best education can just lie back and let the rot continue? My God, you're such a reactionary.

Noor: Me?

Mohsen: Oh, that's right, you're the progressive.

Noor: What?

Mohsen: You bleed for all the right causes and turn up at the right rallies to wave your banners. But get asked to do something that might actually change things and you're not there. A man locked up in prison for speaking his mind doesn't want you to bleed for him; he wants you to *break down the door*. He wants you to stop feeling sanctimonious and actually do something to *free* him. He wants *everything* changed.

Noor: You mean, let's remake everything into the image of this country? Like you've done to yourself, and made yourself into a fool? I mean, look at you, with this fake accent you've adopted; and manners and idiotic martinis and airs.

Mohsen: You really can't stand that I've made something of myself.

Noor: You're a *fake*. There should be a warning label on you: fake Arab, don't believe anything he says.

Mohsen: Better a fake Arab who's ready to lay his life down and bring about change than a spoilt bitch who has her head buried up her ass. Why they're wasting their time on you, I've no idea. Your willful ignoring of facts is *killing* people. Which makes you a goodwill ambassador to savagery. Yes, *you* are; you have blood on your hands and someone needs to call you on it. How dare you even think to criticize me, you, whose denial of everything that's wrong with us is killing us as much as the lunatic who straps on bombs and slaughters people.

Pilgrims Musa and Sheri
in the New World
by Yussef El Guindi

CHARACTERS: SHERI, an American waitress; MUSA, a cab driver from Egypt

PLACE: Musa's apartment in NYC

CIRCUMSTANCE: The morning after hooking up. Musa is engaged to be married to another woman.

(SHERI *emerges from the bathroom, dressing. She goes to get her handbag, ready to leave. She looks at* MUSA *asleep in the bed. Beat. She makes a decision: she sits on the bed and wakes him up.*)

SHERI: Musa. . . . Musa, wake up. (*Shakes him.*) *Musa.* (*He wakes.*) Sorry. It looked like a nice dream.

MUSA: (*Getting his bearings.*) Hello.

SHERI: I need to ask you something.

MUSA: Now it is nice dream.

(*He tries to pull her towards him.*)

SHERI: (*Resists.*) I need to ask something.

MUSA: After you come back to bed.

SHERI: It's important.

MUSA: More important than love?

SHERI: Well, that's what I need to talk to you about.

MUSA: What? Something the matter with the way I—

SHERI: What?—No.

MUSA: (*Continuing.*) Make love?

SHERI: No, no.

MUSA: I do something wrong?

SHERI: You were fine.

MUSA: Fine?

SHERI: You were great.

MUSA: You not just saying that?

Sheri: You were fantastic.

Musa: I can change.

Sheri: Two thumbs up.

Musa: Because you are . . . never mind.

Sheri: What?

Musa: You—never mind.

Sheri: *What?*

Musa: You first American woman for me.

Sheri: Oh. . . . *Really?* I thought maybe in your—job.

Musa: You could not tell?

Sheri: No. You give off this—been-around-the-block vibe.

Musa: Maybe because I drive a taxi?

Sheri: Not that kind of block.

Musa: I think maybe you used to more—skills. Men with more . . . experience. I shut up now.

Sheri: Good idea.

Musa: Let's do it again.

Sheri: I need to ask this. I know what I said before: "no strings, and let's just do it" and calling you a pussy, etc.

Musa: You say unkind things. Not nice to hear.

Sheri: (*Continuing.*) And I know I should just say, "I'll see you later," and either we do or we don't, but that's not me. In spite of what I said. Yes, I understand the stupid saying about no guarantees; God, I hate that saying. But you know, I just think in your thirties you've earned the right to speak your mind, because the bounce you had in your twenties when you could just move on when something sucked, that's gone. Now when something sucks it feels like a life choice.

Musa: You look lovely like this. No need for candles. You are the light in the room now.

(**Sheri** *goes and turns on the overhead light. She will stand directly under the bare light bulb.*)

Sheri: Okay. So this is me. Makeup gone. No nice lighting. I'm no model. Perhaps not even pretty.

MUSA: Very pretty.

SHERI: If you could hold off saying the right things until I ask my question.

MUSA: Ask, then come to bed.

SHERI: (*Takes a breath, then:*) Can you see yourself in a long-term relationship with me?

(*Slight beat; not understanding the question,* **MUSA** *is about to respond but is interrupted.*)

Forget everything I said before. Though I'm certainly not suggesting marriage and kids, so don't freak out. I certainly can't decide that after what'll probably be a one-night stand. But could you—*imagine that?* How can you answer that; of course you can't. I'm like the girl you banged in less time than it takes to make popcorn. I couldn't answer that, I mean, *who are you?* I don't know if I'd want *your* kid.

MUSA: You are asking what?

SHERI: (*Partly to herself.*) I'm doing it again. Unbelievable.

(*She starts to go.*)

MUSA: Ask me again so I understand.

SHERI: I'm a nut case. I should be locked up.

MUSA: Sheri, stop.

(**MUSA** *starts putting on his clothes.* **SHERI** *turns back from the door.*)

SHERI: You know what it is: it's my life. Not yours, mine. And at this point it's still too early for anything to suck with you. And I want to leave before that happens. Because you will disappoint me and I want to end this while I still think there's hope for us.

MUSA: Sheri, please, sit. I want to understand.

SHERI: How could you possibly understand when I don't even know what I'm talking about half the time.

MUSA: (*Leading her to a chair.*) What are you asking? Speak slowly so I follow.

(*Slight beat. She hears the sincerity in his voice, sees the concentration in his look.*)

SHERI: I—I saw something. When we were making love. I wasn't expecting it. A look. Your whole face was—lit up by it. And it wasn't a—it didn't just come and go. It came on and—like—stayed on. And you were lovely to look at then. I'm not talking about the way you moved. Though that was nice too. It's like I think I saw your . . . a little more of you than you might care to show normally. And you looked so—different then; and vulnerable. You can go through a whole relationship and not see that.

Musa: (*Slight beat.*) You are a very strange woman.

Sheri: You know what the scary thing is? I try not to let it all hang out when I first meet someone.

Musa: (*Trying to understand.*) You saw my . . . what?

Sheri: You could've just been hitting my G spot. I've seen stuff before.

Musa: What is G spot?

Sheri: I just wasn't expecting to like you this much.

Musa: You want to have serious relationship?

Sheri: Am I asking that? . . . Yes.

Musa: With me?

Sheri: You're the only one in the room.

Musa: I am nobody.

Sheri: What does that have to do with anything?

Musa: I have no money. Sometimes none at all.

Sheri: I'm not looking for an ATM machine. I do have a job.

Musa: Like boyfriend, girlfriend? Engagement?

Sheri: Oh God, no. Engagement? No. I don't know; no. Maybe.

Musa: Maybe?

Sheri: Probably not.

Musa: But you think of future?

Sheri: I should tell you I'm a little older than you, I think, if you haven't guessed already.

Musa: You—like me?

Sheri: I'm implying that, yes.

Musa: Because I think I like you too.

Sheri: Don't sound so enthusiastic.

Musa: I am. Enthusiastic. I like you very much.

Sheri: Not just for a one-night stand?

Musa: For many-night stand. Sheri—I like you a lot.

(*Slight beat.*)

SHERI: We don't have to rush things. We can just see where it goes.

MUSA: You and me.

SHERI: If it doesn't work out, it doesn't. No pressures.

MUSA: I am glad you come to my place.

SHERI: I wish I could be casual about things. My mother was like that. Then again she married five times and died with her mouth around a bottle.

(*He starts to kiss her. Interrupts him:*)

Oh. Skeletons in the closet. We should get those out of the way. My family's a disaster but you'll never see them, I don't. And I have a brother in prison but he's never coming out. But he did get his GED recently, which I think proves that in my family it's in our genes to try and do your best regardless. What about your skeletons? That I should know about.

MUSA: Now? Just you. You are my skeleton.

(*Slight beat.*)

I make joke about how thin you are.

SHERI: Musa? Small request. Don't screw this up right away. Not for a long time.

MUSA: (*Serious.*) I will not.

(*He leans in to kiss her, but is again interrupted.*)

SHERI: Your friend. *That's* what I dreamt about. (*She points to the calendar picture of the Ka'bah.*) Your friend. Dressed in white. I don't know what he looks like but in this dream he was like—definitely your roommate, and he was in—a boat. That sank. There was a boat with all these pilgrims. On its way to that place. But there were like too many people on it and it—it sank. And instead of bodies floating, there were—suitcases. Everywhere. Hundreds of suitcases, floating. All the belongings of these pilgrims. But it wasn't a sad dream. Because your friend was like talking, and he was kind of funny. Made me laugh in the dream.

MUSA: You see my friend dead?

SHERI: No. He was talking, so . . . he seemed fine. I'm sure he's okay.

MUSA: He take plane to Mecca. Not boat.

SHERI: Then I'm sure he's okay.

MUSA: He call me from airport yesterday.

Sheri: Then it was just a funny ol' dream. No accounting for them. (*Perhaps puts arms around his neck, or comes close to him.*) Must mean I'm already getting comfortable in your world—if I'm dreaming about stuff like that.

Musa: So . . . I was good in bed, huh?

Sheri: Don't get a big head about it. There's always room for improvement.

Musa: We start my improving lessons now.

(*He leans in to kiss her.*)

Pilgrims Musa and Sheri
in the New World
by Yussef El Guindi

CHARACTERS: **GAMILA**, an Egyptian American in tune with traditional Muslim faith and Musa's fiancée; **MUSA**, a cab driver from Egypt

PLACE: Musa's apartment in NYC

CIRCUMSTANCE: Gamila recently discovered Musa has been unfaithful during her visit to his parents.

GAMILA: Have you come to break up with me? (**MUSA** *doesn't respond.*) You have that look of someone who is about to say something that divides the world into before the thing was said and after the thing was said. That thing that you wish didn't have to be mentioned.

MUSA: *Ana . . .* (*Not knowing how to start.*) *Ana asaf.*

GAMILA: Oh, don't. Don't put me in this position and then apologize for putting me in it. God. Men can be such cowards.

MUSA: Gamila. Sit down, we talk.

(**GAMILA** *is perhaps shaking her head in disbelief.*)

GAMILA: This is so cheap. Feels so—

MUSA: (*In Arabic.*) Please, let us talk. (*Argukee, laazem nitkallem.*)

GAMILA: (*Continuing.*) Really. I feel like one of those women in your kitschy novels. (*Picks up a book.*) This silly way you've chosen to learn, instead of the classes I suggested. Really the wrong influences. It's why your family loves me. They think I'll keep you on the right path.

MUSA: (*In Arabic.*) Can we sit for a moment? (*Moomkin nu'ad shwaaya?*)

GAMILA: I can't do Arabic when I'm upset. Except I'm not going to get upset. What?

MUSA: We sit. We talk.

GAMILA: Have you come to break off the engagement?

MUSA: I want to tell you what's happened.

GAMILA: I don't want to understand what's happened. I don't want your side of the story. I don't want to sympathize with you and go oh you poor boy, falling into bed with another woman, and feeling so guilty about it. Let me pat you on the back and tell you it'll all be alright, I forgive you. It happens, betrayal. Just tell me something, was this the first time you did this while we were engaged? Or have you been with other women?

Musa: No. You think I sleep around?

Gamila: Don't act so indignant that I asked.

Musa: This is not something I think would happen. It was a mistake.

Gamila: A mistake? You're leaving her?

Musa: (*Hesitates.*) No. (*Slight beat.*) A mistake in the beginning. But then— we . . .

(*Slight beat.*)

Gamila: Oh. Well. That's an answer. *I* won't feel so bad for dumping you then. . . . I wasn't going to marry you after this anyway.

Musa: It would not be right if you did.

Gamila: Hard to make up with someone when there's a knife sticking in your chest. Just the physical mechanics of getting close when there's a metal object between you.

Musa: I'm sorry. . . . You find better man than me. A good man. A good Muslim. Someone you be proud of. Who live up to what you want. I fail in this. I know I do. I feel it now. With you. I am . . . I am always failing a little with you.

Gamila: What do you mean? I make you feel this?

Musa: No. You are too good a person to make me feel this. You find someone better. You are too nice, and—I am not.

Gamila: Musa: If this is the you're-too-good-for-me excuse, skip it. Don't back out of this by shoving me off with compliments. Did you ever, I mean ever really want me?

(**Musa** *looks at her, surprised by the question.*)

Really. I'd like to know. Please don't do the Middle Eastern thing and pour sugar and compliments to make the crap stink less. Did you? Ever find me attractive? Or were you just fulfilling some family obligation?

Musa: I walk in now and think you are more beautiful than before you left.

Gamila: Musa. Please.

Musa: This is what I think.

GAMILA: I've been traveling for fourteen hours. I've had two babies screaming on either side of me denying me even a little beauty sleep. Could you show me *some* respect by telling me how you really feel for once?

MUSA: I walk in and think you are more beautiful than before you leave.

(*She looks at him, noting his sincerity.*)

GAMILA: Is all this because we haven't had sex yet? (**MUSA** *reacts to the question.*) It's a legitimate question. Maybe you're a little giddy from going to bed with this woman. And aren't thinking with the tool God gave you to think with.

MUSA: *Argukee*, Gamila, please don't speak like this.

GAMILA: It happens. They say a chemical is released when a woman has sex that binds her with the person she just did it with. Maybe an equivalent happened with you. Especially if this was your first, or first since coming. I mean, she's very—fleshy.

MUSA: Gamila, I do not want to speak of this with you.

GAMILA: You can act like this but I can't speak of it? Really, tell me. Did she do something special that you think I can't do when we're married?

MUSA: *Argukee.*

GAMILA: (*Continuing.*) You put me on a pedestal too much, you really do, I think that's the problem. I do have a vagina underneath this, you know.

MUSA: Gamila!

GAMILA: Just so we're clear.

MUSA: Stop this, please.

GAMILA: Among my many attributes, I possess one. And a pair of these. (*Refers to her breasts.*) You should know that up front. One thing I like about our religion is that it's very frank about sex. Doesn't pussyfoot around that subject.

MUSA: None of this has anything to do with sex.

(**MUSA** *goes to a drawer, which might be one of those plastic file drawers, and takes out a shirt.* **GAMILA** *continues speaking during this.*)

GAMILA: I find that hard to believe.

MUSA: It does not.

GAMILA: I can see why you'd go to bed with her. If I was a guy, I might. She has a nice body. If you're into that type. That not-short-of-food look. And sexy underwear. (**Musa** *looks at her.*) Don't look so shocked. It was there on the floor when I walked in.

Musa: (*Exiting into the bathroom.*) I take you home after I dress. This is not—you do not need to speak like this.

(*He closes the bathroom door behind him.*)

Gamila: You're the one who started it.

(*She opens the bathroom door.*)

Too late to close the barn door on that pony.

(*He tries to close the door; she keeps the door open.*)

So what if I see you bare chested. There's nothing like a breakup to create an intimacy that was obviously lacking when we were engaged.

Musa: (*Appears at door, his shirt off.*) Gamila: You are tired. I will drive you home, let me change.

(*He tries to close the door, but again she won't let him. He retreats back into the bathroom a couple of lines into her next speech.*)

Gamila: What am I protecting? My reputation as a good Muslim girl? I already feel like I've been dragged into bed with the two of you; and I've never even kissed you before. It's really unfair to pay the price of this humiliation without ever having experienced the pleasure.

(*He reenters buttoning up his shirt.*)

Musa: (*Irritated.*) You should not have come without calling.

Gamila: You're putting this on *me* now?

Musa: You must call first, even Americans do this.

Gamila: And you never even invited me up? I stick my head in once, but she gets to decorate? *Her* little touches, I'm not given the chance? Not even a photograph of me? Are these hers? These stupid flowers?

(*She picks up the flowers and throws them out the window.*)

Musa: Gamila!

Gamila: And this can't be your vase. It's too crappy.

(*She picks up the vase, ready to throw it out too. **Musa** stops her, grabbing back the vase.*)

Musa: *Inti magnoona?*

Gamila: And this horrible-looking bed cover, that has to be her taste.

(*She goes to sweep off the bed cover, but* MUSA *grabs that out of her hand as well.*)

MUSA: Stop this, you are not a crazy girl! Stop it!

GAMILA: No. No, I'm not. And if I am, why would I be now? For what? You? I don't even know why we got engaged or what I saw in you in the first place.

MUSA: I don't know what you saw in me too!

GAMILA: Who are you that I should care about?

MUSA: Yes, you will find better, I was wrong to pick.

GAMILA: Don't belittle my judgment in wanting to marry you! I wasn't an idiot when I saw something in you. Now I see I was wrong but I wasn't then!

MUSA: Now you see the light, *Al Hamdulilah!*

GAMILA: Oh, shut it! Damn it! Why? Why are you picking *her*? *Of all people?* I don't get it. *She's* an improvement? Because of what? The *sex*? Because she puts out?

MUSA: No!

GAMILA: What else could it be? It must be one helluva blow job she's giving you.

MUSA: Stop it!

GAMILA: What else then?

MUSA: Because I can be what I want with her! For first time. I can't live in this world you want me to.

GAMILA: *What* world?

MUSA: *This* world. The one you always—and my family as well, what they want. It's like I'm in it always, up to my eyeballs, and I can't see anything else. Why did I—why did I come to this country? So I can stay in this same world? I am like a fish in a bowl and what has changed? I look out on America in my taxi instead of Cairo but it is still the same fish bowl I am in, the same story. What is the point?

GAMILA: What are you talking about?

MUSA: What my family expects of me, what you—the way you look at me, I feel I am supposed to be someone I'm not!

GAMILA: What someone?

MUSA: What you expect of me! Like I am . . . Why you want to marry me? Because you think you keep in touch with back home? With our religion?

I am a terrible Muslim. I go to the mosque to see friends, not God. Of course God. But God is not happy with me. I fail Him too.

GAMILA: What are you saying, that you can't—? *What?*

MUSA: *Ana mishader atnafas!*—I can't breathe in this—this life that I know we will have. How it will be, the routine, it is very clear. What we will have in this life together, the things that we will say is *muhim*, that we will repeat is important. You want to keep in touch with your roots? I don't want roots! I want things I know nothing about. I want a life where I don't know where it goes. With us, the story it would be—it would be very clear—and customs and tradition and family; and this is who we are and where we started and this is where we are going. All the way to when they bury me. I don't want the rest of my life to be what I know. This story where I know beginning, middle, and end. Yes, Sheri is not you. She is a very strange and perhaps wrong for me, but maybe that is what I need. The wrong woman. Maybe I need the wrong woman in my life.

(*From above, a thud, then:*)

MAN'S VOICE: (*Offstage.*) Hey! Wrap it up down there! Some people are trying to sleep!

MUSA: (*Looking up.*) I do not believe it. They are telling us to shut up? (*To the man above.*) You shut up!

MAN'S VOICE: (*Offstage.*) You shut up!

MUSA: You shut up! The loudest people in the building telling us to keep quiet! That is too much! Go to hell!

MAN'S VOICE: (*Offstage.*) You go to hell!

GAMILA: (*Slight beat.*) This is how you've felt? . . . Since I've known you?

MUSA: No. Only . . . No.

GAMILA: Why didn't you say anything?

MUSA: Because I *didn't* know how I felt.

GAMILA: (*Slight beat.*) Now you get in touch with how you feel? . . . Where were you these past ten months?

MUSA: Better now than many years into marriage with kids and too much to walk away.

(*Slight beat.*)

GAMILA: (*Half to herself.*) This is how you've felt?

Musa: I didn't know. Until . . . recently.

(*Slight beat.*)

Gamila: If you'd gotten a clue just one month earlier. Before your mother and me sat down like two generals figuring out how to do this wedding.

Musa: I will—I will talk with her. (*A laugh from* **Gamila.**) What? . . . What is funny?

Gamila: What you said. . . . This is how I've sometimes felt with you. That you had these expectations of *me*. I felt I needed to behave a certain way around you. I . . . I thought you expected certain things of me. I felt trapped in that too. Worrying the American part of me would spring out and shock you. And that I'd better behave like the well-brought-up Muslim girl that perhaps you were used to.

(*Slight beat.*)

I probably did want to marry you to keep some link with back home. What's wrong with that? It can get pretty lonely and confusing living here.

Musa: I want confusing.

(*Slight beat.*)

Gamila: You got it. (*Then:*) And just to be clear . . . I also found you not bad-looking. You had that going for you. It wasn't just some desire to keep in touch with back home. I do like you. Just to be clear.

Musa: And I you.

(*Beat.*)

Gamila: Well . . . (*Slight beat.*) I'd better . . . (*Slight beat.*) I guess I'd better get back home. And crash.

Musa: Have some *ammar adeen*. Since you make it.

Gamila: No, I'd—I'd better go.

Musa: Stay a few minutes. I drive you back. Please.

Gamila: (*Considers, then:*) Well . . . what I'd really like—if you're inviting, is that *k'ahk* your mother sent you. That would be the perfect sugar rush to keep me going.

Musa: Where is it, we eat it now.

Gamila: In that bag.

(*They go to one of the bags.*)

Musa: How is she?

Gamila: Oh, you know. Her neck, her back, her shoulder. I think she looked forward to the idea of having a nurse in the family. If it's alright, I'd like to speak to her myself. Tell her it's off. I got to really like her, and your family.

Musa: You do not have to be a stranger to them. Yes, call them. I will tell them it's my fault.

Gamila: No. We don't have to get into all that, do we? I just want to—I'd like to keep in touch with them.

Musa: Yes. Please. I go get plates.

Gamila: Oh, don't bother; we'll be careful.

(*She has found the box of* k'ahk—*which are very similar to Russian tea cookies. They will sit at the table.* **Gamila** *takes off the veil that covers her hair.*)

I hope you don't mind. It's been a day and a half since leaving Cairo. A bath and a hairbrush would feel so good right now. Even before collapsing into bed.

(*She runs her fingers through her hair for a moment. He looks at her.*)

Well, taste one.

(*He extends the box to her first, she takes a k'ahk. They both eat.*)

Gamila: Hafiz has to find a way of importing these or find someone to make them in his store. You can't find these here.

Musa: I have asked everywhere, but nothing is like this.

Gamila: Nothing beats the foods from back home. (*Re: the discarded shirt.*) Did you spill coffee on yourself while driving? That's quite a stain.

Musa: (*Hesitates.*) Sheri. When I meet her earlier. She—threw coffee at me. (**Gamila** *lets out an inadvertent laugh.*) It was not funny at the time.

Gamila: No; I imagine it wasn't. Did you . . . ? Are you both still . . . ?

Musa: I don't know . . . I don't know yet.

Gamila: (*Slight beat.*) She seems nice. Genuinely. I'd find her fun if I'd just met her. And she's very respectful of the religion, or seems so, and curious. And she really likes you. Said some nice things about you. She certainly seems to have brought you to life. I have to give her that. It's clear in your eyes. There's this excited . . . conversation going on inside you now. I think I get it. I really do.

(*Slight beat. He begins to extend his hand to wipe some powdered sugar from the side of her mouth, but stops. Instead just indicates.*)

Oh. You've got some too. Other side.

(*She wipes the side of her mouth.*)

(*He wipes.*)

(*She extends her hand to wipe the side of his mouth. After a couple of wipes, he takes her hand and places it against his mouth. She lets him. He leans across the table and kisses her. It's a somewhat chaste kiss but it lingers. They break. Slight beat.*)

These are hands down the best tasting cookies. I wish I could find them here.

(*They kiss again.*)

Splinters

by Emily Schwend

CHARACTERS: SAM (17 years old); CONNER, her best friend (16 years old)

PLACE: Conner's basement; early morning

CIRCUMSTANCE: Sam's younger sister has been missing for over a year.

(SAM *and* CONNER *are asleep on his couch. Various articles of clothing are strewn about.* SAM *wakes. She looks around, disoriented. She carefully sits up. She pulls on her shirt.* CONNER *continues to sleep.* SAM *extracts herself from the blankets on the couch. She picks through the clothing on the floor, searching for her uniform skirt.* CONNER *wakes up. He watches her.* SAM *finds her skirt. She pulls it on.*)

CONNER: Hey.

SAM: Oh. Hey. (*A beat.*) I woke up and I thought I'd let you sleep, or . . .

CONNER: I'm awake. Now. So . . .

SAM: I should go before your parents . . . whatever.

(CONNER *gets up, pulling on his pajama pants.* SAM *frantically searches the floor for her shoes.*)

CONNER: Yeah, okay, let me just get changed and we can get—

SAM: I'm just gonna go home. Okay? You can sleep or—

CONNER: I'm awake now.

SAM: —go back to sleep or—

CONNER: I don't want to sleep.

SAM: Then don't. Sleep. But just . . . I have to go.

(SAM *continues searching for the missing shoes.* CONNER *approaches her and gently touches her with his hand.*)

CONNER: Hey, it's—

(SAM *jerks away.*)

SAM: I can't find my shoes. And I can't, like, drive home barefoot.

CONNER: Hey, chill. They'll turn up. Hang out for a bit.

SAM: I can't wait for them to, like, magically appear two weeks from now in some random part of your basement, okay? I can't drive home barefoot and, like, waltz into my house with no shoes.

CONNER: Okay. I'll look. Calm down, all right?

SAM: I am calm.

(*They search in silence.* **CONNER** *finds a shoe in the couch.*)

CONNER: Hey . . . look.

(**SAM** *reaches for the shoe.* **CONNER** *holds it away.*)

SAM: Um, are you kidding me?

CONNER: Why're you, like, bolting out of here?

SAM: (*Grabbing at shoe.*) Give me my shoe.

CONNER: Hang on a sec. Just—

SAM: Give it to me!

(**SAM** *snatches the shoe from* **CONNER.** *A beat.*)

CONNER: I just want to hang out for a bit. With you. Because I like hanging out with you and so . . . yeah.

SAM: Look, can you not go all, like, whatever, touchy-feely emotional on me? I still have to find the left one. Because this is just the right shoe and I can't go home with one shoe. That's, like, worse than not having either.

CONNER: What's going on with you?

SAM: Nothing. I just want to go home and . . . whatever. Just go home and go to bed. Before my parents—

CONNER: Look, last night was weird for me too, okay, but—

SAM: Can we not talk about it? Like, really, just not talk about it?

CONNER: We have to talk about it.

(**SAM** *says nothing. She continues looking for the other shoe.*)

So, okay, yeah, it was weird, but it wasn't . . . bad weird. Right? It was good weird. New, but . . . good weird. The whole . . . us. Felt . . . and if that scares you, the you-and-me thing, then we can—

SAM: You think I'm scared?

CONNER: Well, I mean, yeah. Because it's a big, I don't know—

SAM: It's not about you and me, okay?

CONNER: That's what I'm saying, it doesn't have to be, like, this whole thing, this whole . . . "Hey, now we're dating" type thing, 'cause we can just—

SAM: Look, I don't know what happened last night. But I didn't mean for . . . that to happen and I don't—

CONNER: But it did happen. Right? And that means something. And if you're too scared to . . . to admit that, then . . . Because you know it'd be good. Us. If you let it. It could be really good.

(*He clumsily tries to hold her hand. She pulls away.*)

SAM: God, can you just, not? Okay? I don't want you all, like, touching me and giving me, I don't know, like, more-than-friend looks because that's not how I feel, okay?

CONNER: What am I supposed to do then? Pretend like there's nothing there?

SAM: There's no . . . something there and there wasn't ever something there except whatever fantasies you were, like, entertaining in the back of your mind and—

CONNER: I wasn't entertaining fantasies.

SAM: Then stop, like, making this into some whole thing.

CONNER: You're just tweaking out 'cause you're—

SAM: I'm tweaking out 'cause I don't want you all over me, okay? 'Cause this? Between us? Whatever you think happened, like some new opportunity that opened up . . . that's so just not what happened. And it's never going to happen because when I think about last night and what we did, I feel bad. Like gross and awful bad and—

(**CONNER** *kisses her. Sam violently pushes him away.*)

Just . . . don't! I don't want you to and I don't like it and I don't want to think about you like that! I feel disgusting. Looking at you right now makes me feel worse than I can remember. Like I'm this disgusting person. Okay? So I don't feel, like, some bond between us or some new, deep, soul mate intimacy or whatever you think is there that isn't. I don't want you all touching me or talking about it or looking at me like that, okay? I feel bad. Last night made me feel bad. And, yeah, you make me feel bad. Like that gross, uncomfortable, like, claustrophobic whatever. Okay? Like I did something wrong. So when you kiss me or touch me, I mean, I can't even . . . I've never felt so, like, bad about myself. Okay? You . . . and this . . . I feel disgusting and bad inside.

(**CONNER** *looks at her, deeply hurt.*)

CONNER: Worse than when you left your sister alone to get kidnapped from an empty Target parking lot?

(**SAM** *stares at* **CONNER**. *She grabs her keys and jacket and exits through the window.* **CONNER** *stands alone in the room. He starts to clean up the blankets on the couch. He finds the other shoe in the cushions. He throws it on the ground. He punches the couch again and again.*)

Strike-Slip
by Naomi Iizuka

CHARACTERS: ANGIE, Korean American, first-generation American; RAFAEL, Mexican American, second-generation American (both 17)

PLACE: A rooftop in downtown Los Angeles; late night

CIRCUMSTANCE: Angie is watched closely by her rigid father. Rafael does not want to end up like his thuggish father.

(*RAFAEL touches ANGIE's palm.*)

ANGIE: *Son-ppa-lak.*

RAFAEL: *Son-ppa-lak.*

(**RAFAEL** *touches* **ANGIE**'*s face.*)

ANGIE: *Ul-gool.*

RAFAEL: *Uf-gool.*

(**RAFAEL** *touches* **ANGIE**'*s eyes.*)

ANGIE: Noon.

RAFAEL: Noon.

(*RAFAEL touches ANGIE's mouth.*)

ANGIE: *Eep.*

RAFAEL: *Eep.*

(**RAFAEL** *touches* **ANGIE**'*s lips.*)

ANGIE: *Eep-sool.*

RAFAEL: *Eep-sool.*

(**RAFAEL** *and* **ANGIE** *kiss.* **ANGIE** *pulls away.*)

ANGIE: Why do you want to learn Korean? It's not like you're not going to remember. You're going to forget.

RAFAEL: No, I'm not. (*Touching* **ANGIE**'*s palm:*) *Son-ppa-lak.* See? I remember.

ANGIE: Not bad. (*Beat.*) I like this place. You feel like you're on top of the world. It's like you can see the whole city down below and it's all like twinkling. Look at all those cars. They look so tiny from up here. Think about all those people just like in their own little worlds. Like they don't even think about what's out there. It's like they're trapped, you know. And they think that's all there is. It's like their worlds are so small and they never wonder what else there is out there.

Rafael: (*Beat.*) What? What is it?

Angie: Nothing.

Rafael: No. You're like, you're like thinking about something. It's cool. Just say it.

Angie: Rafi, I want to go away.

Rafael: What do you mean?

Angie: I mean, I want to go away.

Rafael: Like go where?

Angie: I don't know. Fiji—

Rafael: Fiji?

Angie: It doesn't matter. It doesn't matter where. Just somewhere else, anywhere else. Let's just go, Rafi, just you and me.

Rafael: Angie, you know I want that. You know that. I want that more than anything. After we graduate, we can take off, I promise. We can go anywhere—

Angie: No. Now, tonight. I want to go tonight.

Rafael: Tonight? Where are we gonna go tonight?

Angie: It doesn't matter. Somewhere else. Somewhere far away. It doesn't matter where. Rafi, please.

Rafael: Angie—

Angie: What? Say it. Just say it.

Rafael: Listen. Listen to me—

Angie: No, don't.

Rafael: Angie—

Angie: No, I don't want to hear it.

Rafael: Come on.

Angie: No, 'cause we talk about these things, we talk about all these things. And you tell me this stuff, you tell me that you love me, you tell me that we're going to have this life, that we're gonna go and have this whole life together, but you don't mean it. You don't mean any of it.

Rafael: That's not true. You don't know. You read your books and you go to school and you don't know how it is.

Angie: You asked me what I want and I'm telling you.

Rafael: You need money to live. You can't just go. You can't just leave with the clothes on your back. Not in real life.

Angie: I can get money.

Rafael: Where?

Angie: It doesn't matter.

Rafael: Angie—

Angie: What?

Rafael: It's not just that.

Angie: What then? What's stopping you?

Rafael: I can't just leave, Angie. I can't do that.

Angie: Fine. Do what you want.

(**Angie** *starts to go.*)

Rafael: Angie. What are you doing, where are you going, wait. (**Rafael** *stops her.*) What's wrong with you? Did somebody do something to you? Did somebody hurt you? Who hurt you, Angie? Tell me who.

Angie: Why? What are you going to do about it?

Rafael: I will kill anyone who hurt you.

Angie: No, see, don't say things you don't mean. That's your problem. You're like a kid.

Rafael: I'm not a kid. I'm a grown man.

Angie: A grown man does what he says he's gonna do. A grown man doesn't talk just to hear himself talk. It's like you say things, but you don't mean them.

Rafael: That's not true.

Angie: You don't even know what I have to live with. You have no idea.

Rafael: Angie, please. I love you.

Angie: If you love me, then let's go. Let's go tonight.

Rafael: Angie—

ANGIE: 'Cause otherwise we're done. It's over. You're never gonna see me again. (*Beat.*) Yeah? Is that how it's gonna be? All right then.

(ANGIE *starts to go.*)

RAFAEL: Wait. Angie, wait. We'll go. We'll leave tonight.

ANGIE: For real?

RAFAEL: Yeah. Just go back home. Get your stuff together. I'll meet you there. It's going to be OK.

(RAFAEL *and* ANGIE *kiss.* ANGIE *goes.* RAFAEL *remains.*)

The Crowd You're in With
by Rebecca Gilman

CHARACTERS: MELINDA (mid-30s), wife of Jasper; JASPER (mid-30s), spouse of Melinda

PLACE: A backyard of a two-flat on the north side of Chicago; early evening on the 4th of July, 2007

CIRCUMSTANCE: Melinda and Jasper have been trying to conceive a child. Their landlords make it clear that they'd like them to find another residence before a baby is born.

JASPER: I'll clean all this up. Go to bed if you want.

MELINDA: It's, like, eight o'clock.

JASPER: Right.

(JASPER *starts cleaning up.* MELINDA *watches him. He looks at her and then forces a laugh.*)

Some Fourth of July, huh?

MELINDA: What is wrong with you?

JASPER: Because I yelled at Dan?

MELINDA: Because what is wrong with you.

JASPER: The guy gets on my nerves sometimes.

MELINDA: Maybe he has a different kind of intelligence than knowing who George Eliot is.

JASPER: Meaning?

MELINDA: He's your best friend.

JASPER: No, Dan is married to your best friend.

MELINDA: And he's your best friend.

(*Beat.*)

JASPER: Well, that's depressing because the guy is really bad for my mental health.

MELINDA: You expect too much from him.

JASPER: I don't want to live an unexamined life.

MELINDA: Neither do I.

JASPER: I want to lead a meaningful life.

MELINDA: Do you not think we do?

JASPER: I just—I don't want to have a baby because they are.

MELINDA: What makes you say that?

JASPER: Just, like, a lot of times you and Windsong buy the same purse and stuff.

MELINDA: That's the stupidest thing I ever heard.

JASPER: You do everything together.

MELINDA: If it's happening at the same time, it's only because we're both thirty-five.

JASPER: Thirty-four.

MELINDA: I'm turning thirty-five in November.

JASPER: I know. I'm sorry.

(*Beat.*)

Maybe the thing with Dan is just—you know—do I look like him? Like, one of those guys?

MELINDA: What guys?

JASPER: The hipster dads. In the Converse sneakers and the baseball caps and the doofy, untucked shirts. Pushing their kids in the strollers, trying to act all engaged. "Look, Tyler. See the doggie? See the doggie with the bum? Hey, Tyler! Did you notice? Daddy's losing all sense of self!"

(**MELINDA** *regards him.*)

MELINDA: Who's Tyler?

JASPER: He's a fictional kid—

MELINDA: In a hypothetical world, but we're talking about real things.

JASPER: And that's just it—I keep seeing real things that completely freak me out. Like little things keep jumping out at me like they're on a spring or something. Like the other day, I was walking down Wilson and I walked by one house, and on the post, at the end of the banister, on the porch steps? There was this little toy giraffe sitting there. It was, maybe, four inches tall. Then the very next house, there was a jump rope wrapped around the banister and the handles were painted to look like ladybugs with a little face and wings?

(*He looks at* MELINDA *to see if she is following him. Small beat.*)

And then I noticed both houses had the same sort of ornamental shrubs, like, little evergreen trees that are trained to sort of droop over in a certain way? You'd think they were dying if you didn't know they were really expensive.

MELINDA: And?

JASPER: And everyone had the same thing in their yards, and if you have the kids, does that mean you have to buy the shrubs, too?

(MELINDA *doesn't answer.*)

You're not following me, are you?

MELINDA: I think I am.

JASPER: And?

MELINDA: We don't have to buy the shrubs. We don't have to do anything the way anybody else does it. We can do it however we want. (*Picking up a plate of food.*) Do you care if I put all of this in one container?

JASPER: Am I not allowed to have doubts?

MELINDA: No, but . . .

JASPER: What?

(MELINDA *doesn't answer.*)

What?

MELINDA: Do you think this is why . . . ?

JASPER: What?

MELINDA: The other night . . . ?

JASPER: It was one time.

MELINDA: But maybe this is why.

JASPER: It was one time.

MELINDA: But I'm afraid it's because you're not sure.

JASPER: That's what I've been trying to say.

MELINDA: But we decided.

JASPER: No. You said you wanted to go off the pill and see what happened. And I said if you go off the pill, you'll probably get pregnant. Which is what you want, right?

MELINDA: But I want it to be what you want. Not something you go along with.

JASPER: But if I don't want it, what would you do? Go back on the pill?

MELINDA: (*Alarmed.*) You don't want children ever?

JASPER: I didn't say that.

MELINDA: Then what are you saying?

JASPER: I'm only trying to tell you I'm scared. That's all. I'm scared.

(*Beat.*)

MELINDA: I'm scared, too.

JASPER: See? Thank you. Right there. That makes me feel better, just to know. Because you seem so sure.

MELINDA: I seem so sure because you seem unsure. I feel like I have to be the rock.

JASPER: I don't want you to be a rock.

(*Small beat.*)

What are you afraid of?

MELINDA: I don't know. I mean, for a while I was afraid that it would mess up our lives, but lately I've been feeling like I kind of know what our life is now and I wouldn't mind if it was messed up.

JASPER: Thanks.

MELINDA: Don't you think we need a change?

JASPER: Couldn't we just paint the bathroom?

MELINDA: (*Regarding him.*) This is the other thing I'm afraid of. That you'll be a jerk.

(*Small beat.*)

I really appreciate that you're so smart and that you like to analyze things. But this isn't something you compile evidence for—

JASPER: It's a huge decision.

MELINDA: I know that. But sometimes it feels like we analyze things to death and we don't act. But we can't analyze this forever because there actually is a clock and if we wait too long we won't be able to have our own child. And that's what I want. Because I look at you and there are so many things I love about you, and our baby would have all those things. I think a kid that had all your best traits and whatever good traits I might have would be a really great kid. And maybe all our good traits would cancel out all the bad ones. I don't know, but think how much fun we'd have finding out. Because kids are, like, something new. Every day. Every day they discover some new thing, and it's probably something you've completely come to take for granted, but then they see it for the first time and it's brand-new and it's *so cool.*

(*Beat.*)

And then all the crazy things they come up with. Like when we took Skip to the beach and he wouldn't stop talking about motors? "What would happen if you put a Lamborghini motor on a Jet Ski? What would happen if you put an outboard motor on a pickup truck?"

JASPER: "What if you took a lawn mower and welded it to a canoe?"

MELINDA: And I kept looking at him, thinking he's so much like your brother and Julie, and what a kick is that? To have more of the people you love in the world,

(*Beat.*)

JASPER: I'd love to have another one of you.

MELINDA: And I'd love to have another one of you.

(*Beat.*)

But what if I never get pregnant?

JASPER: It's only been five months.

MELINDA: Everybody keeps saying that, but what's the problem? I'm young. I'm healthy.

JASPER: Which is all good, right?

(*Beat.*)

MELINDA: I thought I was pregnant this morning, when I woke up.

JASPER: You did?

MELINDA: It was total wishful thinking. But I felt funny and my boobs were all sore and I was really happy. Then I got my period.

JASPER: Why didn't you say something?

MELINDA: I wanted to surprise you at the fireworks. I thought it would be romantic.

JASPER: It's going to happen. We just have to be patient, okay?

(**MELINDA** *nods.*)

Nobody's ever said they wanted another one of me in the world. That's like the nicest thing anyone's ever said to me.

(**JASPER** *puts his arm around* **MELINDA***. They sit.*)

Do you have cramps?

MELINDA: Yeah.

JASPER: Why don't you go inside and put on your pajamas and get the heating pad out?

MELINDA: No . . .

JASPER: I'll clean up out here and then we'll see if there's a good movie on. Okay?

MELINDA: It's not like I can't walk—

JASPER: It's okay.

(**JASPER** *kisses* **MELINDA***.*)

Go lie down.

MELINDA: You sure?

JASPER: Yeah. Go on. Or a baseball game. Or the election returns from Wisconsin.

(**MELINDA** *smiles.*)

MELINDA: (*Conceding.*) Okay. That was stupid. (*Starting to leave.*) Everything's going to be fine.

JASPER: I know.

The Good Counselor
by Kathryn Grant

CHARACTERS: VINCENT, an African American public defender (30s); EVELYN, a single white mother (20–30)

PLACE: an interview room

CIRCUMSTANCE: Evelyn is currently a suspect in the death of her infant.

VINCENT: This is how we do it. I will be you.

EVELYN: How can you be me?

VINCENT: It's pretend. Role-playing. Just listen to me being you.

EVELYN: What's the point?

VINCENT: To help us get a handle on each other.

EVELYN: (*She leans back in her chair.*) I get you. But you don't get me.

VINCENT: Oh yeah?

EVELYN: Yeah.

VINCENT: Oh, I may not be as thick as all . . . (*Changing his tack.*) Well, you know what, maybe I am a little thick. You wouldn't be the first to take note of that. So maybe this could help me.

EVELYN: How does it work?

VINCENT: I have your statement to the police investigators. (*He hands it to her.*) Do you want to read it?

EVELYN: (*Handing it back.*) No. I know what I said.

VINCENT: I also brought some questions the prosecutors will ask and some statements made by some witnesses.

EVELYN: (*Tries to grab the papers.*) What the hell are people saying about me?!

VINCENT: We will get to that in just a minute. Relax.

EVELYN: I'm relaxed. I'm relaxed. (*Grabbing at him again.*) Let me see the motherfuckin' papers.

VINCENT: I will in time, Evelyn. But not till you calm down.

EVELYN: Okay.

VINCENT: (*He breathes in deeply.*) Now, I am going to tell your story. I'm just going to repeat the things that you said in this report and other things you have told me here in this room.

EVELYN: Yeah?

VINCENT: Then I am going to put you in the power seat.

EVELYN: What?

VINCENT: You'll be the law.

EVELYN: How can I be the law?

VINCENT: You'll be the prosecutor. You'll listen to my story and try to figure out if it makes sense.

EVELYN: I think I could do that.

VINCENT: I think so, too. And I want you to be tough on me, Evelyn. Poke holes in the story when you can.

EVELYN: So I am being tough on myself, huh?

VINCENT: Yeah, actually, yeah.

EVELYN: Nothing new.

VINCENT: (*Handing her a sheet.*) I'm going to give you a little cheat sheet to kind of get you started in your role as prosecutor.

EVELYN: (*Looking at the sheet.*) These are things the other lawyers will ask me?

VINCENT: Right.

EVELYN: Okay.

VINCENT: Ready? (**EVELYN** *nods.*) So . . . I've taken the stand, sworn to tell the truth, etcetera, etcetera. Now you ask me the first question.

EVELYN: (*Reading from a paper.*) "Describe events as they occurred on the evening of March 16th."

VINCENT: I cleaned up some decorations from Christina's birthday party and made dinner around 6:30. After we ate, I did the dishes while Christina watched David. Then I gave David a bath in the kitchen sink. Okay so far?

EVELYN: Okay. Keep going.

VINCENT: So then after the baby was bathed and put in his pajamas, I tried to feed him. First I tried—I tried to feed him using my breasts.

EVELYN: No one says it that way! Jesus! Say, "I nursed him!"

VINCENT: Okay. Okay. "I nursed him."

EVELYN: Better.

VINCENT: Thanks. But he wasn't sucking. He hadn't been sucking the last few days. So after I tried a few times, I gave up and I gave him a bottle. (*Dropping out of his character.*) How do I sound?

EVELYN: I believe you.

VINCENT: Good. So then he fell asleep and I put him to bed. (**VINCENT** *waits for her response.*)

EVELYN: (*Looking down at the paper.*) Is it my turn? (**VINCENT** *nods. She reads.*) Where did you put David asleep?

VINCENT: He slept on the bed. A single bed. Where all three of us slept. (*Pause.*) Now come on, Evelyn. What would the prosecutor say to that?

EVELYN: I don't know.

VINCENT: Look on the sheet.

EVELYN: (*Reading.*) "Why didn't you put the baby in a crib or a bassinet or a cradle?"

VINCENT: I wanted to. But the one I had for Christina got ruined in storage when the basement was flooded at the old house and I didn't have the money to buy another. And I didn't want to put him in a drawer on the floor because we had mice.

EVELYN: That's true. (*She gets up and starts to pace around the room.*) But, Jesus Christ, do you have to say that about my not having money?

VINCENT: I think it's an important part of your story, Evelyn.

EVELYN: I worked my whole life, except for a few weeks after the babies were born, and I don't want no one feeling sorry for me.

VINCENT: Why is it so bad for people to feel sorry for you?

EVELYN: You don't want people to feel sorry for you, do you?

VINCENT: No, I guess not.

EVELYN: You better than me?

VINCENT: I have had a different kind of life, that's all.

EVELYN: I have a right to my privacy—

VINCENT: You lost that right, Evelyn—

EVELYN: There you go. Just like the fuckin' cops!

VINCENT: Sorry, sorry. I lost my concentration. I forgot. I'm Evelyn. I'm Evelyn Laverty and I—

EVELYN: —don't want no one feeling sorry for me.

VINCENT: That's right. I don't want no one feeling sorry for me. But I am going to mention that Social Services made an agreement with me to get me some proper equipment for the baby. How's that?

EVELYN: That's okay. They fucked up.

VINCENT: I won't say it like that. I'll say, "They failed to live up to their promise."

EVELYN: That's true.

VINCENT: Next question.

EVELYN: What did you do after you put David to bed?

VINCENT: I cleaned up the apartment and helped Christina with some homework. I made her brush her teeth and clean up. She got into bed next to David and fell asleep.

EVELYN: I read her a story first!

VINCENT: Oh yeah! I read her a story. Sorry!

EVELYN: Whatever.

VINCENT: Then I went outside. I was tired and feeling a little shut in after a long day with the children. So I had a couple of beers and a cigarette to take the edge off.

EVELYN: Wait a minute! Wait a minute!

VINCENT: Evelyn, Counselor. I have some explaining to do here. People may be offended at the idea that a breast-feeding mother was drinking beer on a stoop.

EVELYN: So don't mention it.

VINCENT: Jack Hoover is going to testify that you were getting plastered on your stoop after you put the kids to bed. (*He shows her a statement.*) Look!

EVELYN: What the fuck! Busybody!

VINCENT: He said he saw you drinking.

EVELYN: Two beers!

VINCENT: And smoking, for that matter! And he says after the kids were asleep, some nights you partied with friends.

Evelyn: I have a right to a little relief—

Vincent: Yes you do! I mean, yes I do! I'm stuck in this moldy dump out here on the edge of town, next to a bean field, trying to be responsible, trying to be all that I can to my kids. But what the hell, I'm a young woman—

Evelyn: I'm a human being. Not some breast-feeding machine!

Vincent: And sometimes in the middle of the night I get a little crazy thinking about what my life is and what it might have been! So yes, I have a drink or two, or a cigarette so that I can have one moment in the day when I feel free of all that.

Evelyn: That doesn't mean I'm a bad mother.

Vincent: (*Slowly. He is not sure.*) No, it doesn't.

Evelyn: Okay, then. That's okay, I guess. (*Pause.* **Evelyn** *looks at* **Vincent**.) You're getting into being me, huh?

Vincent: (*Shakily.*) It's my job . . . to try and see things . . .

Evelyn: You have kids?

Vincent: No.

Evelyn: But you have a mother.

Vincent: (*Slowly.*) Yes. I have a mother who struggled like you.

Evelyn: Yeah?

Vincent: And she's proud like you, too.

Evelyn: She have a lot of kids?

Vincent: Four.

Evelyn: They all smart and professional?

Vincent: No. But they do okay. (*He coughs for a moment.*) Let's get back to your story.

Evelyn: Your mother didn't get herself in the mess I am in now, though, huh?

Vincent: Oh, she got herself into some pretty bad fixes.

Evelyn: Like what?

Vincent: (*Sliding into a dark place.*) Oh . . . my brother . . . was difficult. Now you would probably say he was sick.

Evelyn: Is he okay now?

VINCENT: No.

EVELYN: (*Pause.*) That's too bad. I'm tired.

VINCENT: (*Resolutely.*) Me too. But we got to push through this, Evelyn. There are some important points we have to clear up.

EVELYN: What?

VINCENT: Read this. It's a statement from an investigator.

EVELYN: "Footprints were discovered leading up to the spot in the Montrose bean field where—David Laverty's body was discovered."

VINCENT: Finish reading the statement, Evelyn.

EVELYN: I can't believe this shit—

VINCENT: (*More forcefully.*) Read it!

EVELYN: "The footprints in question—"

VINCENT: Finish it, Evelyn. We're gonna hear it in court.

EVELYN: Jesus Christ! (*She picks up the paper and continues.*) "The footprints in question . . . matched the soles of boots found in Evelyn Laverty's apartment. The boots, discovered hidden behind the apartment stove, are size six and a half, the defendant's shoe size, and have bits of clinging vegetation consistent with vegetation at the site where the baby's body was found."

(*Pause. The truth hangs in the air for a moment.*)

VINCENT: (*Abruptly, piercing the silence.*) I don't know how that happened. It's a frame-up. Some one set me up. Maybe that motherfucker, Jack Hoover, did this to me. He wanted to sleep with me and I told him off.

EVELYN: That sounds like bullshit!

VINCENT: Someone stole my shoes to take the baby to the bean field and then afterward put them behind the stove.

EVELYN: That's even worse. This is stupid. (*Throwing down the papers.*) Look, I want to stop this now!

VINCENT: No, we can't, Evelyn. We are going to get through this. How can I answer this piece of evidence? What can I say?

EVELYN: Don't say anything.

VINCENT: (*Shaking his head.*) Come on!

EVELYN: Don't!

Vincent: Yeah, don't say anything. That's what I'll do. I just won't say anything! Yeah, that works. Just don't say anything. That's great! I don't bug my doctor when he blows me off, 'cause he's the doctor and he should know. I don't hound social services for a crib for my baby, 'cause someone might feel sorry for me! I don't ask my babies' fathers for help 'cause they might disappoint me! What gives, Evelyn? You think that if you keep all that shit inside you that no one's gonna notice how spun outta control the situation is. But look at the mess you're in!

Evelyn: Get the hell out of here. I want a new lawyer!

Vincent: Evelyn—

Evelyn: You're just like the rest of them.

Vincent: Yeah, that could be. But just because I'm an asshole, one of the hundreds of assholes that you have had to deal with, doesn't change the fact that you have got to speak up for yourself.

Evelyn: Nothing you say is going to matter!

Vincent: (*Driving. He gets up and pursues her around the room.*) So what! So what! (*Finally.*) I am going to try. I am going to look for some words that are going to stand in for something real that has happened to me. I may not get it right, I might offend some people, some people might misunderstand me, twist my words, but fuck it, I am going to speak.

Evelyn: (*Softening. The despair beneath her defensiveness starts to surface.*) What are you gonna say that'll change anything?!

Vincent: I will tell them about my life with my children.

Evelyn: What difference—

Vincent: And I will tell them how I struggled—

Evelyn: No one cares.

Vincent: And I will tell them about the bed.

Evelyn: What?

Vincent: The bed where I rested with my babies.

Evelyn: (*She sits slowly.*) No. Uh-uh. It's my bed. It's my life—

Vincent: (**Vincent** *stands behind her.*) I never thought anything bad could come of that bed.

Evelyn: No, I didn't.

Vincent: It was warm in that bed—

EVELYN: Not ever. No.

VINCENT: After the days I had, it was like crawling into paradise.

EVELYN: It was . . .

VINCENT: When I lifted the covers to join my children, the heat rising from their sleeping bodies . . .

EVELYN: Warm. So warm.

VINCENT: The smell washed over me . . .

EVELYN: (*Trance-like.*) Before I fell asleep that night . . .

VINCENT: Before I fell asleep that night.

EVELYN: I said a prayer . . .

VINCENT: I said a prayer.

EVELYN: . . . that I would become bigger and stronger and smarter. That I would become the mother that my children deserved.

VINCENT: And then?

EVELYN: I fell asleep. Christina was on one side next to the wall and I was on the other. David was between us.

VINCENT: And then?

EVELYN: I don't know. Oh yeah, I had a dream.

VINCENT: Tell me about it.

EVELYN: We were all together, Christina, David, and me . . . and this is crazy, we were flying through the air . . . in that bed. And we were over the sea and it was nice, but then the sky started getting darker, so I was starting to feel a little panicky, but then I saw an island. And as we got closer, I saw that there were people lined up standing by the shore. And they were dressed in purple robes. Their hands were lifted as though they were trying to catch some rain. Then as we came closer, the people looked up. And I thought, "Look at that! All the people, they're waiting for us. They're waiting!" And then . . .

VINCENT: Yes . . .

EVELYN: I woke up.

VINCENT: And . . .

EVELYN: It was gray in the room. A faucet was dripping. And the bed had gone cold. Even the sheets felt stiff. I'm thinking, "Shit, it's another motherfucking day." And I reach out for David. Thinking that I can maybe stand to get out of bed and start breakfast if I can just hold him for a bit. Even when me and Christina were cold, his body would be hot like a toaster and I wanted to warm myself with him. One minute, God, that's all I'm asking for. One minute with him while he is peaceful. One minute while he is still dreaming of the life he may have. One minute before he wakes up and becomes just this thing who needs me. (*She is shivering.*) But when I reach out for him, he's not there. But there's something underneath me . . . underneath me . . . and it's hard . . . like a stone . . . and the stone is David.

VINCENT: Gone?

EVELYN: (*She gasps as the weight of her awareness hits her.*) Gone. Gone. Oh no. Oh God! He's gone.

VINCENT: Evelyn—

EVELYN: My boy gone. I won't live through this. You can't make me live through this—

VINCENT: I can get you out of here, Evelyn. We can get your daughter back. Christina still needs you.

EVELYN: (*Looking for a place to escape her grief, she paces the room.*) Get out! Get away!

VINCENT: Just because your baby—

EVELYN: (*Holding her head in her hands.*) I'm to blame.

VINCENT: SHHHHH! Evelyn! (*Whispering.*) This is a defensible case. They can't prove you intended this. Even if you did something that hurt the baby—

EVELYN: He wanted to breathe and I—Oh my God, where can I go? I got to get out!

VINCENT: There are things you don't know. There are things beyond anyone's control—

EVELYN: Not one thing right—

VINCENT: You have to listen. He was a sick baby, Evelyn.

EVELYN: —my entire fucked-up life—

VINCENT: He had a serious condition—

EVELYN: —no matter how hard I try—

VINCENT: We don't know if he would have survived. Evelyn, we can help you!

EVELYN: (*Sobbing.*) Not one thing right! (*She grabs at him.*) I'm going under.

VINCENT: I've got you, Evelyn. Hold on.

EVELYN: I can't. I can't live anymore. I can't. I'm going under.

VINCENT: I'm holding on. Holding on to you.

(*He contains her in his arms, trying to keep her from blowing apart.*)

Time Stands Still
by Donald Margulies

CHARACTERS: SARAH, a photojournalist who covers wars and global strife; JAMES, Sarah's partner and a freelance journalist (both late 30s–early 40s)

PLACE: Their loft in NYC

CIRCUMSTANCE: James fled Iraq before Sarah was severely hurt by a roadside bomb.

EDITOR'S NOTE: The playwright uses a slash (/) to indicate where the next actor is to begin her line; the asterisk (*) cues the actor to continue his line so that it is spoken simultaneously with the dialogue that comes between it.

(JAMES *gathers bowls and mugs and rinses them at the sink. Mid-conversation.*)

SARAH: When did he tell you?

JAMES: When we went down for ice cream.

SARAH: He didn't want me to know?!

JAMES: He said I could tell you, he just didn't want to get into it while they were here.

SARAH: Why not?

JAMES: He was protecting Mandy.

SARAH: From what?

JAMES: From you.

SARAH: Was I really so horrible?

JAMES: You were pretty bad.

SARAH: We were buddies by the time they left . . .

JAMES: He was afraid of what you might say.

SARAH: What, that having a child at his age is the most ridiculous, irresponsible thing / I've ever heard?

JAMES: *Something* like that, yeah.

SARAH: Did he talk about the morality of depriving a kid of a father?

JAMES: How's he depriving a kid / of a father?

SARAH: He's too old! He'll be lucky if he lives to see the kid go off to college.

JAMES: What, young men don't die? Come on, Sarah, you know better than *that . . .*

SARAH: (*Abashed.*) You're right.

JAMES: Anything could happen, to anyone, anytime. You're living proof of that. A crane could come crashing down on us right now. If he's up for this, at this stage of his life, more power to him.

SARAH: So what are they going to do?

JAMES: He's going to marry / her and they're going to have this baby.*

SARAH: Oh my God.* Poor Richard.

JAMES: Why "poor Richard"? The man is ecstatic; I've never seen him like this. He can't believe his good luck. To tell you the truth . . . When he told me . . . (*A beat.*) I was jealous.

SARAH: Why, you wanted to get Mandy pregnant?

JAMES: Ha-ha. No. (*A beat.*) I wished we were getting married.

(*Pause.*)

SARAH: Seriously? (*He nods. A beat.*) Oh, honey . . .

JAMES: Why not?

SARAH: I thought we didn't need marriage.

JAMES: We didn't.

SARAH: I thought we agreed. / It wasn't our thing.

JAMES: We did. But things are different now.

SARAH: Why, because I almost died?

JAMES: Yes. (*Pause.*) When you were in the hospital, I had no legal relationship to you whatsoever. Every catheter, every procedure, permission had to come from your asshole father! Do you realize how frustrating that was? I was right there! They had to get him on the phone from Palm Springs! (*A beat.*) We've been putting ourselves in dangerous situations for years and never stopped to think what would happen if one of us got hurt. We didn't have a plan.

SARAH: So being married would've made medical management a lot easier.

JAMES: Yes.

SARAH: That's got to be the most romantic marriage proposal I've ever heard.

(**James** *laughs. Pause. He gets down on one knee and takes her hand.*)

James: Sarah . . .

Sarah: (*Outraged.*) Get up. Get up! You're changing the rules on me!

James: I'm not changing the rules, the playing field changed.

Sarah: You know how I feel about this! You can't lay this on me all at once! / It isn't fair!

James: I didn't mean to.

Sarah: What do you expect me to say, "Sure, honey, let's do it"?

James: Of course not. (*A beat.*) I had a lot of time to think about this while you were in the hospital, you know. I got to play out your death almost every single day. You were out for most of it, so you have no idea how close you came. (*A beat.*) When a couple gets to be our age, and has been together as long as we have, it's time to call this what it is: a marriage. (*A beat.*) We are not your parents.

(*Pause.*)

Sarah: Can I think about it?

James: (*Deadpan.*) No. Of course you can think about it. (*He kisses her.*) Take all the time you need.

(*He resumes washing dishes. Silence.*)

Sarah: James? (*He can't hear her over the running water.*) Jamie?

James: Yeah?

Sarah: Come here a minute.

James: One second. . . . Let me just . . .

Sarah: Now. Please.

(*He turns off the water, wipes his hands, and joins her.*)

James: What is it?

Sarah: If we're going to do this . . . If we're really going to take this marriage talk seriously . . .

James: (*Bracing himself.*) Okay . . .

(*Pause.*)

Sarah: When I was there . . . After you left . . .

James: I know what you're going to say.

SARAH: What do you mean you know?

JAMES: I know.

SARAH: You don't know what I'm going to say.

JAMES: He's dead. It happened. It's over.

(*He kisses her brow and returns to the sink. Pause.*)

SARAH: (*Nonplussed.*) What the fuck just happened?

JAMES: I'm saying it's okay, I understand, I forgive you.

SARAH: You forgive me? You forgive / me?

JAMES: Look . . . Whatever happened . . .

SARAH: I thought you knew what happened.

JAMES: Sarah. All I'm saying is . . . You're alive, you're here, we're together. . . . That's all I care about. That's all that matters.

(*Pause.*)

SARAH: Who told you?

(*He makes a sound of amused exasperation.*)

People knew. Friends there knew.

JAMES: What difference / does it make?

SARAH: I want to know who told you.

JAMES: No one had to tell me. I just knew.

SARAH: How?

JAMES: Please, Sarah, leave it alone? / Please . . . ?

SARAH: Did I let something slip?

JAMES: Why are you pursuing this?

SARAH: I need to know.

(*Pause.*)

JAMES: Subtle things.

SARAH: Like . . . ?

JAMES: The tone of your voice on the phone.

SARAH: What?

JAMES: Changed.

SARAH: My tone.

JAMES: Yeah. Your voice kinda . . . flattened out. Sounded farther away. Like you were holding something back.

SARAH: I was angry with you.

JAMES: I know / you were angry.

SARAH: That's what you heard in my voice: / I was mad at you.

JAMES: I know. But it wasn't just anger. I recognize your anger, believe me.

SARAH: That was it? My tone?

JAMES: (*A beat.*) There was this e-mail you sent.

SARAH: When?

JAMES: I don't know, like a week after I came home?

SARA: Yeah . . . ?

JAMES: You wrote me about all the checkpoints you hit, how insane it was. Something like that. Remember?

SARAH: Vaguely. So?

JAMES: The thing was . . . you wrote "I" instead of "we."

SARAH: What do you mean?

JAMES: In your e-mails. Whenever you described things you did, you always said "we." "We went here . . . We saw this . . ."

SARAH: I don't understand what that has to do / with anything.

JAMES: One day it was "we," like it always was, the next day it was "I." (**SARAH** *looks quizzical.*) "I." As if you were alone.

SARAH: I was alone. / You were gone.

JAMES: No, no. You weren't alone; Tariq was with you. You knew I knew Tariq was with you; you knew I knew he was with you; that was no secret.

SARAH: So?

JAMES: Something must have happened. Overnight. The status of your relationship had changed. You weren't a photographer traveling with her fixer anymore. "We" took on a whole new meaning. Got way too intimate. You thought you could hide behind the first person singular. Instead you gave yourself away.

(*Pause.*)

SARAH: Wow. I'm impressed.

JAMES: Look . . . These things happen.

SARAH: These things.

JAMES: We both know what it's like covering a war. It's pure adrenaline. Bombs bursting in air, death everywhere. We had some amazing sex, you and I.

SARAH: You think this is about sex?

JAMES: Well . . . ?

SARAH: I didn't just sleep with him.

JAMES: What do you mean?

SARAH: I didn't just sleep with him, James.

(*He's perplexed. She averts her eyes. He understands.*)

JAMES: (*Stunned, hurt; to himself.*) Oh my God.

SARAH: (*Reaches for him.*) Jamie . . .

JAMES: You were in love with him? (*Suddenly emotional.*) How could you have fallen in love with him, Sarah? / How could you have done that?!

SARAH: I don't know!

JAMES: Why?

SARAH: After you left, I was so . . .

JAMES: Do you think I wanted to leave you? / Do you?

SARAH: Of course not.

JAMES: I was a mess! Don't you remember what a mess / I was?!

SARAH: Yes . . .

JAMES: I was shell-shocked! *

SARAH: I know.

JAMES: * That was real, / that wasn't an act.

SARAH: I know it was real.

JAMES: Those women, those girls, blew up right there, right in front me! *

SARAH: I know.

JAMES: * Their blood and brains got in my eyes! In my mouth!

SARAH: I know.

JAMES: I freaked out! I had to get the hell out of there! Where were you for me?!

SARAH: I couldn't leave with you!

JAMES: Why, because you were fucking Tariq?

SARAH: No! Because I had a job to do! You said you'd be okay / without me!

JAMES: What was I supposed to say?!

SARAH: You told me to do what I had to do!

JAMES: What a joke! I leave you with our trusty fixer! "Tariq'll take care of you." Hell, that's what we paid him for! Two hundred bucks a day! Tell me something: Did you continue to pay him? Even after you started fucking him? (*Long pause.*) Y'know . . . ? That terrible night, when I got the call . . . that you were hurt . . . ? And he was dead . . . ? You know the first thing that went through my head? (**SARAH** *shakes her head.*) I thought, "Oh, good! Now I can redeem myself for wimping out."

SARAH: You didn't / wimp out.

JAMES: "I'll prove to Sarah how much she needs me. I'll show her!" Isn't that fucked?

SARAH: No . . .

JAMES: You'd just gotten blown up and I'm thinking, "Oh, good! A second chance!" (*A beat.*) Never thought I'd be competing with a dead man.

(*He grabs his jacket.*)

SARAH: Where are you going?

JAMES: (*Softly.*) I gotta get out of here. (*He starts to go.*)

SARAH: (*Calls.*) James! (*She stands to go after him, and falls.* **JAMES** *rushes to her aid.*)

JAMES: Oh, shit . . .

SARAH: I fell.

JAMES: Yes. You did. You okay?

SARAH: I think so. (*He helps her up and carries her to the bed.*) I'm okay. I'm okay. (*Pause.*) You sure you want to marry me? Like this?

JAMES: (*Smiling.*) Are you kidding? Especially like this: I can outrun you for once. (*Pause. His smile fades.*) I'm so sorry.

SARAH: Shhh . . .

JAMES: I should have stayed, I should never have gone home. (*She kisses his mouth to silence him. Their kissing becomes more intense. They whisper between kisses.*) I missed you.

SARAH: I missed you, too.

JAMES: I missed this.

SARAH: Me too. (*Modestly.*) Can we, uh . . . ? (*Gestures to the lamp.*) I don't want you to see me.

JAMES: I want to / see you.

SARAH: (*Insisting.*) Please. (*He turns off the light.*)

JAMES: Are you okay with this?

SARAH: Yes.

JAMES: You sure? 'Cause if you're not / ready . . .

SARAH: No, no, I am. I want to.

(*In the semidarkness, they begin to make love. We see her face: her mind is elsewhere.*)

Time Stands Still
by Donald Margulies

CHARACTERS: Sarah, a photojournalist who covers wars and global strife; James, Sarah's husband, is a freelance journalist (both late 30s–early 40s)

PLACE: Their loft in NYC

CIRCUMSTANCE: James fled Iraq before Sarah was severely hurt by a roadside bomb. After years of cohabitating, they have married.

EDITOR'S NOTE: The playwright uses a slash (/) to indicate where the next actor is to begin her line; the asterisk (*) cues the actor to continue his line so that it is spoken simultaneously with the dialogue that comes between it.

> (JAMES, *lit by the television, reclines on the sofa watching a movie. He has a pad nearby on which he occasionally makes notes. The volume is low. Unseen by him,* SARAH *is sitting up in bed with* JAMES's *computer on her lap, illuminated by its screen, quietly seething. Soon, She looks around for a cigarette.*)

JAMES: (*Startled.*) Whoa! (*He cracks up laughing.*) Didn't see you. (*He mutes the volume.*) What are you doing?

SARAH: Gotta be a cigarette around here somewhere . . .

JAMES: What do you want a cigarette for?

SARAH: I want to smoke it.

JAMES: Don't. You haven't had a cigarette in months.

SARAH: I want one now . . .

> (*He watches her look through drawers, pockets, etc.*)

JAMES: I thought you were sleeping.

SARAH: Never got there.

JAMES: If this was keeping you up . . . You should've told me . . . I would have made it lower.

SARAH: What is this? (*Meaning on TV.*)

JAMES: *Invasion of the Body Snatchers.* The original. 1956. Research. You know: for the horror-movie piece. Come sit down. (*He makes room; She continues looking.*)

SARAH: Why do you watch this shit?

JAMES: What?

SARAH: Why do you watch / this shit.

JAMES: This isn't shit . . .

SARAH: (*Re: Netflix envelopes.*) *Saw II . . . Saw IV . . .*

JAMES: It's an allegory for the McCarthy era. All about the Red Scare—honey, there are no cigarettes.

SARAH: This is your idea of escapism? Replacing real horror with fake horror?

JAMES: Yes. Exactly. It gets me out of my head. So, yeah; whatever it takes. (*A beat.*) Look, I know you think movies are a waste of time. / You've always thought movies were a waste of time. *

SARAH: That's not true. * I think most movies are a waste of time. I think writing about shitty movies is certainly a waste of your time, legitimizing crap like this . . . ! (*She rummages through her camera bag, finds a lone, broken cigarette, then searches for a match.*)

JAMES: Look, what the fuck are you so . . . ? I said I was sorry I woke you.

SARAH: You didn't wake me. I was up. Reading.

JAMES: What were you reading?

SARAH: The thing you wrote. For the book. (*She smokes the cigarette. Pause.*)

JAMES: Where did you, uh . . . ?

SARAH: It was on your laptop.

JAMES: What were you doing on my laptop?

SARAH: It was on the bed! I couldn't sleep 'cause of all the screams coming from your fucking movie . . . *

JAMES: I said, if it was too loud, you should have said something.

SARAH: * . . . so I thought I'd go online.

JAMES: You went poking around / my laptop?

SARAH: "Poking around"? I opened it up! There it was! Right on the screen! If you didn't want me to see it, why'd you leave it up? (*Pause.*)

JAMES: How much did you read?

SARAH: The whole thing.

JAMES: It's not finished.

SARAH: Bullshit.

JAMES: I'm still working / on it.

SARAH: Isn't Richard expecting it tomorrow?

JAMES: Yeah, but / I . . .

SARAH: Then it's finished.

JAMES: I was going to give it another pass in the morning.

SARAH: Were you ever going to let me see it?

JAMES: Yes. In the morning. (**SARAH** *scoffs.*) This was hard, Sare. You have your pictures. You can hold them and move them around. I have to replay everything in my head so I can write about it. I needed to process it on my own.

SARAH: "Process it?" You mean like put it through a blender? Pulverize it?

JAMES: I needed to make sense of it. / Okay?

SARAH: Was erasing history part of your process?

JAMES: What?

SARAH: How could you do that to him? After all that man went through . . . !

JAMES: What are you talking / about?

SARHA: Tariq. How could you annihilate him all over again?!

JAMES: "Annihilate" him? How did I "annihilate" him?

SARAH: You wrote him out of our story!

JAMES: No, I didn't.

SARAH: * Deleted him! Like he never existed! Like the old Politburo days: when they'd white out the undesirables till there was no one left in the picture!

JAMES: He's there . . . I mention him . . .

SARAH: Mention! Yeah! In passing! Like the scenery!

JAMES: He's not what interested me.

SARAH: (*Incredulous.*) He's not?!

JAMES: Not primarily, / no.

SARAH: My God! And you call yourself a journalist?! He's the story! The indignity that man endured! His entire life! And still had such humanity! Such grace!

JAMES: Christ, you make him sound like a saint!

SARAH: Maybe he was! Maybe he's what being a saint is really about!

JAMES: You mean fucking other men's women? *

SARAH: Is that what I am? (*Mock macho.*) Your "woman"?

JAMES: He was a scrappy opportunist just like everybody else you meet / over there!

SARAH: You just can't bear the thought that he and I were lovers, / can you?

JAMES: Don't say "lovers."

SARAH: So what do you do? Delete him! Poof! He's gone!

JAMES: You know what I think? I don't even think it was Tariq you fell in love with.

SARAH: Oh, no?

JAMES: No. It was his suffering. His victimhood. The romance of his wretched history. Holy cow! What a turn on! You were fucking Oppression itself!

SARAH: That's a shitty thing I to say . . .

JAMES: If he been just another brown-skinned New York cabbie, you wouldn't've looked twice at him / in the rearview mirror.

SARAH: If I met you in the bar on the corner, who's to say I would have looked twice at you?

JAMES: At least you and I had things in common . . . ! / We knew where each other was coming from . . .

SARAH: You think that's all it takes, having things / in common?

JAMES: Some kind of common ground. Something. His English wasn't even that good; / he wasn't even that good a translator.

SARAH: His English was very good! You know, you're beginning to sound like some fucking imperialist!

JAMES: "Imperial / ist"?!

SARAH: Yes! There's a hint—more than a hint—of racism here, / you know that?

JAMES: Oh, really, and your fascination with his exoticism, that isn't a kind of racism? Gunga Din? The "noble savage"?

SARAH: Fuck you! (*A beat.*) Fuck you.

(*Silence. He reaches toward her in a conciliatory gesture.*)

JAMES: Sarah . . . (*Pause.*) Can't we just . . . ? The hell with it. The hell with all of it. I want us to move on now. Can we? Please?

SARAH: I can't.

JAMES: Oh God, is he going to haunt us the rest of our lives?

SARAH: I'm not talking about Tariq. (*Pause.*) I'm talking about this.

JAMES: What?

SARAH: This life you want. I can't do it; I thought I could / but I can't.

JAMES: Wait a minute, wait a minute. This life I want? What do you mean this life I want? If I remember correctly, we just got married. (*She says nothing.*) Hello? (*Pause.*)

SARAH: I could never have gotten through this without you. I mean it. (*He scoffs.*) I'll always be grateful.

JAMES: Fuck that.

SARAH: What?

JAMES: "Grateful." I don't want you to be "grateful."

SARAH: Why not? You didn't have to take this on; you could've walked away.

JAMES: No, I couldn't have. I did what a person does. That's all. It's what you do. (*A beat.*) Is that why you married me? Because you were grateful?

SARAH: You wanted it so much . . .

JAMES: Oh, for fuck's sake . . .

SARAH: And I wanted to make you happy . . .

JAMES: I don't believe this . . .

SARAH: I thought marriage would change me. If I said and did all the right things . . . I would feel it; it would be so. But . . . (*She shakes her head. Pause.*)

JAMES: So having kids . . . ? That was just . . . ? (*She averts his gaze.*) Jesus . . .

SARAH: Do you see me pushing a stroller and going to playdates? Honestly, Jamie, / do you?

JAMES: You said you were ready!

SARAH: I thought I was!

JAMES: You fucking lied to me!

Sarah: I didn't lie to you! If I lied to you, I lied to myself! (*Silence.*) I'm not what you want anymore.

James: Don't tell me what / I want.

Sarah: You want a playmate. That isn't me. You want a Mandy. *

James: That is not what I want.

Sarah: * Someone young, and adoring, who will give you all the babies you want. You'll find her. You should have the life you want.

James: All I want . . . all I ever wanted . . . was a life with you.

Sarah: I wish I could kick back and watch movies with you, I really do. But I can't. There's too much going on. I can't sit still.

James: What am I supposed to do? Pack you off to hell whenever you need your adrenaline fix, and hope you'll come home in one piece? Is that what you expect me / to do?

Sarah: I don't expect you to do anything. I'm telling you I can't do this. (*Pause. Posing a question.*) You've seen the things I've seen . . .

James: Yeah . . .

Sarah: How can you live with yourself, knowing what goes on out there?

James: How? Because I know what goes on out there—and on, and on— whether you and I are there to cover it or not. (*Pause.*) So you actually believe what you do can change anything.

Sarah: It's got to. (*Silence. He smiles to himself, shakes his head ironically.*) What? (*He makes a dismissive gesture.*) What were you thinking?

James: You'll laugh at me.

Sarah: No I won't. (*A beat.*)

James: *Days of Wine and Roses.* Blake Edwards. 1962. Jack Lemmon, Lee Remick, drinking themselves into oblivion; he hits the wall, goes on the wagon, but she . . . can't do it. She needs the buzz more than she needs him. (*A beat.*) Well, here I am: Jack Lemmon on the wagon. But you . . .

Sarah: I'm a drunk?

James: You need it. The whole fucking mess of it. The chaos, and the drama. You need it. (*A beat.*) More than you need me.

Sarah: Not more than I need you. (*They sit in silence. He nods.*)

Part 2

Male-Male Scenes

9 Circles
by Bill Cain

CHARACTERS: L<small>AWYER</small>, civilian defense attorney (40s); R<small>EEVES</small>, an Army private on trial for rape and murder (19/20 years old)

PLACE: A federal prison

CIRCUMSTANCE: Reeves was honorably discharged after 10 months of fighting in Iraq. A month ago, Reeves was notified of his potential execution.

(R<small>EEVES</small> *is in restraints throughout.*)

L<small>AWYER</small>: What's harder these days, Daniel? Not eating or not sleeping?

R<small>EEVES</small>: *Cramps*, sir. I can't *shit*, sir. It's the medication. I killed the hajjis, sir. We went to their shack and I killed them. I'm *guilty*.

L<small>AWYER</small>: Prove it.

R<small>EEVES</small>: *Sir?*

L<small>AWYER</small>: Prove it.

R<small>EEVES</small>: I was *there*, sir. I *know* what I *did*.

L<small>AWYER</small>: (*A moment, then—*) Mr. Reeves, if I wanted to know what you did, you would be the last person I would ask. We know very little of ourselves.

R<small>EEVES</small>: Maybe you don't know *yourself*, sir.

L<small>AWYER</small>: The one thing I am certain of is that we are not who we think we are.

R<small>EEVES</small>: *Sir*, I was warned about you. You'll turn everything upside down. You're a lawyer, *sir*.

L<small>AWYER</small>: Who warned you about lawyers?

R<small>EEVES</small>: A preacher, sir.

L<small>AWYER</small>: Preachers usually turn things upside down. Did he? (*A nod.*) Well, then, I'm just putting things back.

(*The* L<small>AWYER</small> *takes the Bible from* R<small>EEVES</small> *and places it on the ground.*)

R<small>EEVES</small>: (*Fighting going mad.*) Don't play with me, sir. People always play with me. They say they'll come back and they don't. They say, "Say 'not guilty,'" then they throw me in jail. They swear me in and then throw me out. I think it's driving me insane. SIR.

LAWYER: Mr. Reeves—I'll plead you guilty.

REEVES: Thank you, sir.

LAWYER: If you will just give me one shred of evidence that you were involved in a crime.

REEVES: Like what?

LAWYER: Spent cartridges, semen stains, blood samples, a murder weapon. A dead body would help.

REEVES: SIR, you may not have NOTICED, SIR, but I am in RESTRAINTS in a Cell in a FEDERAL PRISON. Where am I going to get any of that *SHIT*?

LAWYER: Where is *anybody* going to get any of that shit? That's what I'd like to know. There is no case—at least not in the conventional sense—against you.

REEVES: I'm *guilty*, sir.

LAWYER: (*OK, then*—) There is one thing I think I can prove you guilty of.

REEVES: Sir?

LAWYER: There was an incident with a dog.

REEVES: A dog?

LAWYER: You threw a dog off a roof?

REEVES: *Fuck the dog, sir.*

LAWYER: A surprising number of people saw you do that. If you want to be guilty of something, I suspect I can prove you guilty of that.

REEVES: *Fuck the dog!*

LAWYER: The dog—

REEVES: Fuck the dog!

LAWYER: OK, if it upsets you. Let's—let's talk about the girl you killed.

REEVES: (*Easy with that.*) Alright.

(*Puzzled by* REEVES's *lack of upset*—)

LAWYER: It doesn't bother you to talk about her?

REEVES: Sir, no, sir! I don't give a fuck about the girl.

LAWYER: That surprises me. I thought that's what you were guilty of. (*Preempting.*) I'm not playing with you, this is the crime. What happened with the girl. That's what this trial is about. What you demand to be guilty for. And yet you don't feel bad about her?

REEVES: She ruined a lot of good men's lives, sir.

LAWYER: *She* did.

REEVES: By her, I mean all of them in their fucked-up country, sir. She fucked up a lot of good men's lives.

LAWYER: She was fourteen.

REEVES: She doesn't *matter*. She really doesn't *matter*.

LAWYER: Well, if she doesn't, who does? Who are you so anxious to give up your life for?

REEVES: (*Looking him over, then—*) You were never in the military, were you, sir? (*No.*) Then you wouldn't understand.

LAWYER: The brotherhood. The camaraderie.

REEVES: (*His deepest belief.*) Sir, yes, sir.

LAWYER: You feel bad for the men you left behind. The ones who were beheaded and mutilated—because of what you did to the girl.

(**REEVES** *can scarcely bear hearing this. He struggles against his restraints.*)

Mr. Reeves—*they* don't matter.

REEVES: *The fuck they don't.*

LAWYER: You are not being tried for their deaths.

REEVES: (*Violent bottom line.*) *I'm guilty.* I will tell them I'm guilty!

LAWYER: (*Violent bottom line.*) I will *not* let you testify *against yourself*. Not in *court*. Not in *here*. (*Finger on* **REEVES**'s *forehead.*) And not in *here*.

(*A long moment of contact.* **REEVES** *takes that in.* **LAWYER** *removes his finger.*)

REEVES: (*Simple and sad.*) I did it, sir. I'm guilty.

LAWYER: One remarkable thing about a trial is—even if a person is guilty, if his story can be presented in such a way as to make the *reason* for his actions comprehensible—no matter how strange they might seem in the cold light of day—if they can be shown to have made sense at the time to the person doing them—people tend to understand. (*Then—*) I think that's wonderful.

REEVES: A sympathetic reaction.

LAWYER: Yes, exactly.

Reeves: I've had them, sir. Twice.

Lawyer: Just twice?

Reeves: Sir, I think that's more than most.

Lawyer: Well, we only need *one*. One member of the jury who understands your story. But to tell the story in that way—I will have to know who you are—exactly who you are—in the story—what you did—why you did it. (*Then*—) Now, would you like people to understand what you did?

Reeves: I'd like to understand it myself .

Lawyer: Just answer my questions, OK? (*A nod, then seriously.*) Tell me about the dog.

Reeves: (*Instantaneous.*) *Fuck the dog.*

Lawyer: Why did you throw the dog off the roof?

Reeves: *Fuck! The dog!*

Lawyer: *You want to be guilty about something? Start here.* You *did* this. Why? *Why did you throw the dog off the roof?*

Reeves: I thought it was—(*What?*)—funny.

Lawyer: Funny. Funny? Killing a dog? Did other people find it—

Reeves: Other people *freaked*. That's funny, right?

Lawyer: Not to the dog.

Reeves: Really? You know what a dog thinks? *You* do? You can *prove* the dog *didn't* think it was funny? Who knows—maybe the dog thought it was funny. Dogs think *everything* is funny. Maybe the dog thought it could *fly*—what the *fuck* are we *talking* about? Look, am I being charged with *cruelty* to *animals*?

Lawyer: You and your buddies are being charged with rape and murder. Capital crimes.

Reeves: How are they pleading?

Lawyer: Guilty.

Reeves: How come they get to plead guilty and I don't?

Lawyer: Because they got a deal. Plead guilty and live.

Reeves: Get me the same deal.

Lawyer: I can't.

Reeves: Then get me a new lawyer.

Lawyer: It doesn't have to do with me. You can't do what they're doing.

Reeves: What?

Lawyer: They're testifying against you, Daniel. They are *lining up* to testify—they are *falling over themselves* to testify against you. They're going to nail your hide to the barn door, Mr. Reeves, your brothers-in-arms. See, they know who *they* are in the story. They're the ones who are out on parole in ten years—all because they are willing to throw you off the roof, Daniel.

(**Reeves** *struggles with his restraints*—)

It doesn't have to be that way. (*Then*—) All they have are fifteen photographs of the crime scene. That's *all* they have, and those photographs were used as proof that the killings were the work of insurgents. *Everyone* up and down the line signed on to that. Fifteen photos and the testimony of your squad-mates—every single one of whom is seriously and repeatedly *perjured*. They've got *nothing*. There is no evidence against you.

Reeves: You want evidence against me—dig up the girl.

Lawyer: Daniel—

Reeves: *Dig up the girl.*

Lawyer: (*With sudden edge.*) Please don't talk about "the girl." She has a name. Khorsheed. It means "sun."

(*Sensing his sympathy for the girl*—)

Reeves: You know I'm guilty. Don't you?

Lawyer: I am trying to understand what happened *inside* you.

Reeves: I don't know.

Lawyer: OK. Let's figure it out. You walk into the room and you see the girl being held down on the floor. Was she struggling? Was she crying?

Reeves: Crying. Screaming. It was embarrassing.

Lawyer: Why were you embarrassed? What did she scream?

Reeves: She said, *"Sa'dny."*

Lawyer: *Sa'dny?* What does *Sa'dny* mean?

Reeves: I don't know.

Lawyer: You know some Arabic. You talked to the locals in it. What did she—

REEVES: I don't know. "Fuck you, Americans."

LAWYER: (*Driving.*) I don't think so. You would have understood that. What does *Sa'dny* mean?

REEVES: *How am I supposed to know?*

LAWYER: Well, what did you *feel*? That's the important thing—

REEVES: I have a personality disorder. I don't feel things.

LAWYER: Of course you do.

REEVES: I DON'T FEEL—

LAWYER: Mr. Reeves, you feel so many things, they had to restrain you. You are pumped full of pharmaceuticals just to keep you functioning. You walked into a room and saw a girl struggling. Two people, your brothers, are holding her down. A lovely fourteen-year-old girl: You look at her and you felt—

REEVES: *Nothing.*

LAWYER: Did you think it was funny?

REEVES: Are you sick?

LAWYER: You thought killing the dog was funny.

REEVES: Killing the dog wasn't the funny part.

LAWYER: What was?

REEVES: FUCK THE DOG! IF YOU WANT PROOF AGAINST ME— DIG—HER—UP.

LAWYER: Even if Islamic law allowed it, I don't think it would prove anything.

REEVES: I WAS THERE. What happened, *happened*. We *raped* and *killed* a girl.

LAWYER: Prove it. (*Then*—) Source of Information 3 isn't sure about what he did. He says he attempted to rape the girl but—(*His notes.*)—"he was not sure if he had done so." (*Then*—) SOI2 says the same. I am not saying this wasn't horrific, but I do not think it is what it seems to be. What happened? Are you *sure* you raped that girl?

REEVES: (*Enough of this.*) I'm sure I killed the bitch.

LAWYER: (*Enough of this.*) But then again—(*The heart of the matter.*) You're also sure you caused the deaths of three men at a checkpoint.

REEVES: SIR, YES, SIR.

LAWYER: Prove it.

REEVES: Huh?

LAWYER: *Prove—it.* Prove one event had any connection whatsoever with the other. (*Then—*) That's what you really feel guilty for? That's what you want to die for—not the girl? OK, I get that. Just *prove* it.

REEVES: (*Baffled.*) Sir?

LAWYER: At the time they—your buddies—at the time they were killed, when their bodies were put on display—when the videos were made and shown? Nobody said a word—not a word—about the girl or her family. The story didn't come out for *weeks.* Then Al-Jazeera combined the two stories and created a propaganda bonanza. Why would they sit on a story that was *that* good if there was *any* truth to it *at all?* People believe it because it is a *terrific* story. (*Then—*) You believe it because it flatters your ego. It makes you important—tragic even. It gives you something easy to confess to.

REEVES: Easy? EASY?

LAWYER: It's always easy to be guilty of something you *didn't* do. It makes *you* the victim instead of the girl—but there is *no proof* the events are *related.* I do not believe that they are, or we would have heard about it the *instant* it happened.

REEVES: Are you lying to me?

LAWYER: I'm a lawyer, Mr. Reeves. That is an awkward question.

REEVES: DO NOT PLAY WITH ME.

LAWYER: The good news is I do *not* think you are responsible for the deaths of your squad-mates at the checkpoint. The bad news is your other squad-mates are shopping you for reduced sentences. The simple *truth* is you are what you have always been—an individual human being with a story to tell. Now tell it to me. There is nothing to hide. Tell me, Daniel. You walk in and you see her on the floor, you look in her eyes—

REEVES: They're testifying against me?

LAWYER: Yes, Daniel. I am sorry, but they are.

REEVES: (*With growing anger.*) I am not the dog.

LAWYER: Good.

REEVES: I am NOT the dog! I AM NOT—

LAWYER: Tell me about the dog.

REEVES: We were up to our asses in *dead bodies*. We were wearing *full-body armor*, carrying *automatic weapons* walking around looking for *people* to kill, and everybody went *nuts* when I threw a *dog* off a *roof* (*Amused.*) "He killed the dog! There's something wrong with him—he killed the dog." (*Then, laughing.*) The *dog*.

LAWYER: Go on.

REEVES: And it's *funny*. I mean, all this shit is going on, bombings and body parts—and they point at me and say, "Look at *that*! What *he* did? *That's* wrong. He killed a *dog*." It's *funny*. But it's not. Is it? I mean, not to the dog. You think I'm the *dog* off the *roof* AND IT'S NOT—FUCKING—FUNNY!

LAWYER: Daniel, please believe I never thought that. You are not the dog.

REEVES: Who am I then?

LAWYER: (*With growing enthusiasm.*) That's the other thing I can prove. I can prove that you are the person—the *only* person in this whole affair who said, "Something is wrong here." You are the *only* one who sought help—*before* the event—to get out of this mess. You sought help and they said—Well, we don't know what they said because the psychiatrist you went to won't say *what* she said. She won't testify.

REEVES: She won't?

LAWYER: Not without a grant of immunity.

REEVES: What does that mean?

LAWYER: (*Driving forward.*) It means she thinks she did something *very* wrong. Something that she *does—not—want* on the record. But you went on the record. In a culture in which seeking help is the *last* thing you do, you sought help. And I need to know what went on in that conversation. What did she say?

REEVES: It's confidential.

LAWYER: What did she say that was so terrible?

REEVES: It's confidential.

LAWYER: I need to know, Daniel, or there is no second story to tell at your trial.

REEVES: Dig her up. I'm guilty. DIG HER UP.

Lawyer: There would be no point, Daniel. She's dead. Her family is dead. All that's left of that girl is in here. All that's left of this whole incident is in here. (**Daniel**'s *head.*)

Reeves: (*Wild.*) I—AM—THE—DOG. I—AM—THE—DOG.

Lawyer: What did you tell the shrink, Daniel?

Reeves: (*Wilder.*) I TOLD HER I WANTED TO KILL EVERYBODY.

Lawyer: And what did she say?

Reeves: (*Wildest.*) SHE SAID I WAS NORMAL!

9 Circles
by Bill Cain

CHARACTERS: Reeves, an Army private on trial for rape and murder (19/20 years old); Pastor, folksy, carries a Bible

PLACE: Federal prison cell

CIRCUMSTANCE: Reeves was honorably discharged after 10 months of fighting in Iraq. A few weeks ago, Reeves was notified of his potential execution.

PASTOR: Son, you raped a girl, led others to do the same, and then you killed her and her whole family.

REEVES: You're sure I did that?

PASTOR: I am. Then you set fire to that girl's body and tried to put the blame on others. If you swore while you were doing it, you broke all ten of the Lord's commandments at one crack and broke 'em hard. Son, that *lawyer* was the wrong tool for the job. You need Jesus.

(*A smile.*)

And I'm going to take you to him.

(**REEVES** *looks at the* **PASTOR** *with anger. Thinks better of it. Smiles.*)

REEVES: (*Self-containing.*) I'm not going to get mad at you. I'm not going to shout. I'm not going to do that anymore. Fuck the act. (*Then, matter-of-fact.*) You want to talk about breaking commandments? You know what they did to my friends after I left? They cut off their dicks, put them in their mouths, cut off their heads and then took pictures of themselves— laughing. That's what those people are like.

PASTOR: All of them?

REEVES: Close enough so it doesn't matter. (*Then—*) One day there was a kid—walking towards us. Couldn't have been more than eleven. Hot, *hot* day and the kid is wearing an overcoat.

PASTOR: You shoot him?

REEVES: We don't do things like that. We got him to take off the coat.

PASTOR: You speak Arabic?

REEVES: Enough to make ourselves understood. And so he took off his coat, then his shirt, and there he was—in his underwear—covered in explosives. They strapped munitions onto an eleven-year-old boy.

PASTOR: I never met an eleven-year-old boy didn't have munitions strapped to him . . . I suspect you had more than most strapped on you.

REEVES: Look, why don't you go over there and bother them. If *anybody* needs Jesus, *they* do.

PASTOR: They aren't baptized. The minister from the base called me when he saw your picture in the papers. He told me he baptized you.

REEVES: Well, it didn't work.

PASTOR: Maybe he should have held you under longer.

REEVES: A few seconds more and it would've been waterboarding. Didn't work.

PASTOR: Worked on me. Made you my responsibility. (*Then*—) Speaking of lawyers. Your father hired a lawyer. It was in the paper.

REEVES: Really? (*With growing hope.*) Now why didn't anybody tell me that?

PASTOR: Why should they? The lawyer wasn't for you. He hired a lawyer to speak for him. Somebody he went to school with.

REEVES: (*Fuck it.*) Wouldn't have done me any good anyway.

PASTOR: Not a good lawyer?

REEVES: Good enough if you're buying a house.

PASTOR: Son, I don't know who you have at this point but Jesus.

REEVES: (*Restraint failing.*) *Fuck* Jesus. OK. *Fuck* Jesus. Where I was—the Tigris and Euphrates?—that's Bible land and there was no sign *anywhere* that *anybody* was one *bit better* for the *Bible*—and they had it *first*, OK? (*Then*—) No. I'm not going to shout.

PASTOR: (*I understand. In fact*—) I was like you once. Didn't even believe Jesus lived. Till I read one verse. One verse changed my life.

REEVES: God is love?

PASTOR: (*No.*) "Back off, you Syrian bitch."

(*Silence. Then*—)

REEVES: I don't recall ever hearing that one. And I had the book read to me when I was little.

PASTOR: (*Admittedly*—) It's a loose translation. . . . Woman comes up to Jesus. Says, "My daughter's dead. My little girl's dead. Can you bring her back to life?" And Jesus says to her, "Get away from me, you Syrian bitch." (*Then*—) At least, that's the sense of it.

Reeves: You are one fucked-up minister.

Pastor: Actually, he says, "You don't give the master's meat to the dog under the table." Called her a dog. A female dog. It's in the book. . . . I expect that Arabs had been calling Jesus names for a long time and this Syrian woman asking him to perform a miracle for her—that was his limit.

Reeves: (*?*) Out of *all* the verses in the Bible—*all* the miracles—all the *healings*—*that* saved you?

Pastor: Who said I was saved? I'm a recovering alcoholic with an Internet porn addiction I'm working on. Sometimes I think I walk through life just exchanging one addiction for another. I'm a weak and shallow vessel but I believe in Christ Jesus the Lord.

Reeves: Because he said, "Back off, you fucking Syrian bitch"?

Pastor: See, the thing is—nobody would put words like that into the mouth of their Savior and Lord. Would they? (*Then*—) I mean, who would dare add his own darkness to the Savior's blinding light. *Nobody* would make that up. Nobody could.

Reeves: Guess not.

Pastor: (*Exactly.*) He had to be *real* to say that. And if he was real, why— there is hope for us all.

Reeves: You know, you're the first pastor I ever met I might be able to talk to. . . . Maybe we should go back and start over with our area of common interest.

Pastor: And what is that?

Reeves: Internet porn.

Pastor: Son, read the book and prepare yourself for the shit storm that is about to hit you. There is a fair amount of shit repellent in here. It'll help when the storm comes your way.

(**Reeves** *takes the bible. Then*—)

Reeves: The girl—she wasn't dead.

Pastor: The paper said you shot her dead.

Reeves: No, not her. The Syrian girl. In the story. I know that story. She wasn't dead.

Pastor: No—matter of fact—she wasn't.

Reeves: Girl in the story was possessed by a demon. The mother asked Jesus to drive the demon out. You changed that part of the story.

Pastor: Yes, I did. Out of respect for you.

Reeves: You think I'm possessed, Pastor?

Pastor: It would be a comfort to me to think you were. Otherwise—we're just talking about plain I-don'tgive-a-fuck human evil and even God himself is helpless before that. Are you?

Reeves: Am I what?

Pastor: (*Taking courage to ask*—) Are you evil, son?

Reeves: (*Amused.*) Well, I'm not possessed. No voices in here. No distractions and 20/10 vision. I think I could have been a sniper. (*His head.*) It's quiet in here. Lonely sometimes. Might be good to have a voice or two to talk to.

Pastor: Voices in your head aren't interested in conversation. I knew a young man killed himself.

Reeves: Voices?

Pastor: (*Yes.*) There was some discussion as to whether he should be buried in consecrated ground or not.

Reeves: Well?

Pastor: What?

Reeves: Was he? Buried in consecrated ground?

Pastor: Do funerals interest you, son? . . . Maybe that's where I should've started. Maybe that's our area of common interest. Paper says you came here to see a funeral.

Reeves: I don't want to talk about that.

Pastor: (*Understanding.*) Because those three men who just got buried— they died for you.

Reeves: Well, that's a funny way to put it, but I believe—had I been there— they'd still be alive. I. (*Then*—) I don't want to talk about them.

Pastor: Would you care to talk about the rape?

Reeves: It's the rape that interests you, isn't it?

Pastor: It doesn't bother me unduly. Tell you the truth, I'm not sure I believe in consensual sex. I mean, somebody always wants it more, right? It's rare that need and desire are equally matched.

Reeves: You are the god-damnest minister.

Pastor: I suspect I am.

REEVES: You're enjoying this, aren't you?

PASTOR: Tell the truth, you scare the shit out of me. I'm scared to be here with you. Scared to say what I have to say. Still, it's my duty to bring you to the Lord. Even at the end.

(*Then, with new seriousness—*)

REEVES: I don't want a funeral. When I'm dead, leave my body on a couch in a vacant lot. Let dogs come and eat it. I'd like that.

PASTOR: Really?

REEVES: (*No, then for real.*) I'd like to get shot and go out on a Hummer hood.

PASTOR: You don't have to punish yourself, son. God will do that for you.

(**REEVES** *appreciates this. Amused—*)

REEVES: He already has.

PASTOR: Yes, he has. More than you know.

(*A moment—*)

REEVES: What don't I know? (*No response.*) What?

PASTOR: (*A risk.*) They're saying now—it was done for revenge.

REEVES: Really?

(**REEVES** *laughs.*)

Well, that's a relief. I knew somebody would figure that out. See, we all figured some hajjis—they killed the girl for revenge. Maybe an honor killing. That's what they do over there. Nothing but revenge.

PASTOR: I wasn't talking about the girl.

REEVES: Who then?

(*Very careful. Very delicate.*)

PASTOR: Your friends. The soldiers. The ones just got buried. They're saying now that they were killed for revenge.

REEVES: Revenge? For what? (*No response.*) What?

PASTOR: For the rape of a young girl.

(*Silence. Then* **REEVES** *laughs with relief.*)

REEVES: Now that just shows your ignorance. They would never have anything to do with something like that.

(*The* **PASTOR** *lays this out carefully.*)

PASTOR: Maybe it didn't matter. (*Then, feeling at risk.*) Maybe the family of the girl wanted revenge. (*Then—*) That's how they are, after all. According to you. (*Then—*) Maybe they saw your friends, your brothers—three American soldiers in a Hummer unprotected. They weren't the soldiers they wanted—they *wanted* you—they wanted the man who raped their child—but maybe any Americans were close enough, so it didn't matter.

(*Then—getting what the* PASTOR *is laying out—*)

REEVES: Are you saying—?

PASTOR: I am.

REEVES: Are you saying it was because of *me* they got killed?

PASTOR: If you killed that family. Did you, son?

REEVES: No. (*Then, attacking him.*) And you're a sick fuck to make that up.

PASTOR: But I didn't make it up.

REEVES: Where'd you get it then?

PASTOR: Internet.

REEVES: You know, there's a lot of bullshit on the Internet.

PASTOR: True enough, but I believe this.

REEVES: Yeah? Why?

PASTOR: Because it's like that story.

REEVES: Which?

PASTOR: Of the Syrian woman. (*Then—*) It's one of those stories you just couldn't make up. (*Then—*) Don't think anybody could.

(*The implications begin to shake* REEVES.)

They were killed for you, son. They died for your sins. Somebody had to and you wouldn't let Jesus do it for you.

REEVES: I don't believe it.

PASTOR: I didn't either. At first. But it makes sense, doesn't it, when you think about it. I mean, the violence of their deaths—that feels *personal*. The kind of thing, oh a father might do—

REEVES: I want a lawyer.

PASTOR: (*Pleased.*) Wrong tool for the job.

REEVES: They did *not* die for me.

Pastor: The thing that worries me is—what were they thinking as they were dying—your friends. Did they think they were dying for their country?

Reeves: They had their parade. Nothing can hurt them now.

Pastor: Or did one of the Iraqis know enough English to make it clear what they were dying for? Did somebody make it understood to them that they were dying for you. For Daniel Reeves and his demons.

Reeves: (*Deep denial.*) You'll say anything—anything at all—to get me to come to Jesus.

Pastor: Have I disturbed the quiet of your mind?

Reeves: Is that what you wanted?

Pastor: Yes, I believe so.

Reeves: Jesus drove demons out. He didn't drive them in.

Pastor: No, he didn't. But there's no confusing me with Jesus, is there? (*Then*—) Well, I'll be going now. I'll just leave the Bible in case you want to take a look. I've marked that story.

Reeves: You want voices—you want voices telling me to kill myself like that boy in your story, don't you?

Pastor: Oh, the voices didn't tell him to kill himself.

Reeves: No?

Pastor: The voices told him to kill his family. . . . That's why he killed. So when they asked if that boy should be buried in consecrated ground, I said there was no worry there: Wherever that boy was buried would be consecrated ground. He was a hero in death. And that's what I want for you, boy. Same thing you want for yourself. You want to be a hero, don't you, boy?

Reeves: Man, why are you doing this?

Pastor: (*Truth.*) The girl.

Reeves: I thought that didn't bother you.

Pastor: Not so much the rape, terrible as that is.

Reeves: What then?

Pastor: The fire. You set fire to her body. See, that's where your sin collides face to face with my addiction. I can't stand to see beauty vandalized.

Reeves: (*Powerful truth.*) I didn't do that.

PASTOR: Don't deny it, son.

REEVES: (*Very strong and sure.*) I told them not to. I didn't do that.

(*A moment. Then—*)

PASTOR: No, you probably didn't, the man who did that was ashamed of what he did. . . . But you did the rest, didn't you, son?

(**REEVES** *grows increasingly agitated as the* **PASTOR** *prepares to leave.*)

Don't lose heart, son. Let it be a call. Even Jesus needed a call. The woman said to him, "Maybe I don't get the meat from your table, but even dogs can have a crust of bread." And he threw her a crust. He drove out the demon. There is hope. For us all.

Detroit
by Lisa D'Amour

CHARACTERS: KENNY, fresh out of substance abuse rehab; BEN, Kenny's neighbor, recently laid off from his job

PLACE: The front steps of Ben's house; afternoon

CIRCUMSTANCE: Ben's severance is about run out. Plus his financial-planning website hasn't taken off.

(*They are each drinking a beer, like a Budweiser. They are quiet for a couple seconds.*)

KENNY: Well, whatever new job I get they're gonna garnish the paychecks.

BEN: Have you ever thought of sitting down with a credit specialist?

KENNY: I thought *I was* sitting down with a credit specialist.

BEN: And how much do those specialists usually cost? When you pay full price?

(*Silence for a moment.*)

I'm not asking for a lot of money. I just need to place some value on my time. Services cost money. If you offer something for free, it is seen as having less value. My book told me this.

KENNY: How is $25 going to make a difference to you right now?

BEN: It's the principle. I've got to stick by my principles.

(*They both take a sip of beer.*)

It's not a lot of money.

KENNY: Let's see, we'll see. I've got a court case I'm waiting on in Arkansas. It's gonna save us, if it comes through.

BEN: In Arkansas?

KENNY: I slipped and fell in a supermarket a few years ago. That's how I hurt my back. That's why I have to wear the weightlifting belt. The belt that cost me my job.

BEN: Right.

KENNY: When I get that settlement, I'll give you your $25 and you can give me more "advice."

BEN: Alright.

(*A few seconds.*)

Are you supposed to be drinking that?

KENNY: One is OK.

(*They sip.*)

So are you ready to start taking "real" clients?

BEN: I better. I have one more month of severance pay.

KENNY: One more month and you'll be just like me.

BEN: I guess so, yeah.

KENNY: Bruh-thaaaz.

(**BEN** *and* **KENNY** *clink beer cans.*)

How much you want to bet they're gonna call us any minute. Ah! There's snakes! There's roaches!

BEN: I don't know that their cell phones work out there.

KENNY: "Come out here! It's dark!" And you know what, we're not gonna go.

BEN: Well—

KENNY: No, really, they're out there in nature, sitting in the menstrual hut, eating crickets, whatever, that's what they want, and we have to honor that. We have to let the women be women.

BEN: They better not come back wanting to burn that . . . that . . .

KENNY: Sage stick.

BEN: Yeah! I went to a wedding once where they did that. So weird.

KENNY: That stuff stinks.

BEN: Wearing feathers and a deerskin skirt.

(*They both laugh.*)

KENNY: So whaddaya say, brothah? Boys' night out. There's Dan's Place and Déjà Vu and Temptations and Barely Legal.

BEN: I don't know—really?

KENNY: I've only been to Dan's Place and Déjà Vu. Déjà Vu is upscale but Dan's Place is traaa-shee!

BEN: I mean, really I should work.

KENNY: Work? It's Saturday. Our wives are away—

BEN: I know but maybe—

KENNY: We're just embracing our human nature, man—

BEN: But, Kenny, those clubs are expensive.

KENNY: We're just relaxing after a hard week's work.

BEN: The drinks alone are like nine bucks. And it's usually a three-drink minimum. It adds up, and then what?

KENNY: Aw, man. Aw, man, is that what this is about? You think it's irresponsible? For us to have a night out? For *me* to have a night out?

BEN: No, I didn't say that. It's just . . . it's just one night . . . if we take a step back for a second—

KENNY: Oh God, that fucking book!

BEN: I have. . . . I have a vision for my life, Kenny.

KENNY: So do I, douchebag.

BEN: Hey, hey, hey. This is coming out wrong. I mean, I don't even know how . . . can we . . . can we just drink, please?

KENNY: Hmph.

(*Both men take a sip.*)

You're a good man, Ben.

BEN: I don't know.

KENNY: No really, you are.

BEN: In a parallel universe I'm a good man.

KENNY: I'm an asshole.

BEN: No, you're not.

KENNY: I'm like, "You too good for yellow mustard!?" right in the middle of the store.

BEN: You're under a lot of stress.

KENNY: I'm an asshole, and it's too late for me.

(**BEN** *doesn't know what to say. The two men sip their beers.*)

BEN: I think this might be against the law.

KENNY: What?

BEN: Drinking beers in the front yard.

KENNY: You own your house, right?

BEN: Of course. Well, I mean, the bank owns it—

KENNY: Shit then, private property. You gotta hang on to that house, Ben.

BEN: Of course.

KENNY: Don't let anyone take it from you.

BEN: No, no, we're fine. I mean, we haven't even dipped into our savings and I don't think we'll have to. We're not . . . we're not anywhere near that yet.

KENNY: Hang on to that house. That's what my grandfather always used to say to my dad.

BEN: And did he hang on to it?

(**KENNY** *doesn't say anything. It is obvious his dad did not hang on to the house. Silence. Sound of the suburbs. Kids in the distance on bikes. A plane overhead. The compressors for several central A/C units. Maybe hovering a little closer than usual, pressing in.*)

(**BEN** *contemplates boys' night out.*)

I mean, I've got this leg.

KENNY: I bet it could get you a sympathy lap dance.

BEN: I don't know.

KENNY: I'll drive.

BEN: It's just such a hassle to *go* anywhere.

KENNY: We deserve it, Ben.

(*A few moments of silence where they kind of sit and watch and sip. Then* **BEN** *finishes his beer and crushes his can.*)

BEN: Alright, let's do it.

KENNY: Serious!

BEN: Yeah, you decide where we're going and you have to drive. Except I've been to Dan's too and it really is too skankified, so not there.

KENNY: You've been?

BEN: Sure, for an, um, bachelor party.

KENNY: Yeah right.

BEN: So maybe one rung up the ladder.

(**Ben** *looks down the street.*)

Kenny: Temptations then, let's try Temptations.

Ben: Should we get dinner first?

Kenny: Nah, man, let's just eat something here.

Ben: We've got nothing in the house.

Kenny: Fuck it, let's scrounge. I've got a can of Manwich.

Ben: I think we have hot dogs.

Kenny: Yeah, we'll chop 'em up, mix 'em around.

Ben: Spaghetti? Over Spaghetti?

Kenny: Oh man, no, I think maybe no—

Ben: Alright we might have some white bread.

Kenny: My brothah, we're good to go! Chow down and get there in time for happy hour.

Ben: I think it's two-for-one naval shots.

(**Kenny** *kind of dances and sings that line from the song "Hey-Ya" by OutKast.*)

Kenny: awright, awright, awright—

Ben: That's what they advertise, anyway.

(*This next speech cracks* **Ben** *up.*)

Kenny: See! For two brothahs on a budget! For two *men* whose wives are out playing survivor. For two men in need of a little R and R after a tough couple of weeks. For two men in search of a little good clean fun. For two men in need of a boys' night out. For two men who appreciate God's gift to this green earth. Who appreciate that special titty talent of the special titty dancer. For two men who want to feel more connected to their bodies and to the world. Who want to get out of the house and live a little. For two men who aren't afraid to have a good time even though their financial lives are swirling around in some kind of homemade toilet bowl—

Ben: Come on—

Kenny: For two men who are men. For two men who are going to have a great fucking night. For two men who are going to have a fucking great fucking night on the town, not far from their house. For two men who can take one night to not worry so much, to go out on the town and engage with the night life, with the life of the night, who want to see what kind of good clean fun is out there and if in the process they get their hands a little dirty, well, hey, it was in the name of good clean fun. For two men who, oh shit . . . oh shit . . . oh shit . . . oh shit . . .

(**KENNY** *sees something down the street.* **BEN** *looks.*)

BEN: Oh shit.

KENNY: Oh shit.

(**BEN** *takes the beer cans and tosses them behind the bushes.*)

Oh shit. Shit.

(*Sharon and Mary walk up.*)

Edith Can Shoot Things and Hit Them
by A. Rey Pamatmat

CHARACTERS: **KENNY**, a Filipino American; **BENJI**, his friend (both 16 years old)

PLACE: School library; early 90s

CIRCUMSTANCE: An amorous relationship is blossoming between Benji and Kenny. Benji's mother does not approve of the relationship.

(**KENNY** *has a few books.* **BENJI** *has his usual gigantic, overstuffed backpack.*)

KENNY: Come over.

BENJI: I'm not supposed to.

KENNY: I liked it better when she'd given up on you.

BENJI: Me too. At least we were getting laid. Dad says it's not punishment; I'm just not allowed to leave because we all need to spend more time together. But when he goes to work, Mom barely speaks to me, because to her it *is* punishment. And my stupid brother is just a dick. He tries to push or kick or hit me, and then he says something lame to piss me off like, "Fag!" or "Pussy!" or "Jesus saves!" And she lets him. So I tell him to quit touching me or he'll get my gay cooties. And then he walks around like some big stud being all "I'm not queer. I screwed Jemma Lieber." And I actually think, as of two days ago, he is screwing Jemma. But my mom won't say a word, because it comforts her. Like her oldest son is more of a man because he's boning a brainless perpetual shopping machine.

KENNY: God.

BENJI: So then I go, "You know what makes you a man? Taking it up the butt—if you can do that, you can do *anything*."

KENNY: WHAT?!

BENJI: Yeah. And then my brother punched me in the gut. And my mom locked me in my room. My mom will never let me go to your house again.

(**BENJI** *takes the sleeve of* **KENNY**'s *shirt between his fingers, trying to look casual.*)

But we'll always have pre-calc.

KENNY: So romantic.

BENJI: And maybe . . . My dad. He's taking me to dinner on Thursday. Just me and him. To A&W. I like the curly fries. Do you want to come?

KENNY: With your dad?

BENJI: Yeah.

KENNY: Why?

BENJI: Why? Because he . . . wants to meet you. "He's your boyfriend. Shouldn't I meet your boyfriend?"

KENNY: Are you serious?

BENJI: You called me your boyfriend. When we got ice cream. I didn't—you said it, and I . . .

KENNY: Oh.

BENJI: I shouldn't have taken it so seriously. You were freaking out, but I . . .

KENNY: Okay.

BENJI: Yeah?

KENNY: Thursday. A&W. Will you pick me up, or should I drive?

BENJI: We'll pick you up. And he'll probably pay for everything, so . . .

KENNY: So . . . another date.

BENJI: Yeah. Sort of. With a chaperone. What did your dad say? He saw us that night, so he knows.

KENNY: Yeah. He asked who you were. I told him. And he just . . . stared at me. Blankly. Like he . . . he didn't care.

BENJI: He's such a jerk.

KENNY: He's my dad.

BENJI: Can't you just say he's a jerk? Why do you defend him?

KENNY: Now you sound like Ed. Whatever. I don't care what he thinks. It's better if he doesn't care. If he leaves us alone.

BENJI: Your dad doesn't care enough. My mom cares too much.

KENNY: Yeah, right? Anyway, what's important now is Ed. I need to get her out of there, but I don't know how. I used to leave her alone, Benji. And now I'm there alone, and it's so quiet. Edith used to watch the same stupid movies over and over again—like this gnome musical thing. And I never knew why. But now I know. Without her there's nothing there. But what can I tell my dad so he'll take Edith out of that school? Nothing I come up with seems good enough to do the job.

BENJI: That's your answer. There's nothing to come up with. There's no story to tell.

KENNY: I can't just leave her there.

BENJI: Don't. Tell him that he can't leave her, because . . . he can't. You need to help your sister. And you need to stop telling stories to pretend your dad's not a jerk or to avoid confronting people or just to get your way.

KENNY: No, I have to at least . . . I can't stop—

BENJI: Kenny, if you don't, then you will one day, eventually, lie to me.

KENNY: No, I won't. (*Pause.*) I won't!

BENJI: Tell him the truth, Kenny.

KENNY: I . . . I don't know how to do that.

BENJI: You'll figure it out. You take it up the butt, remember? You can do anything.

(**BENJI** *tugs at* **KENNY**'s *shirt again.*)

KENNY: I think about how you smell. Is that weird?

BENJI: How do I smell?

KENNY: Like Ivory soap. And dryer sheets.

BENJI: I think about your hand on the back of my head. Your fingers in my hair. I really want to kiss you, Kenny.

KENNY: Your brother might see. He'll tell your mom.

BENJI: She can't treat me any worse than she's already treating me.

KENNY: Benji, let's at least—we'll go somewhere, or—

(**BENJI** *kisses* **KENNY**.)

BENJI: I don't want us to hide. I don't want you to hide. Tell him the truth. They threw us out, or threw us away. They have no right anymore to tell us what to do.

Equivocation
by Bill Cain

CHARACTERS: CECIL, King James's right-hand man; SHAG, Shakespeare

PLACE: Cecil's Office

CIRCUMSTANCE: Shag has been asked to write and produce a play about the gunpowder plot.

(SHAG *waits nervously in Cecil's office, which has in it the King's robe, crown, and scepter—displayed museum like. As* SHAG *goes to touch them,* CECIL—*in a good mood—enters on a run.*)

CECIL: (*Playful.*) Hands off or your head's off. (*As* SHAG *steps away.*) I keep them here so James's children can't play with them. Don't you start.

(CECIL *limps briskly past* SHAG, *removes the manuscript from under* SHAG'S *arm.*)

See. I told you it wouldn't take long. (*After paging though the text.*) This isn't the play.

SHAG: No. It isn't.

CECIL: Well? Where is it?

SHAG: Barely begun.

CECIL: You're not . . . What's the word for a person who waits till the last minute? A . . .

SHAG: Writer?

CECIL: Procrastinator. From the Latin. *Pro eras.* "For tomorrow." "Tomorrow" is my least favorite word.

(CECIL, *a busy man, gets to work at his desk as the conversation goes on.*)

SHAG: I work well under pressure.

CECIL: Is that what you've come here for—pressure?

SHAG: No. I've come here to . . . (*Hesitation.*) After considerable discussion with the company . . . (*Hesitation.*) And I say this most regretfully—

CECIL: (*Still working.*) Come, come, more matter with less art.

SHAG: Again, it is with great regret that I say that we cannot—(*Dead stop.*) "More matter with less art?" (*Then—*) That's from *Hamlet.* So—(*Then, a victory.*)—you *have* seen my plays!

Cecil: (*Brilliantly articulate while still working.*) There is a ship in the harbor—captured from the Spanish—containing all God's riches in small, easily pilfered quantities—gold bracelets, ivory carvings, spices. Not only do I know what is still in the hold—I know where the stolen items are—down to the last grain of pepper.

Shag: When do you sleep?

Cecil: I don't. (*Looking up at* **Shag**.) I could give you the same details on every ship in the harbor—even though I haven't been in their stinking holds—(*Rising.*)—and I can tell you about every one of your plays even though I haven't been in your cesspit of a theater. I am well informed.

Shag: Are you?

Cecil: I am. I have been informed you are here to tell me you won't do my play.

Shag: Easy guess.

Cecil: Is it? Then perhaps you would like me to inform you about your family. (*A file on his desk.*) Would you like me to tell you about your dead son, your foolish father, and your endlessly rutting wife? (*This silences* **Shag**.) Now, if you do not have my play, what are you doing here?

(*Provoked,* **Shag** *goes on the offensive. His anger goes into the details of his work—not unlike* **Cecil**.)

Shag: I've come to find out about the *dirt*.

Cecil: Dirt? What dirt?

Shag: *Dirt.* Men tunneling under Parliament must have brought out a huge amount of *dirt*. Where did it go?

Cecil: (*Are you insane?*) In a time of national crisis, nobody's going to care about the dirt.

Shag: *Does this play matter to you?* (**Shag** *has* **Cecil**'s *attention.*) Because there will be seven hundred penny-a-place standees at every performance, all of whom make their living with their hands, and if there's *anything* they will want to know about, it's *the dirt*. (*Preempting* **Cecil**.) And the water. The tunnel's by the river. Water would have seeped in. How did they get rid of it? Who ran the pumps? It's a long tunnel. Where did the wood come from to build the supports to hold it up? Was one of them a carpenter? Which? Who knew how to support a mine shaft? (*Before CECIL can speak.*) It's the details that sell the story. People tend to trust you on the big things if you get the small ones right—and this play is going to require more trust than usual.

CECIL: Why?

SHAG: Working people know nothing neat-as-this-piece-of-nonsense can possibly be true. This—(*Tossing the manuscript.*)—is a shoddy piece of work.

CECIL: *The King* wrote a shoddy piece of work?

SHAG: *Whoever* wrote this wrote a shoddy piece of work. Was it you?

CECIL: I remind you. When you speak to me you are speaking to the King. Do you understand that?

SHAG: I understand more than that. When I am speaking to you, I am speaking to the man who made an English king out of wee James of Scotland. It could not have been easy.

CECIL: And if the King walked in now, you would find a way to flatter him too, wouldn't you? (*Disgusted.*) Probably at my expense . . . Now, what's the precise problem with this?

SHAG: (*Escalating.*) There's nothing wrong with *it*. It's what's wrong with *me*. I'm a *playwright*.

CECIL: And?

SHAG: (*Escalating.*) You don't want a play. You want a *propaganda* story. I don't do that.

CECIL: (*Outraged.*) Don't do propaganda? *You?* You're the man who gave Richard the Third his *hump*.

SHAG: He was a murderer.

CECIL: They're *all* murderers! *He* balanced the budget. People have *no idea* how hard that is! (*Outrage building.*) You made the Yorks *hideous* so that the people would love the Tudors and, in return, the Tudors made you *rich*! And now that you have your *land* and the *second largest house in Stratford*—now—NOW you *don't do* PROPAGANDA?

SHAG: No, I don't do *story*. . . . You were right about that. I am not an *original writer*. I find stories. I "dialogue" them. *Modify*. Sometimes improve, *but I need material and this*—

CECIL: —*is a shoddy piece of work! Fine! FIX it!*

(CECIL *returns to his work, but* SHAG *won't be ignored.*)

SHAG: I can't! It isn't dramatic. Nothing *happens*.

CECIL: Nothing—? *A group of thirteen fanatics plot to blow up Parliament*—

Shag: And *don't! Even my actors see the problem! There is no plot!*

Cecil: (*Rising, enraged.*) It is *treason* to say so!

Shag: Treason? . . . Treason? . . . It's—(*What?*)—literary criticism.

(*Silence. Then, getting it—*)

Cecil: Ohhhhhhhhhhhhhhhhh—no *plot.* (**Cecil** *gets the irony. Releases the tension. Then—a new start.*) Concerning your plays—

Shag: (*Done with this!*) I'd ask you not to criticize them further until you have actually *seen* one of them!

Cecil: (*An admission.*) I have never seen your plays, but I have *heard* them. Here at court.

Shag: I've never seen you.

Cecil: You've never looked behind the arras. Your plays—move me. I cannot be seen to be moved. Your words are—(*Almost sexual.*)—extraordinary. They have a quality that I admire very much.

Shag: And what is that?

Cecil: Power. (*Then—*) Since the time of Henry Eight we have lived in a divided country. We have had two religions—Catholic/Protestant—old faith/new—petty theological differences have been tearing this country apart.

Shag: Petty?

Cecil: Do you think God cares if we pray in Latin or English? If there are seven sacraments or three? Surplices or chasubles? We all worship one God, do we not?

Shag: Many lives were sacrificed for those "petty" differences. The Law of Religious Uniformity saw to that.

Cecil: My father was the architect of that law. He was trying to bring about national unity. What my father didn't understand was—you can't *legislate* a soul into a country. For that, you need a story—a moving story—a story everyone can believe in. William—you are the one person who can make this work.

(*Before* **Shag** *can respond—*)

(**Voice** *offstage, heavy Scots accent: "Beagle!"*)

Cecil: (*Awkward pause, then—*) I must go.

Shag: Who's that?

(**Voice** *offstage:* "*Beagle, laddie!*")

Shag: The King? The King is looking for his—

Cecil: (*Packing papers.*) For the dirt and pumps, the priests—Jesuits—they are the arithmeticians of the religious world and, as the power behind the plot, I'm sure they found ways of working it out.

Shag: Then I need to speak to the priests.

Cecil: As do I, but I haven't been able to find them.

Shag: I thought you were well informed.

Cecil: I am, but they have an advantage of me in that I am not in league with the devil.

Shag: You don't expect me to believe that.

Cecil: Which part? That the priests are in league with the devil or that I'm not? Because I assure you *I'm not* or I would know where the devil they are.

Shag: (*Leaving.*) Well, send for me when you find them.

Cecil: You know, it's a shame your father isn't alive. He knew priests, didn't he? Knew them well. (***More than a hint of threat.***) He entertained Jesuits? Had them in his home? Your home? Didn't he?

Shag: Is that what this is about? *My* father?

Cecil: (*Truth.*) It can be.

Shag: My father was not a spiritual man. He was a leather worker. It's easy to cheat with leather. It stretches. He liked the priests because they never changed their measure.

Cecil: I will give them this. You can stretch them a full foot taller and they will still give you nothing. (*Then—*) Well, shall we do what no one since Henry has been able to do and restore unity to this nation?

(**Cecil** *offers his hand.* **Shag** *declines.*)

Shag: What you want is a sermon, not a play. (***Handing back the money.***) Your world has rules—so does mine. Comedies end in weddings; tragedies in deaths; histories in battles. This—(*The manuscript.*)—just ends.

(**Voice** *offstage:* "*Beagle!*")

Cecil: (*Rushing, writing* **Shag** *a pass.*) Speak with the remaining conspirators in the Tower. Let us say Thomas Wintour. Perhaps he can provide the details you need.

SHAG: I don't think they'll be of help.

CECIL: Why not?

SHAG: I read Tom Wintour's confession. He wrote it?

CECIL: Dictated it.

SHAG: But it's his signature?

CECIL: Sworn and witnessed.

SHAG: Odd, he misspelled his own name.

CECIL: He was under some *pressure* at the time. You work well under pressure. How much pressure do you need? Enough to make you forget how to spell your name? Because it *can be provided.*

   (**VOICE** *offstage:* "Beagle! Beagle, I say! . . . BEAGLE!")

SHAG: He *is* calling his *dog,* isn't he?

CECIL: I must go. Get writing.

   (**CECIL** *starts out.*)

SHAG: GOD SAVE THE KING! (**CECIL** *stops. Turns.*) What—no a*men*?

CECIL: You—even you—must find *some* things stick in your throat.

Inana
by Michele Lowe

CHARACTERS: EMAD, an Iraqi, chief of the Mosul Museum; YASIN, Shali's father, an Iraqi artist

PLACE: Emad's art studio

CIRCUMSTANCE: Prior to the invasion of Iraq, Yasin attempts to preserve Inana, a treasured statue, by enlisting the help of an expert forger, Emad.

EMAD: I must apologize for the mess. I've been working on a terra-cotta plaque. I haven't gotten the dragon quite right and it was supposed to be finished last week.

YASIN: I won't keep you.

EMAD: On the contrary, it's an honor to have you here.

YASIN: Then you know who I am?

EMAD: You're the curator. You're a friend of AbdelHakim Taliq.

YASIN: For many years.

EMAD: I shall miss his collection when it's gone to Tehran.

YASIN: I think he's wise.

EMAD: I don't know if he's wise but he's very careful with his treasures. Very protective. No doubt like you.

YASIN: Yes.

EMAD: Yes.

(*A beat of awkward silence.*)

YASIN: Is there somewhere we can speak without being interrupted?

EMAD: No one comes around here. Too much dust.

YASIN: You have a reputation for making objects that are so beautiful we see them in museums all over the world.

EMAD: But not in yours.

YASIN: No.

EMAD: You hope.

YASIN: I'm quite positive.

EMAD: You have the Waru urn don't you?

YASIN: On the first floor, yes.

EMAD: (*Slyly.*) It's a lovely piece, isn't it?

(*Silence.*)

YASIN: Some would think you mean to tease us.

EMAD: Not at all. My vessels and vases are at best minor works of art inspired by the greatest antiquities. They aren't copies. Anyone familiar with the original would know that. They couldn't be for a thousand reasons. They're merely interpretations.

YASIN: Then how is it they wind up on display in so many venerated institutions?

EMAD: I don't keep track of what I sell. Once it leaves here I have nothing to do with it. If people misunderstand my handiwork and think it's valuable, if they say it's come from an Egyptian excavation or Syrian temple, I can't do anything about that.

YASIN: You don't like museums.

EMAD: Everything is so neat and orderly entombed in those glass cases. Who comes to your museum? Not the people in the neighborhood.

YASIN: They're welcome to.

EMAD: They're not your kind of people and they know it. You mock them. You put their history behind glass and then you ask them to pay to see it.

YASIN: If we didn't house the objects, we couldn't study them.

EMAD: Can't we just say they're beautiful and be done with it?

YASIN: Beauty itself means nothing. It needs to be put into historical context.

EMAD: Why not let them exist on their own, as objects here and now?

YASIN: If you don't believe in history, why copy an antiquity?

EMAD: Because I'm not that talented and they're far better than anything I could think up.

YASIN: You're an antiquarian at heart with a modernist viewpoint.

EMAD: My wife says my biggest problem is that I was born three thousand years too late.

(**EMAD** *has taken a pair of scissors and paper into his hands. He is cutting out shapes.*)

YASIN: What are you making there?

EMAD: My wife calls it my busy work. Years ago we went to Paris and saw Matisse's paper cuts. I loved them; they're the only contemporary art I like. I'm not very good at the execution, but I'm not paid to be. My fingers need to move, so I give them paper and scissors and voilà, something happens. You fold here, cut there. I try not to get too involved in the mechanics. If I think of a bird while I cut, quite soon there's a sparrow sitting in my palm. Or something that resembles a sparrow. Here.

(*He hands* YASIN *the paper and scissors.*)

YASIN: I'm clumsy at this sort of thing.

EMAD: Even my wife can do it.

YASIN: I wouldn't know where to begin.

EMAD: Think of an object, the lines it has, the soft spots, the way it looks from a particular angle. Don't close your eyes, you'll poke yourself and bleed. I've done it.

(YASIN *tries but gives up.*)

YASIN: Nothing's coming.

EMAD: Try it again. Try it in that office of yours, only make sure the door's closed.

YASIN: You've been to the museum?

EMAD: Many times.

YASIN: Are you familiar with the statue of Inana?

EMAD: Yes, of course. I've studied her at length. Oh, don't worry, I haven't done anything based on her. Yet.

YASIN: I've been instructed to make a copy of her. In this case you'd be authorized to do so.

EMAD: By whom?

YASIN: By me. I assure you it would be completely legal. The copy of the statue would be displayed and we'd keep the original in the main vault.

EMAD: And you'd be fooling people into thinking she was the original.

YASIN: We don't want to deprive the public from seeing her; however, we don't want her at risk either.

EMAD: Why now? Because of the Americans?

YASIN: I've been thinking about doing this since the Gulf War. We haven't lost her yet. I don't want this to be the time our luck runs out. Do I have your attention yet?

EMAD: Very much so.

YASIN: Shall we move on to more mundane subjects then?

EMAD: Money?

YASIN: And time.

EMAD: A job like that would take approximately six months to execute, providing I agreed to do it.

YASIN: I'd need it sooner.

EMAD: As I mentioned to you before, I'm already behind. I have another commission due in less than three months and another one after that. But if you're prepared to wait a year—

YASIN: I'm not.

EMAD: Then I'm afraid I can't help you. I can recommend someone to you in Rome. He's excellent.

YASIN: It has to be you and it has to be done as soon as possible.

EMAD: I've been known to make special arrangements.

YASIN: What if your schedule was clear and you could put all your resources behind it?

EMAD: You mean in a perfect world?

YASIN: Yes.

EMAD: I could have it to you in eight weeks. But as I told you—

YASIN: My benefactor has very deep pockets.

(*Beat.*)

EMAD: Four million dinars.

YASIN: (*Shocked.*) Four million?

EMAD: For the statue of Inana in eight weeks' time, yes, four million dinars.

YASIN: Is that number negotiable?

EMAD: Not at all.

YASIN: (*Shocked.*) Four million?

EMAD: Dinars.

YASIN: I don't have anywhere near that much.

EMAD: Then I'm afraid I can't help you.

YASIN: Is there some other arrangement we could make?

EMAD: Such as?

YASIN: We're both creative men.

(*Beat.*)

EMAD: Then let us both think on it another night.

YASIN: I have little time to waste dwelling on the impossible.

EMAD: I assure you it's not the impossible I seek. Perhaps there's something else you can give me, something with a value greater than money.

YASIN: It would have to be something extraordinary.

EMAD: I was thinking the same thing.

The problem is that you want something from me that you can't afford. It's a dilemma, isn't it? How do you satisfy a craving for something completely beyond your reach? You can kill it so it's out of your mind. That often works.

YASIN: Not in this case.

EMAD: Or you can bend things to fit, turn the pieces until they fall into place. I've given it some thought and I've discovered there is something you can give me. Something with a value greater than money.

YASIN: I can't give you anything from the museum.

EMAD: That wasn't what I had in mind.

YASIN: What is it then?

EMAD: I want you.

YASIN: Me?

EMAD: Our friend Abdel-Hakim tells me that he's looking for a bride for you.

YASIN: Out of the goodness of his heart, but not at my request.

EMAD: I have the perfect girl. If you agree to marry her, I'll make you the statue within two months' time for nothing at all. Money doesn't enter into it.

YASIN: Are you mad?

EMAD: Not at all.

YASIN: You want me to marry a girl in exchange for the statue?

EMAD: Not only marry her but leave the country with her as soon as possible.

YASIN: You are mad.

EMAD: Only delirious with joy. I have found a solution to both our problems.

YASIN: What is your problem?

EMAD: She is my daughter.

YASIN: Do you love her so little?

EMAD: On the contrary, I favor her above all my children, but she's too smart for her own good. She's talking about teaching women to read, groups of women, in secret. Too dangerous. I want you to take her wherever you like and never come back.

YASIN: You can't be serious.

EMAD: If you return, I'll tell the world that I created a copy of the greatest statue in Iraq for your museum at your request.

YASIN: This isn't at all what I was thinking.

EMAD: It's a very creative idea. I'm so pleased with it, I'll even buy the travel tickets.

YASIN: What if I could come close to getting you the money you requested? What if I paid you over time?

EMAD: I don't want money. I like these terms much better.

YASIN: But they're impossible.

EMAD: Why?

YASIN: I don't know anything about your daughter.

EMAD: What kind of woman are you looking for?

YASIN: I'm not looking for a woman. I don't want to get married.

EMAD: Do you want to be alone for the rest of your life?

(YASIN *does not respond.*)

Then you must get married. This is the perfect opportunity for you, Yasin. You get a wife and your statue. In fact, I think you come out much better in the end than I do.

YASIN: How would it look for me to marry the daughter of the biggest art forger in the Middle East?

EMAD: A month before you wed, I'll announce that I'm giving up my business. I'll close the studio. That'll be my very public wedding gift to you both.

YASIN: You'd do that?

EMAD: When you have children you'll understand better. Besides, after I make your statue, how could I possibly follow that?

Perfect Mendacity
by Jason Wells

CHARACTERS: **Peoples**, a polygraph consultant, Black American (40s); **Walter**, a microbiologist and defense contractor, White American (50s).

PLACE: Peoples's office

CIRCUMSTANCE: Walter is being investigated by his employers over an incriminating memo that was leaked to the media.

EDITOR'S NOTE: Slash marks (/) indicate where the lines are to overlap.

>(**Peoples** *sits at the desk, just out of* **Walter**'s *periphery. Makes a few clicks on the laptop and studies the screen.*)

Peoples: Here we go. Is your name Walter Krootzer?

Walter: Kreutzer. Yes.

>(*There is a fifteen-second pause after every answer.*)

Peoples: Are we in the United States of America?

Walter: Yes.

Peoples: Have you ever violated your own code of ethics?

Walter: No

Peoples: Have you ever brought a confidential memo home from work?

Walter: No.

Peoples: Are we sitting outdoors?

Walter: No.

Peoples: Have you ever lied to your supervisors about anything?

Walter: No.

Peoples: Did you show a confidential memo to your wife?

Walter: No.

Peoples: Did you ever say the holocaust was exaggerated?

Walter: What?

Peoples: Did you tell a bunch of white supremacists that the holocaust was an exaggeration?

WALTER: (*Rattled.*) That isn't one of the questions.

PEOPLES: Did you?

WALTER: This is not a question that we discussed! They're not going to ask a question that wasn't discussed ahead of time. That's not how it works.

PEOPLES: Well, surprise then, I guess. You don't know *what* they might do.

WALTER: There's *no* test. . . . There's *no* test that uses surprise questions.

PEOPLES: Maybe I'm some crazy cowboy, runnin' off on his own, no respect for the guidelines of the American Polygraph Association.

WALTER: You have to stick to the questions!

PEOPLES: I don't have to do diddly-nothin', except discover your mendacious propensities by any means I choose.

WALTER: Wait a minute. Are you supposed to be in character?

PEOPLES: Huh?

WALTER: Are you speaking / for yourself, or preten—

PEOPLES: Yes. No, I'm pretending to be the examiner, Walt. You know how this works.

WALTER: I want you to stop . . . checking *up* on me! Just stop . . . running / checks on me!

(*Tries to extricate himself.*)

PEOPLES: Be careful with that equipment.

WALTER: Get me out of here. / Just—just—

PEOPLES: Whoa, whoa. Don't pull on that stuff. You're gonna mess that up.

WALTER: I want my money back;

PEOPLES: Pardon me?

WALTER: You heard me.

PEOPLES: I'm not giving you your money back. I've put a lot of time into this, and I've shared my secrets with you. / Now, just sit still.

WALTER: Your secrets are worthless. Blue buttons and red buttons . . . /*White . . .*

PEOPLES: Red Buttons? Remember him?

WALTER: What?

PEOPLES: Red *Buttons.* I never made that association before.

WALTER: I don't know what you're talking about. Just unhook me. Now.

PEOPLES: You don't think this'll work? You never lied to yourself before? 'Cause that's all you're doing.

WALTER: You're trying to . . .

PEOPLES: What?

WALTER: You're trying to FUCK ME!

PEOPLES: Whoa, hold on. Now, why would I do that?

WALTER: You know why.

PEOPLES: No, I don't. You paid me cash. To do what I do. This is what I do. Why would I want to undermine my livelihood?

WALTER: Because you don't like me.

PEOPLES: Walt. Hm. Walt. Were you pushing your buttons just now? During the test?

WALTER: Yes.

(**PEOPLES** *turns the laptop so* **WALTER** *can see it.*)

PEOPLES: Look how you freaked out, here, when I mentioned that holocaust business. You see that? You got all flustered; forgot how to lie to yourself. See?

WALTER: Yeah.

PEOPLES: But look here: The other questions. Your baseline is high and steady. Your relevant responses are shaky—I guess I'd have to give you a DI, but I'd puzzle over it first. It's that close. And we're just getting started. So, now, you don't have to care if I "like" you or not. You only have to understand that I'm your *friend.* Your *friend* did this for you, Walt.

WALTER: I'm not paying you to do research on me.

PEOPLES: I'm done with that. I just needed something to work with. That's all. We gotta rehearse everything. We even gotta rehearse the surprises. You want to be good at this, don't you?

WALTER: Yes.

PEOPLES: Then trust me.

WALTER: We're supposed to be working on the Comparison model. Comparison Test doesn't have surprises.

PEOPLES: Walter, you ain't trying to get a job at Office Depot. You are a scientist at a defense business. You think they're not gonna assume you studied this stuff? They are going to seek to mess you up. They're gonna attack you on the pre-test. They're gonna attack you on the test. They're gonna attack you on the post-test. You know why? Because they're mercenaries. We got an adjective for them: *mercenary*.

WALTER: If they really believe I'm guilty, they'll get me.

PEOPLES: I'm gonna change your attitude. Today. Right now. Now, straighten up. Shake it off. Relax. We're gonna go again.

(*Returns to the desk.*)

Now, this time, really push them red buttons. Now I can't say it without thinking "Red Buttons." Remember him? Never got a dinner? That's alright. You ready?

WALTER: Yeah.

PEOPLES: Here we go: Is your name Walter Krootzer?

WALTER: Kreutzer. Yes.

PEOPLES: Did you say the holocaust was exaggerated?

WALTER: God DAMN it!

PEOPLES: (*Innocent.*) You didn't think I was / gonna ask it?

WALTER: Son of a BITCH!

PEOPLES: I didn't say I wasn't gonna / ask it.

WALTER: It was the *second* fucking *question*!

PEOPLES: It's my Sacrifice Relevant.

WALTER: That's not a Sacrifice Relevant. That's not a Sacrifice fucking / Relevant!

PEOPLES: Walter. Walter.

WALTER: *What?*

PEOPLES: My niece can probably hear you out there.

WALTER: Listen to me: They were a *paying* audience. It was a business arrangement. I'm a *scientist*. If someone wants to know the facts about something, I, I , I—It's an obligation. It is practically an *obligation*.

PEOPLES: You're totally messing up this chart, Walt.

WALTER: Do you hear me?

PEOPLES: Yeah. What were the facts?

WALTER: The, f— They wanted to hear about Leuchter's study of, of Zyklon B residue at Auschwitz. It's a bullshit study, and I as much as said so.

Peoples: This chart says you're lying.

Walter: Goddamnit, are you watching the chart?

Peoples: I'm just telling you . . .

Walter: I thought "only the examiner" could tell I was lying.

Peoples: Well, he's looking at this chart, and he says you're lying.

Walter: You can't use it that way.

Peoples: You gotta stop thinking about how I can use it. I am beholden to no one. Now, you're saying you went all that way to disappoint these people?

Walter: I told them it was inconclusive, alright? Which is true. Okay?

Peoples: Your cardiovascular is allover / the place.

Walter: Of *course* my cardiovascular is all over the place. D'avore. What do you *think*?

Peoples: I'm just trying to get you to calm down.

Walter: No, you *should* be trying to get me to calm down, but you're actually trying to get me *upset*! For some reason. I mean, what are you *doing* to me?

Peoples: I'm helping you.

Walter: You are not helping me.

Peoples: So, you have—and I'm just asking out of curiosity—you have some sort of ethical, uh, *principle*, by which you are obligated to speak to anyone who pays you?

Walter: As long as I don't *lie*, D'avore. Then, yes. As long as they understand that I'm bringing objective, factual . . .

Peoples: Yeah?

Walter: Information, then . . . then . . .

Peoples: It's factual that the holocaust was exaggerated?

Walter: Oh—look. *Look:*

Peoples: Yeah?

Walter: Why did they have to say six million?! That's all. Why not *four*? Isn't four enough?! Four and a half! Why *six*?! "Three to six million," they could say. Even that! I mean, I'm a scientist, that's all. Numbers *mean* something to me. To settle on the highest . . . possible . . . ?

PEOPLES: What difference does it make?

WALTER: That's what I'm saying. That's my point. It's millions. We concede that it's millions. Why do we, why do we have to be held to this . . . this . . .

PEOPLES: Who's "we"?

WALTER: What do you mean?

PEOPLES: Who's "we"? You say "we" concede that it's millions.

WALTER: I mean "everyone."

PEOPLES: And why "concede"? Like you're in an argument about it. Why not just "say"? "Say" it's four million, or whatever. "Concede" sounds like you don't want to say it. Like you're reluctant. Right? If I understand that word.

WALTER: I'm not what you think I am.

PEOPLES: Okay.

WALTER: Those people are idiots. I understand that. I just—I just—I have to make a living.

PEOPLES: (*Studying laptop screen.*) Magic Eight Ball says, "Yes." You have to make a living.

WALTER: Please stop pretending that you have any legitimate scientific basis for reading that thing right now.

PEOPLES: But you're not a history expert, are you?

WALTER: I'm a scientist. Statistics is a science.

PEOPLES: But you're not a statistics scientist, are you? You're a micro . . . botanist . . . / or . . .

WALTER: Biologist.

PEOPLES: What I'm saying is, if my Klan meeting was looking for a speaker . . .

WALTER: It wasn't a Klan meeting.

PEOPLES: No, I'm saying . . .

WALTER: And they didn't call themselves white supremacists. If they had called themselves something, I wouldn't have gone.

PEOPLES: They didn't *call* themselves nothin'?

WALTER: They were the Truth in . . . Public . . . Something Society, or some bullshit.

Peoples: So I'm saying if my Truth Society was having a meeting, I'd hire a speaker I knew was, you know, sympathetic.

Walter: I never professed sympathy. *Please.* I had some experiences in Rhodesia—interesting . . . political. . . . . These were eventful, complicated times. / Look . . .

Peoples: Rhodesia?

Walter: Zimbabwe. It's Zimbabwe now.

Peoples: They got a lot of Jews down there? In Zimbabwe?

Walter: No. Please. These were racial conflicts I had nothing to do with. Except I happened to be there at the time. That's all.

Peoples: So, black folks and white folks.

Walter: Yes.

Peoples: Which side was the Truth Society on?

Walter: Okay, that's it. Unhook me, or I'll do it myself. I'm done here. Keep the money, but I'm done with you.

Peoples: Hold on, Walter. Why you taking this so personal?

Walter: You've *made* it personally. Personal. *You* have. You've got some kind of problem with me, and you're gonna waste the whole afternoon *interrogating* me about every little . . . / every little . . .

Peoples: *They* are going to interrogate you.

Walter: Not about *this* stuff. Not about this. You think they care? You know what kind people they have working there?

Peoples: What kind?

Walter: Well. *All* kinds. All, different kinds. Is all I'm saying.

Peoples: I try not to judge people, Walter. Everybody's got a story, you know?

Walter: Um. I could take that two ways.

Peoples: I don't follow.

Walter: People say, "Everybody's got a story," to *dismiss* that story. See? But, but . . .

Peoples: Huh?

Walter: Sometimes people have an actual, *actual story* . . .

Peoples: Hmm. But my / point is . . .

WALTER: Worthy of acknowledgment. Some sort of . . .

PEOPLES: My point . . .

WALTER: . . . the benefit of the *doubt* . . .

PEOPLES: My point, Walter, my point is, if you don't get / your head together . . .

WALTER: The benefit of the *doubt*. My head? Just leave my fucking head out of it, okay? Just get out of my fucking head completely. Just do your fucking *job*, okay?

PEOPLES: I'm gonna urge you not to take that tone with me.

WALTER: (*Redirecting his frustration.*) *God.* I'm sorry. I'm *sorry.* Please. Can we— This is not . . . This / is not . . .

PEOPLES: Push that blue button.

WALTER: I can't.

PEOPLES: Push the blue button, now. Make these lines go down. Push it.

WALTER: I'm trying. But I don't believe in you.

PEOPLES: Walter . . .

WALTER: Wait.

(*He goes to his "blue" image.*)

PEOPLES: That's it. You're makin' it happen.

WALTER: You can't— You don't know.

PEOPLES: No, no. Hold it down.

WALTER: (*Getting agitated.*) I have something in my head. An insect in my brain.

PEOPLES: What?

WALTER: I mean . . .

PEOPLES: You have a / insect in your . . . ?

WALTER: That's not what I meant. I—that's not what I meant.

PEOPLES: But you s—

WALTER: I was speaking metaphorically

PEOPLES: (*Warily.*) Okay. Let's try to get back to zero. Just look at that white image. Look at that blank page.

WALTER: Okay.

PEOPLES: You see that blank white page?

WALTER: Yes.

PEOPLES: You see it?

WALTER: Yes.

PEOPLES: There ain't an *insect* on it, is there?

WALTER: Goddamnit, / I'm not crazy.

PEOPLES: Alright, / calm down.

WALTER: I'm not crazy. / Don't talk to me like I'm crazy.

PEOPLES: I know you're not. I know. I won't. Just relax.

WALTER: That's what they told Aldrich Ames, you know. Just relax. None of this bullshit, these blue pictures and / red pictures . . .

PEOPLES: He was probably a sociopath. You ain't a sociopath, *are* you.

WALTER: *You* would think so. *Wouldn't* you, D'avore? *You* would goddamn well think so. / *Wouldn't* you?

PEOPLES: No, I wouldn't think so. You want some water, or something?

WALTER: You *experts* don't know what you're talking about.

PEOPLES: That's what I'm sayin', Walt. That's why you gotta beat it by its own rules. Hedge your bets. If you gotta play poker with a guy who's cheating, you gotta cheat him yourself if you want to win. See? You just gotta keep telling yourself, over and over, the machine doesn't know, the machine is flawed, the machine doesn't know. We just want to catch liars, Walt. We all want to do something human beings ain't supposed to do. That's the only reason we keep using this piece of junk. It's all we got. We just want it so bad.

WALTER: You're wrong. You don't know if it works, because you don't *understand* it. You don't get it. I say, respectfully.

PEOPLES: Let me see these lines go down. Make 'em go down. That's good. What don't I get?

WALTER: It isn't the examiner, it's the machine! You think the machine is flawed, but it isn't. It measures the observable, truth. It's perfect. If it says you're lying, you're lying, even if you're telling the truth. If it says you're telling the truth, you are, even if you're lying. The machine is perfect. It's perfect. It's perfect. It's perfect.

PEOPLES: Walter.

WALTER: You're either lying or you're not, but you don't know until the machine tells you!

PEOPLES: (*Skeptical.*) I don't know about that.

WALTER: It's Schrödinger's cat. The observer's paradox.

PEOPLES: Are you seeing a cat here, now, Walter?

WALTER: No, I'm not seeing a *cat*. Schrödinger's cat. You put a cat in a radioactive box with a vial of hydrocyanic acid.

PEOPLES: Push those lines down. That's good.

WALTER: It either killed the cat or it didn't. You don't know, until you, until you open the box and see. Until then, the cat is neither dead not alive. It's neither. It's both. At the same time. Until you open the box.

PEOPLES: *What's* the cat's name?

WALTER: Schrödinger's cat. And no, I don't know the *cat's* name.

PEOPLES: Oh. Well, I really don't think that's how a polygraph works, and also that's a terrible thing to do to a cat. Are you pushing that blue button?

WALTER: Yes.

PEOPLES: That's fine. That's good. Is your name Walter Krootzer?

WALTER: Kreutzer. Yes.

PEOPLES: Are we in the United States of America?

WALTER: Yes.

PEOPLES: Do you work for people who shoot folks in the head and throw them in a ditch like some garbage or something?

WALTER: No.

PEOPLES: Yeah, you're gonna be just fine, Walter. You're gonna be just fine.

Pilgrims Musa and Sheri
in the New World
by Yussef El Guindi

CHARACTERS: Tayyib, a store owner and immigrant from Somalia; Musa, a cab driver from Egypt

PLACE: Outside Tayyib's apartment and cab interior; NYC

CIRCUMSTANCE: Despite being engaged, Musa has fallen for Sheri, an American waitress.

Tayyib: (*Slight accent.*) Musa! My store opens in an hour. You've not earned the right to piss after being this late. You can go in my store. People in this country expect you to open your business on time. Not when you're in the mood. (*To himself.*) Where's the brown bag? And bring—(*Checking to see if it's missing.*)—yes, bring the brown bag. And the backpack beside it.

(Musa *enters carrying suitcases, including the brown bag and the backpack.*)

Did you lock the door behind you?

Musa: And said a prayer that you should find all your possessions when you get back.

Tayyib: You joke. The thieves here have MBAs in being crooks. If you don't lock it up, they think you're giving it away. Please: do I have to see that this early? Your fly, man. It's been open since you come.

Musa: (*Laughs.*) Oh.

Tayyib: Is this why you late picking me up? Your lady friend don't want you to zip it up? Love me some more, Musa?

Musa: Don't be angry just because you don't have a woman.

Tayyib: Me? My friend. I have more women than suitcases. I just don't go smiling like a fool about it.

Musa: What women? Those who stand by the corners?

Tayyib: The difference between you and me? When I go with women, I know what I'm doing. I'm having a nice time. And so are they. I am not falling in love.

Musa: Did I speak of love? When did I speak of this?

TAYYIB: Your face. It has the look of someone who has eaten too much sugar. And just before they crash.

MUSA: It is true, she is sugar. "Sucar," my Somali friend.

TAYYIB: Listen, my Egyptian friend. Have you not come to me for advice before? Have I not guided you a little as you try and settle down in this country?

MUSA: (*Having fun.*) You are wise beyond your years, it is true.

TAYYIB: Have you ever come back to me and said, "Tayyib, that was some stupid shit you said to me"?

MUSA: If I did, I would keep it to myself.

TAYYIB: Well, then, my first advice to you this morning is to please wipe that stupid smile off your face; because if you don't I will delay opening my store to slap it off. It should be a law that people in love should not be seen by other people until the silliness of love wears off and they settle down into a normal relationship.

MUSA: I am not in love. Stop saying this.

TAYYIB: You are, and you know how I know? All lovers have this brain-dead look in their eyes. Scientists report on this. When you fall in love, your intelligence drops. There are studies. You smile for no reason, you hug and laugh at nothing. And you think the whole world has been built just to be a stage for you and your lover. What has not been studied is how annoying this is to the people watching.

MUSA: How long since you been with a woman?

TAYYIB: I tell you, my friend, I make love like a bunny.

MUSA: I mean, not with yourself, with real person.

TAYYIB: All I am saying is take it easy, okay? Slow down. Before you make a mistake you regret.

MUSA: Okay, okay. Do not be this serious.

TAYYIB: (*Continuing.*) A big mistake. I've seen it before and it is difficult to watch.

MUSA: Nothing happen. I am in a good mood. This is not a crime.

TAYYIB: I think to Gamila it might be. Have you thought of this? (*Slight beat.* MUSA *doesn't respond.*) Do you even think of this?

MUSA: She does not need to be mentioned in this.

TAYYIB: Really? I think this is more of this dead-brain quality they talk of. The arrow of love strikes and kills the brain first.

MUSA: My friend, you give whiskey for payment. Who are you to talk of good behavior?

TAYYIB: You are right, neither of us are good Muslims. I with my whiskey, and you having no problem screwing someone when you are engaged. Gamila, this beautiful woman, will come back, and you will stop seeing this Sheri and you will get married? Is this the plan?

MUSA: This is not your business.

TAYYIB: Is she not coming back soon?

MUSA: You go to strips clubs!

TAYYIB: I'm not judging you!

MUSA: You are! I see it!

TAYYIB: If it's a fling, I understand. You are not the first to think screwing behind your fiancée is not a crime. I'm not sure in which book this is okay, but it happens. Men have penises they have to exercise.

MUSA: It is because you have lost yours in one of your suitcases that you lecture me.

TAYYIB: (*Continuing.*) Two weeks ago, you were like a schoolboy bragging. Now, you come with stories about the way she does things. How she wakes up in the morning and makes you breakfast. The way she laughs. This is a man with growing feelings for someone. Am I wrong?

MUSA: I'm sorry I told you anything.

TAYYIB: Musa: Your Gamila is a jewel. And wants you for a husband. Why, I don't know, but she does. She is beautiful. Comes from a good family, and is respectable and religious. She wants to finish school and become a nurse. *And* she's a citizen. You don't need an American to get you a green card.

MUSA: Alright, you've spoken; now we leave it alone.

TAYYIB: Get in the taxi, I want to tell you something.

MUSA: Is there more hot air? Save it for your customers, please.

TAYYIB: Just get in the taxi.

(**MUSA** *rolls his eyes as he reluctantly gets in the taxi.* **TAYYIB** *also gets into the taxi.*)

Listen to me. How long have I been in this country?

MUSA: After this morning with you, it will be too long.

Tayyib: Long enough to know a few things you don't. I know how it is. To come from a country where everything feels like it's one color, and then suddenly you are in this big candy store of a country. Stuff you didn't dream you could have. Women you didn't think you could meet.

Musa: Your store will open in less than an hour.

Tayyib: Shut up and listen. I will tell you something. I found a woman early on. This American woman. Beautiful, sexy. In your fantasies you dream of a woman like this.

Musa: She ran screaming from you, yes? This is the story.

Tayyib: (*Continuing.*) And we were in love. We could not have been more so. We looked into each other's eyes and all the pieces of the world fit together. I believe in love; I do. But any love, it must—any love must have some common sense behind it. A solid ground for real feelings to take root. And not end after the first quarrels. But we, stupid in love, thought nothing could touch us. Because, like all lovers, we thought we were different. But by the end, everything was kicking our behinds. Everything. Small things, and very quickly. My speaking two languages for instance, and how she felt shut out when I invited my friends over and spoke in my own tongue. Or the smells from the kitchen when I cooked my food and how that made my sweat taste funny and could we eat normal food for once. And even that I went to the mosque, or rolled out my mat to pray at home. And all of these were charming to her in the beginning. Don't think they weren't. It was like a little spice for her, and for me, the different ways *she* did things. I loved it. But eventually, she began to miss home. Her idea of what home life should be. And so I did. Musa: You cannot be a foreigner twice in this country. When you are out here, you are a foreigner, but when you go home, you must be allowed to hang up your foreigner hat and be yourself. Do not mistake the woman who gives you pleasure with the woman who will surround you with things that feed you, in here. Gamila is a beautiful woman. *She* will make you feel at home. And without this home, this country will eat you up little by little.

Musa: What happened to this woman—that you were with?

Tayyib: What happens to most lovers. One day you wake up and don't say good morning to the person you once adored. The only difference with us is the reasons that led to this. And the taste it left in my mouth. That I let someone make me feel more of a foreigner than I already was. Where I actually felt embarrassed to be who I was.

Musa: That's your story. It's not mine.

TAYYIB: When is Gamila coming back?

(**MUSA** *doesn't answer, and instead retrieves the backpack and any remaining suitcases.*)

Have you thought ahead at all? Even a little?

MUSA: I will tell you something I said before: it is none of your business.

TAYYIB: The final thing I will say is I went to this diner where your Sheri works. Perhaps our friendship will end after I say this, but I am obliged to tell you that the way she carries on with other men in the diner would make me very nervous. Yes, the women here are whatever, but even American men would have problems seeing their girl sitting on the laps of her customers. And joking and laughing and God knows what else. We all love the free spirit here, that is why we came, but there's free and then there's no morals or anything.

(**MUSA** *stops, stares at* **TAYYIB.**)

MUSA: How dare you—You know nothing.

TAYYIB: I know nothing; very well.

MUSA: Nothing. About her, or anything.

TAYYIB: I spoke as a friend but never mind.

MUSA: Not one thing!

TAYYIB: Very well, I'll shut my mouth.

MUSA: We agree on something, finally!

TAYYIB: And you tell me this is not love.

MUSA: You have the mind of an idiot! You know that? You are like a car that drives on flat tires and gets nowhere, every time. And still you have the nerve to turn on the engine of this big mouth and speak!

TAYYIB: I will forgive you for that. Because you are upset, and the future will prove me right. This conversation never happened, but you will see.

(**MUSA** *angrily starts the engine. The faint sound of music from the car radio is heard. Perhaps the faint sound of another Arabic song.*)

MUSA: How dare you? How dare you?!

(*He changes gears, grips the steering wheel. A long beat.*) (*Then* **MUSA** *turns the engine off. Beat.*)

I'm . . .

(*Slight beat.*)

I am not sure what I'm doing. . . . She's . . . this woman, Sheri, she's . . .

(*Slight beat.*)

She's in my life now.

(*Slight beat.*)

She's in my life now.

TAYYIB: We'll talk on the way. . . . Start the car.

(*He pats* MUSA's *hand.*)

Don't worry. Falling in love is not the end of the world. All you have to figure out is what is important to you. What is most important, in here.

(*Taps his heart.*)

Drive. We'll talk. We'll talk some more.

Strike-Slip
by Naomi Iizuka

CHARACTERS: **RAFAEL**, Mexican American, second-generation American (17); **RICHMOND**, African American (40s)

PLACE: A garage in Boyle Heights

CIRCUMSTANCE: Richmond is an ex-cop making money a different way now. Rafael is about to become a father.

(*RAFAEL is a mechanic. He's working on the engine of a car. He checks his clipboard. RICHMOND joins him. RAFAEL gives him the clipboard and a pen.*)

RAFAEL: If I could get your cell phone number. . . . How've the brake pads been feeling?

RICHMOND: Fine, just fine. Where's Hector at?

RAFAEL: Hector? He, uh, left.

RICHMOND: What do you mean he left? Hector is the guy I work with here. He's the only one I trust to work on my car.

RAFAEL: Well, he's gone. Hector don't work here no more.

RICHMOND: Did he say where he went to?

RAFAEL: Why?

RICHMOND: I'm just asking.

RAFAEL: No, he didn't say.

RICHMOND: So you're the new guy?

RAFAEL: Yeah.

RICHMOND: I hope you know what you're doing.

RAFAEL: I do. It's a nice car.

RICHMOND: Pontiac GTO.

RAFAEL: She's a beauty.

RICHMOND: Yeah, she is. I take good care of her.

RAFAEL: Where do you get a car like that?

RICHMOND: You got to have luck and you got to have cash.

RAFAEL: Just like that, huh?

Richmond: Just like that.

Rafael: You make it sound easy.

Richmond: It's not that hard, really. I guess it just depends on who you are.

Rafael: You mean, whether or not you're lucky.

Richmond: I mean, whether or not you got the cash.

Rafael: Yeah? And where do you get the cash?

Richmond: Are you asking me what I do for a living? Is that the question?

Rafael: Yeah, I guess.

Richmond: I used to be a cop. I'm retired now.

Rafael: Is that right?

Richmond: You got something to say about that?

Rafael: It just surprises me is all.

Richmond: That I was a cop? That surprises you?

Rafael: I just wonder how you afford a car like this on a cop's salary, that's all.

Richmond: Come again, (*Reading his name tag.*) Raoul?

Rafael: It's Rafael

Richmond: Oh, OK, Rafael. I'll try and remember that. Next time I get my oil changed, I'll ask for Rafael.

Rafael: I guess I just want to know how does someone like you get the cash.

Richmond: Someone like me? What is that supposed to mean?

Rafael: You know.

Richmond: No, I don't think I do. Why don't you illuminate me, Rafael.

Rafael: Come on, man. Why you gotta act like that?

Richmond: Act like what?

Rafael: I just look at someone like you and I think you ain't that different from me. How is it you got what you got?

Richmond: Maybe 'cause I ain't like you. Maybe 'cause I work harder. Maybe 'cause I'm smarter. Maybe 'cause luck shines down on me in a way that you will never know 'cause you just don't have what that is, because you will never have what that is.

Rafael: Man, who do you think you are?

Richmond: I'll tell you who I am, Rafael. I'm the fuckin' customer and you're the fuckin' grease monkey who rotates my fuckin' tires. You have a problem with that?

Rafael: Fuck you.

Richmond: OK, see, now you just chose to mess with the wrong person. 'Cause I tell you what: I'm going to walk right over there to your manager and I'm going to personally see to it that they fire your ass right here on the spot.

Rafael: Go ahead.

Richmond: You think I'm kidding?

Rafael: Do it, man. See if I care.

(**Richmond** *walks away.*)

Rafael: Fuck you, man. Fuck you.

(**Rafael** *looks at the clipboard and tears off the pink sheet with* **Richmond**'s *contact information.* **Rafael** *goes.*)

Superior Donuts
by Tracy Letts

CHARACTERS: **FRANCO**, African American, works at the donut shop (21 years old); **ARTHUR**, Polish American, owns donut shop (58 years old)

PLACE: Superior Donuts shop; Uptown, Chicago

CIRCUMSTANCE: Franco is in debt from gambling.

EDITOR'S NOTE: Selection is pulled from two different scenes.

(**ARTHUR** *reaches under the counter, hauls out* **FRANCO**'s *book.* **ARTHUR** *and* **FRANCO** *stare at each other.*)

FRANCO: What?

ARTHUR: I read it.

FRANCO: That was fast.

ARTHUR: It's a quick read.

FRANCO: And?

ARTHUR: It's really impressive, Franco.

FRANCO: You think?

ARTHUR: Yeah.

FRANCO: Really?

ARTHUR: Oh, it's really something.

FRANCO: No. Really?

ARTHUR: No. Really. I'm impressed.

FRANCO: Really?!

ARTHUR: I just think it's great.

FRANCO: Arthur P. You. You just. You.

ARTHUR: Pick a verb, any verb.

FRANCO: You just . . . sit right down and tell me every little thing you can think to say about it.

ARTHUR: It's completely engaging, from start to finish.

FRANCO: Engaging, you mean in the sense you were, what, you were *interested.*

ARTHUR: Yeah.

FRANCO: You were *engaged*, it was *engaging, yes*! Okay, what else?

ARTHUR: From start to finish, I was really swept along by the story.

FRANCO: "Swept along by the story." Arthur P. says: "Swept along by the story."

ARTHUR: The writing, really. I would never believe it was written by someone so young. I just can't think of enough good things to say about it. It's just great.

(*A long moment.*)

FRANCO: Did you like Rocco, the main character?

ARTHUR: Rocco Biggs is just a great character.

FRANCO: Yeah?

ARTHUR: He's funny and smart, and we cheer for him, y'know? We want to know that he's going to be okay. That's what keeps us reading.

FRANCO: Right.

ARTHUR: That chapter about his dad, that's a killer.

FRANCO: Which one, you mean when his—

ARTHUR: Well, the whole section really, at the racetrack, after his dad gets in trouble and you know he has to blow town—

FRANCO: Right—

ARTHUR: And he sits Rocco down and you know this is really the last time they'll ever see each other, and he tells Rocco this is really it. He's not going to be around anymore.

FRANCO: Yeah.

ARTHUR: And that if Rocco wants to survive in America, he's got to just keep hustling, keep, what is it he says? The little mantra he gives him?

FRANCO: "Never stop moving."

ARTHUR: That's it.

FRANCO: "Never stop moving."

ARTHUR: I think you should show this to some people.

FRANCO: What do you mean? Who?

ARTHUR: Get it typed up or put on a computer or whatever, then show it to I don't know, a publisher, or an editor.

FRANCO: No shit?

ARTHUR: No, I'm serious. I mean, you have to clean it up, right, no one wants to go through all these legal pads and—

FRANCO: Right, right, right, right—

ARTHUR: But no, get it cleaned up and then find someone who does this sort of thing.

FRANCO: You know anybody?

ARTHUR: What do you mean?

FRANCO: You know anybody who does that sort of thing?

ARTHUR: You mean the *typing*?

FRANCO: No, man, the publishing. You know any publishers?

ARTHUR: No. How would I know publishers? No.

FRANCO: You don't know anyone like that?

ARTHUR: No. Hey, don't let that stop you. You know what, I get the feeling you won't let that stop you. You'll find someone.

FRANCO: Thanks, Arthur.

ARTHUR: I haven't done anything.

FRANCO: Just that you read it. Y'know? Means a lot.

ARTHUR: Thanks for letting me read it.

FRANCO: You won the bet, fair and square. (*Beat.*) Nah. I wanted you to read it.

ARTHUR: I guess it's not real until someone else reads it.

FRANCO: That ain't it. Just. Well, that's what friends do, right? They share their stories.

(*End of scene . . .*)

(*. . . New scene picks up*)

(ARTHUR *calls into the kitchen.*)

ARTHUR: Franco, I blew it. I was almost there and I was almost there and I tightened up. If James hadn't come in.

(FRANCO *enters with another plate, another donut.*)

FRANCO: You just gotta wade in there, man. If you get knocked around, you get knocked around. No way to protect yourself.

ARTHUR: And how do you know this? You've been knocked around?

FRANCO: I can't complain.

ARTHUR: You can't?

FRANCO: I won't. Now try please. (**ARTHUR** *tries the donut, makes a face: "pretty good."*) It's good?

ARTHUR: I think you nailed it.

FRANCO: Nailed it!

ARTHUR: That's a very good donut.

FRANCO: And that's from *my dough*, too. I made that donut from the group up.

ARTHUR: That's right.

FRANCO: Look out now, I start crankin' out delicious dessert cakes and everyone's just gonna have to get the hell out the way.

ARTHUR: You're on the path to donut greatness. Which reminds me, I had a thought about your book.

FRANCO: What's that?

ARTHUR: I thought of someone we might get to look at your book.

FRANCO: Who?

ARTHUR: Look, this isn't anything, but—I see the look in your eye, and I'm telling you, this isn't anything.

FRANCO: What?

ARTHUR: My ex-wife's brother's . . . partner. He wrote—used to write little restaurant notices for the *Reader*.

FRANCO: And?

ARTHUR: And nothing, that's all I got. A guy used to write restaurant notices, for a free paper. That's as close to a publisher as I can get you. If I can even track him down. But it's a place to start. (**FRANCO** *leaps in the air, screams, dances, pumps his fists.*) Okay, okay—

FRANCO: *Hell yeah!* Look out, Arthur P., 'cause here we come, baby, back from the dead! Ain't no stopping us now, man! Let me tell you how it's gonna be: This man is gonna read *America Will Be* and he'll set me up with the next man I need to talk to and *that* man's gonna put a check in my hand—

ARTHUR: Right, yes, a big check—

FRANCO: And they're gonna print my book and we'll put my book right here in a big display in the window that say "The Great American Novel."

ARTHUR: Very catchy, why not.

FRANCO: And meanwhile you and me are poppin' out the delicious dessert cakes and there's people out the door of this place and down the street, lined up to buy my book and eat our donuts and drink our coffee—

ARTHUR: Yeah, hey, fuck you, Starbucks!

FRANCO: And then wait till we get Poetry Night going—

ARTHUR: The Superior Donuts, uh, Literary . . .

FRANCO: The Superior Donuts Literary Festival and Poetry Jam—

ARTHUR: "It ain't horse fat."

FRANCO: And we get a microphone and a little stage right over here—

ARTHUR: I can serve specialty donuts—

FRANCO: And we'll get all the people from the neighborhood—

ARTHUR: The Countee Cullen Cruller—

FRANCO: My mom and baby sister'll be right over here, eating their donuts and listening to me read from my book.

ARTHUR: You know, I bet James could actually help me get a liquor license?

FRANCO: You can have a little glass of wine with your cop lady friend, right, taking it all in, the King and Queen of Uptown, and your daughter shows up, too, to take her place in the kingdom, all of us together, a real home filled with books and ideas and food and family.

(*Silence.*)

ARTHUR: That's not going to happen.

FRANCO: Why not?

ARTHUR: It's not going to happen because that isn't what happens.

FRANCO: We'll make it happen.

ARTHUR: Life isn't just what you wish for.

FRANCO: You know what life is?

ARTHUR: Derailment.

FRANCO: You're wrong.

ARTHUR: I'm old.

FRANCO: Sometimes good things just happen.

ARTHUR: *I used to know a restaurant critic.*

FRANCO: Like you said, a place to start.

ARTHUR: Dreaming's dangerous.

FRANCO: Dangerous to who? To you?

ARTHUR: You're going to get crushed.

FRANCO: What are you scared of?

ARTHUR: I'm not scared of anything.

FRANCO: Are you serious? You don't talk, you don't vote, you don't listen to music. Why do you bother to get outta bed in the morning? You can't even ask that old lady out on a date.

ARTHUR: That's got nothing to do with this—

FRANCO: You can't even talk about your own daughter.

ARTHUR: You're way outta line.

FRANCO: Right, if I mention her, I'm just an employee.

ARTHUR: You *are* just an employee.

FRANCO: And you're a tight-ass boss.

ARTHUR: Because I know a fantasy when I hear one?

FRANCO: They ain't fantasies, goddamn it, they're possibilities! Don't you even believe in possibilities?

ARTHUR: This conversation is over.

FRANCO: See, you're even scared to fight with me. You just wait and see, old man. Wait and see what happens with this book. I'll show you. I'll prove it to you!

ARTHUR: (*Wheeling on* **FRANCO**.) You'll prove it to me? *You'll* prove it to *me*? Who the hell are you? Come in here with your chewed-up notebooks and your goddamn pipe dreams. Even if I find this joker, and even if I convince him to wade through your frickin' legal pads and even if he pats you on the head, that isn't your ticket. It's just another dead end. They're all dead ends. You don't want to do yourself a favor, do me one: Grow up. Stop acting like a fuckin' clown. (**FRANCO** *exits.*)

Part 3
Female-Female Scenes

Compulsion
by Rinne Groff

CHARACTERS: MRS. SILVER, Mr. Silver's wife (40s); ANNE FRANK, (teenager)

PLACE: The Silvers' bedroom; night

CIRCUMSTANCE: After legal battles in the U.S. over the adaptation of Anne Frank's diary, the Silvers have moved to Israel.

EDITOR'S NOTE: *The scene is intended to be played with* MR. SILVER *voicing a marionette of Anne Frank.*

> (*The Silvers are asleep in bed.* MRS. SILVER *wakes up, startled.*)

MRS. SILVER: Sid. *Mon dieu.* Wake up.

> (*The* ANNE FRANK *marionette sits up in the middle of the bed, looking at* MRS. SILVER.)

Sid, please. Please wake up.

ANNE FRANK: He can't.

MRS. SILVER: Why not?

ANNE FRANK: He's afraid of you

MRS. SILVER: Of me?

ANNE FRANK: That you'll try the whole suicide thing again. How can he tell you anything with that hanging over his head?

MRS. SILVER: What are you doing here?

ANNE FRANK: I've always been here. You know that.

MRS. SILVER: Get out of our bed.

ANNE FRANK: He wants me here. You know that, too. That's why he invited Mr. Matzliach over.

MRS. SILVER: (*Realizing.*) They're not going to do the play.

ANNE FRANK: They're planning a reading. Finally to hear it out loud.

MRS. SILVER: But he promised me.

ANNE FRANK: Promised you what? That he would give up the lawsuits? He did. Sign the agreement? He did. That agreement was a total fraud. The committee of three, with the rabbi, whose decision he agreed to abide by, they never met, not even once. One guy had his lawyer settle it with my father's people.

MRS. SILVER: Does Sid know this?

ANNE FRANK: Of course.

MRS. SILVER: Why didn't he tell me?

ANNE FRANK: Your rule. Don't mention me in this house. Besides it wasn't about who did or didn't meet. He would have done it anyway.

MRS. SILVER: Done what?

ANNE FRANK: A week after the settlement, before he knew all this, he wrote a letter. "Dear Daddy"—except he called him Mr. Frank—"Dear Mr. Frank, while the legal phase of our encounter is over the moral phase is not done. Your behavior will remain forever as a ghastly example of evil returned for good, and of a father's betrayal of his daughter's words."

MRS. SILVER: He can't do that. Part of the agreement was no more accusing.

ANNE FRANK: "Mr. Frank, I realize that your black heart cannot be reached by reason or facts . . . "

MRS. SILVER: Please stop.

ANNE FRANK: You're a writer, too, aren't you?

MRS. SILVER: Yes.

ANNE FRANK: I read the book set during the war. I liked it. You really did all that stuff?

MRS. SILVER: Most of it.

ANNE FRANK: You weren't that much older than me back then.

MRS. SILVER: Old enough to join the Free French Forces.

ANNE FRANK: I wish I was older.

MRS. SILVER: We all do.

ANNE FRANK: You wish you were older, too?

MRS. SILVER: No, you. That you had lived.

ANNE FRANK: Nah, everybody likes me better dead. It's depressing.

MRS. SILVER: I imagine it is. I liked your book, too, Anne. I gave it to him because I liked it so much. Now I hate it. I'm sorry but I do.

ANNE FRANK: Have I been your Hitler and your Stalin?

Mrs. Silver: What? No.

Anne Frank: He told Daddy that Daddy was his Hitler and his Stalin. Do you think your husband has a persecution mania?

Mrs. Silver: I thought it was getting better.

Anne Frank: Is that what his analyst says?

Mrs. Silver: I don't know what his analyst says. Confidentiality. Maybe we should get new analysts.

Anne Frank: What do *you* talk about in therapy?

Mrs. Silver: Denial.

Anne Frank: Like Holocaust denial?

Mrs. Silver: What do you know about Holocaust denial?

Anne Frank: I know they say I didn't write my diary because I used different ink and different paper sometimes, and that's their proof that no Jews were ever murdered in the gas chambers. I didn't know there were Holocaust deniers in the land of Israel.

Mrs. Silver: Little girl, there's everything everywhere.

(*Pause.*)

Anne Frank: I think I'd like to be in therapy.

Mrs. Silver: For what?

Anne Frank: Stuff like when they separated me from my mother at Auschwitz. Or watching my sister die of typhus right before my eyes. Do you think analysis could help with any of that?

(*Quiet.*)

Mrs. Silver: If we do that reading of your play—oh God, oh God—if we do it here at the house, privately, but he could hear it and get what's been, what he feels has been denied to him all these years, will you leave us alone then?

Anne Frank: Oh yes, you have to do a reading here at the house! That will be fun.

Mrs. Silver: But will it cure him?

Anne Frank: That depends. Will lots of people come?

Mrs. Silver: There are lots of characters in the play, so at least that many have to come.

Anne Frank: But I'm the lead, right? I'm the most important one.

Mrs. Silver: Yes. The most important.

Anne Frank: I think it's a great idea. Do you ever let your children spend the night in your bed?

Mrs. Silver: When there's a thunderstorm. Or when they're sick.

Anne Frank: Can I stay here? For just this one night?

Mrs. Silver: *Cherie*, no.

Anne Frank: You think I'm too old for that?

Mrs. Silver: It's not that. It's too painful for me.

Anne Frank: But what about for me? And for my father, too. His pain. The things your husband said to him. So cruel. I see my father's dreams. To this day, torment.

Mrs. Silver: I can imagine.

Anne Frank: You can't imagine. How could you imagine? He made it home only to learn, one by one, how every person in his family had been murdered. He tracked someone down who had seen me in the camps. She told him what I looked like in the end: starving to death, naked, covered in lice. She told him what I said: "Everyone is dead. I'm all alone now." But Daddy wasn't dead. He was even at that moment trying with every part of his being to make it back to his little daughter. To find her and kiss her again. To hold her in his lap and kiss her. The smell of her hair. His precious Anne, his firecracker. But he will never hold her again for all the days of his life. She is gone forever, and nothing can bring her back.

(*Silence.*)

Mrs. Silver: Why do you do that?

Anne Frank: What?

Mrs. Silver: Talk about what he felt. Not what *you* felt.

Anne Frank: Some things are private. Don't you know that? You will never know what I felt in those last days. Never. (*And then—*) If you let me stay, I promise I'll go right to sleep.

Mrs. Silver: I won't.

Anne Frank: No, you'll sleep, too. We'll all snuggle together. It's the only way.

Mrs. Silver: Okay, sweetheart. But you can't make a habit of it. He can only do this one reading, and that has to be the end.

Anne Frank: (*Snuggling in.*) Yes. Just for tonight. That's all. Tonight.

Dead Man's Cell Phone
by Sarah Ruhl

CHARACTERS: JEAN, single, no kids, works at holocaust museum; OTHER WOMAN, Gordon's mistress

PLACE: A café

CIRCUMSTANCE: While at a café, Gordon passes away. But his cell phone will not stop ringing. Jean, at a nearby table, picks up the cell phone and agrees to meet strangers that have a connection with Gordon.

(*The* OTHER WOMAN *waiting in a blue raincoat.* JEAN *enters in a blue raincoat.*)

JEAN: Hello.

OTHER WOMAN: Hello. Thank you for meeting me.

JEAN: Not at all.

OTHER WOMAN: We like the same clothes.

JEAN: Yes.

OTHER WOMAN: I suppose that's not surprising, given the circumstances.

JEAN: I don't know what you mean.

OTHER WOMAN: You don't need to pretend.

JEAN: I know.

OTHER WOMAN: Gordon has good taste. You're pretty.

JEAN: I'm not—

OTHER WOMAN: Don't be modest. I like it when a woman knows she's beautiful. Women nowadays—they don't know how to walk into a room. A beautiful woman should walk into a room thinking: I am beautiful and I know how to walk in these shoes. There's so little glamour in the world these days. It makes daily life such a bore. Women are responsible for enlivening dull places like train stations. There is hardly any pleasure in waiting for a train anymore. The women just walk in. Horrible shoes. No confidence. Bad posture.

(*The* OTHER WOMAN *looks at* JEAN's *posture.* JEAN *sits up straighter.*)

A woman should be able to take out her compact and put lipstick on her lips with absolute confidence. No apology.

(*The* **OTHER WOMAN** *takes out lipstick and puts it on her lips, slowly.* **JEAN** *is riveted.*)

JEAN: I've always been embarrassed to put lipstick on in public.

OTHER WOMAN: That's crap. Here—you have beautiful lips.

(*She hands* **JEAN** *the lipstick.*)

JEAN: No—that's—

OTHER WOMAN: I don't have a cold.

JEAN: It's not the germs. It's—

OTHER WOMAN: Put it on. Take your time. Enjoy yourself.

(**JEAN** *puts on some lipstick.*)

That was disappointing. Oh, well.

JEAN: I'm very sorry about Gordon. You must be—his friend?

OTHER WOMAN: Gordon didn't tell you much, did he?

JEAN: No.

OTHER WOMAN: Gordon could be quiet.

JEAN: Yes. He was quiet.

OTHER WOMAN: He must have respected you. He was quiet with women he respected. Otherwise, he had a very loud laugh. Haw, haw, haw! You could hear him a mile away.

(*She remembers* **GORDON**.)

You must wonder why I wanted to meet with you.

JEAN: Yes.

OTHER WOMAN: You were with Gordon the day he died.

JEAN: Yes.

OTHER WOMAN: Gordon and I—we were—well—You know. (*She thinks the word "lovers"*)

And so—I wanted to know . . . this is going to sound sentimental . . . I wanted to know his last words.

JEAN: That's not sentimental.

OTHER WOMAN: I hate sentiment.

JEAN: I don't think that's sentimental. Really, I don't.

OTHER WOMAN: So. His last words.

JEAN: Gordon mentioned you before he died. Well, he more than mentioned you. He said: tell her that I love her. And then he turned his face away and died.

OTHER WOMAN: He said that he loved me.

JEAN: Yes.

OTHER WOMAN: I waited for such a long time. And the words—delivered through another woman. What a shit.

(*The* **OTHER WOMAN** *looks away. She wipes a tear away.*)

JEAN: It's not like that. Gordon said that he had loved many women in his life, but when he met you, everything changed. He said that other women seemed like clocks compared to you—other women just—measured time—broke the day up—but that you—you stopped time. He said you—stopped time—just by walking into a room.

OTHER WOMAN: He said that?

JEAN: Yes.

OTHER WOMAN: Oh, Gordon.

(*The phone rings.* **JEAN** *hesitates to answer it.*)

OTHER WOMAN: Aren't you going to get that?

JEAN: Yes.

(*She answers the phone.*)

Hello?

(*On the other end: who is this?*)

My name is Jean. Yes, of course. How do I get there?

(*A pause while the mother gives directions.*)

(*To the* **OTHER WOMAN,** *whispering*) *Sorry.*

(*The* **OTHER WOMAN** *shrugs her shoulders.*)

All right, I'll see you then. Good-bye.

(**JEAN** *hangs up.*)

OTHER WOMAN: Who was it?

JEAN: His mother.

OTHER WOMAN: Oh, God. Mrs. Gottlieb? Let me touch up your lipstick before you go.

(*She does.* **JEAN** *puckers.*)

Dead Man's Cell Phone
by Sarah Ruhl

CHARACTERS: MRS. GOTTLIEB, Gordon's mother, wears fur indoors; JEAN, single, no kids, works at holocaust museum

PLACE: Mrs. Gottlieb's house

CIRCUMSTANCE: While at a café, Gordon passes away. But his cell phone will not stop ringing. Jean, at a nearby table, picks up the cell phone and agrees to meet strangers that have a connection with Gordon.

MRS. GOTTLIEB: I don't know why I didn't see you at the funeral.

JEAN: I was in the back.

MRS. GOTTLIEB: Would you say that you tend to blend in with a crowd?

JEAN: I don't know—

MRS. GOTTLIEB: You might wear brighter clothing. Or a little mascara.

JEAN: It was a funeral, so I wore black.

MRS. GOTTLIEB: Fine, fine. That's beside the point. Gordon left his telephone to you?

JEAN: Yes—he left it to me.

MRS. GOTTLIEB: Why?

JEAN: He wanted me to have it. Why did you call him on the phone—*after* the funeral?

MRS. GOTTLIEB: I call him every day. I keep forgetting that he's dead. I do a little errand, take out my purse, and call Gordon while I'm stopped in traffic. It's habit.

JEAN: I'm very sorry. It must be awful to lose a child.

MRS. GOTTLIEB: It is. When someone older than you dies it gets better every day, but when someone younger than you dies it gets worse every day. Like grieving in reverse.

JEAN: I'm so sorry.

MRS. GOTTLIEB: I see it as my job to mourn him until the day I die.

JEAN: Oh—yes . . .

Mrs. Gottlieb: Please, sit down.

(**Jean** *sits down.*)

So.

Jean: So.

Mrs. Gottlieb: Does anyone continue to call Gordon?

Jean: Yes.

Mrs. Gottlieb: Who?

Jean: Some business acquaintances who don't know that he's dead.

Mrs. Gottlieb: And do you tell them he's—? (*She thinks the word "dead"*)

Jean: Yes.

Mrs. Gottlieb: I can't bring myself to tell anyone.

Jean: I understand.

Mrs. Gottlieb: It's so painful, you have no idea.

Jean: No, I don't.

Mrs. Gottlieb: What it's like to lose a child.

Jean: No.

Mrs. Gottlieb: You don't have children?

Jean: No.

Mrs. Gottlieb: Why not?

Jean: I might have them, one day.

MRS. GOTTLIEB : You're getting older. How old are you?

Jean: Almost forty.

Mrs. Gottlieb: Married?

Jean: No.

Mrs. Gottlieb: How do you expect to have children then?

Jean: I don't know. I could—

Mrs. Gottlieb: When you're thirty-nine your eggs are actually forty, you know.

Jean: I could adopt.

Mrs. Gottlieb: It's better to have your own. They resemble—it's the little ticks—the family eyebrow—Gordon's eyebrow—

(**Mrs. Gottlieb** *makes a little line in the air, indicating his eyebrow shape. She tries not to cry.*)

Jean: I'm sorry.

Mrs. Gottlieb: Gordon—and I—had a falling out—you know—after that, he never returned my phone calls—

Jean: He called you the day he died.

Mrs. Gottlieb: What? How do you know?

Jean: Your number was on the outgoing calls.

Mrs. Gottlieb: It was?

Jean: Yes. It said: Mom.

Mrs. Gottlieb: Let me see.

Jean: I deleted it by mistake.

Mrs. Gottlieb: Gordon called me.

Jean: Yes.

Mrs. Gottlieb: He wanted to speak with me.

Jean: Yes.

Mrs. Gottlieb: How did you know Gordon, anyway?

Jean: We worked together.

Mrs. Gottlieb: Really.

Jean: Yes.

Mrs. Gottlieb: No wonder you don't have children.

Jean: What do you mean?

Mrs. Gottlieb: Gordon's line of work was—toxic.

Jean: It could be.

Mrs. Gottlieb: Did you do the outgoing or the incoming business?

Jean: Incoming.

Mrs. Gottlieb: Oh—I see. Why don't you stay for dinner. Gordon's brother will be here. And Gordon's wife—you know—his widow.

Jean: Oh, I wouldn't want to intrude. You must need family time now.

Mrs. Gottlieb: You knew my son. I insist that you stay.

Jean: If it would help.

MRS. GOTTLIEB: Yes, I think it would. You're very comforting, I don't know why. You're like a very small casserole—has anyone ever told you that?

JEAN: No.

MRS. GOTTLIEB: Are you religious?

JEAN: A little.

MRS. GOTTLIEB: I see. We're not religious. Our name means "God-loving" in German but we're not German anymore. Hermia chose a Catholic Mass for Gordon because she likes to kneel and get up. I did not raise my children with any religion. Perhaps I should have. Certain brands of guilt can be inculcated in a secular way, but other brands of guilt can only be obtained with reference to the metaphysical. Gordon did not experience enough guilt. Dinner will be served at seven. Do you eat meat?

JEAN: Um—kind of.

MRS. GOTTLIEB: Good. We'll be having large quantities of meat. I'm a little anemic, you know. I eat a large steak every day and it just goes right through me.

JEAN: Oh, I'm sorry.

MRS. GOTTLIEB: So—seven o'clock.

JEAN: Seven o'clock. Great. I'm just going to run out for a moment—I have an errand—

MRS. GOTTLIEB: Very good, Jean. We'll see you at seven.

Dead Man's Cell Phone
by Sarah Ruhl

CHARACTERS: HERMIA, Gordon's widow; JEAN, single, no kids, works at holocaust museum

PLACE: A bar

CIRCUMSTANCE: While at a café, Gordon passes away. But his cell phone will not stop ringing. Jean, at a nearby table, picks up the cell phone and agrees to meet strangers that have a connection with Gordon.

(HERMIA *and* JEAN *drinking cosmopolitans.*)

HERMIA: Give me another. Don't worry, l can drive home after all, Jean.

JEAN: You think so?

HERMIA: If I drive with my face. Haw, haw, haw! Oh, God, I sound like Gordon.

JEAN: You must have a lot on your mind. Do you want to talk?

HERMIA: Yes, in fact, I would. Lately I've been thinking of the last time I had sex with Gordon. Over the last ten years, when Gordon and I would have sex, I would pretend that l was someone else. I've heard that a lot of women, in order to come, pretend that their lover is someone else. Like a robber or Zorba the Greek or a rapist or something like that. Do you ever do that?

JEAN: No.

HERMIA: But you know what, Jean? I pretended that *I* was someone else, and that Gordon was Gordon, but he was cheating on me with me—*I* was the other woman. And it would turn me on to know that Gordon's wife—me—was in the next room, that I—the mistress—had to be quiet so that I—the wife—wouldn't hear me. You and I both know that Gordon had affairs.

JEAN: Well—

HERMIA: So the last time I had sex with Gordon I wish I could say that I wasn't pretending. That he was really in me, and I was really in him. But I was pretending to be a co-worker of Gordon's. He brought her to dinner once. That night, she was wearing a thong under a white pantsuit. (I never wear a thong. It's like having a tampon in your asshole, don't you think?) Anyway, that last time, I imagined myself in this white pantsuit and his hands under my thong, ripping it off. I pictured what Gordon was seeing—and I picture me, looking back at Gordon. And there is more and more desire, like two mirrors, facing each other—it's amazing what the mind can do. After I met you, I was convinced that you and Gordon were having an affair. So after dinner, I was—you know—and I pretended to be you—and it worked. Isn't that a riot?

JEAN: That's—um—

HERMIA: I wouldn't normally tell you that but I've had a lot to drink at this point.

JEAN: You should know that I didn't have a sexual relationship with your husband.

HERMIA: Then why do you have his fucking phone?

JEAN: I was the last one with him.

HERMIA: And why was that, Jean?

JEAN: A coincidence.

HERMIA: Gordon didn't have coincidences. He had accidents. There's a difference.

(*The phone rings.*)

Give that to me.

(*She rips the phone out of* JEAN's *hands.*)

Oops—missed the call! Is his picture of the Pope still on it? From a business trip to Rome. Those mobs at the Vatican, waving their cell phones, stealing an image of the Pope's dead face, and Gordon among them. I can still hear him laughing, I have the Pope in my pocket. There it is. Dead Pope. Oh, I feel sick.

(*The phone rings again.*)

I'm going to bury it. Like the Egyptians.

JEAN: No.

(JEAN *gestures for the phone. The phone keeps ringing.*)

HERMIA: Yes, in the ground, with Gordon. There was this Belgian man very recently in the news and the undertakers forgot to remove the cell phone from the coffin and it rang during the funeral! Just went on ringing! And the family is suing for negligence, Jean—for *negligesh*—you have to *bury* it, see—to *bury* it—very deep so you cannot hear the sound.

(*The phone stops ringing.*)

Are you ever in a very quiet room all alone and you feel as though you can hear a cell phone ringing and you look everywhere and you cannot see one, but there are so many ringing in the world that you must hear some dim echo. Nothing is really silent anymore—and after a death—an almost silence—you have to bury it, bury it very deep.

JEAN: I'm sorry, Hermia, but I can't let you do that. Gordon wanted me to have his phone.

(**HERMIA** *hands* **JEAN** *the phone.*)

HERMIA: Do you know what it's like marrying the wrong man, Jean? And now—now—even if he *was* the wrong man, still, he was *the* man—and I should have spent my life trying to love him instead of wishing he were someone else. What did Charles Dickens say? That we drive alone in our separate carriages never to truly know each other and then the book shuts and then we die? Something like that?

JEAN: I don't know what Charles Dickens said.

HERMIA: What good are you, Jean. You don't even know your ass from your Dickens. Oh, God! Two separate carriages and then you die!

(**HERMIA** *weeps.*)

JEAN: Hermia. There's something you should know. Gordon wrote you a letter before he died. There were different drafts, on napkins, all crumpled up. The waiter must have thrown them out after the ambulance came, but I read one of the drafts.

HERMIA: What did it say?

JEAN: I forget exactly. But I can paraphrase. It said, Dear Hermia. I know we haven't always connected, every second of the day. Husbands and wives seldom do. The joy between husband and wife is elusive, but it is strong. It endures countless moments of silent betrayal, navigates complicated labyrinths of emotional retreats. I know that sometimes you were somewhere else when we made love. I was, too. But in those moments of climax, when the darkness descended, and our fantasies dissolved into the air under the quickening heat of our desire—then, *then*, we were in that room together. And that is all that matters. Love, Gordon.

HERMIA: Gordon knew that?

JEAN: I guess he did.

HERMIA: Well, how about that.

(*Years of her marriage come back to her with a new light shining on them.*)

You've given me a great gift, Jean.

JEAN: I'm glad.

HERMIA: What can I give you?

JEAN: Nothing.

HERMIA: You gave me back ten years of my marriage. You see, after I learned that Gordon's "business trips to Rome" equaled him, trafficking organs, I couldn't bring myself to—. You know—people never write in to *Cosmo* about how sexual revulsion can be caused by moral revulsion—they just tell you to change positions.

JEAN: Organs?

HERMIA: Oh, yes, Gordon and his organs—that's funny, Gordon rhymes with organs, how is it I've never noticed that—Gordon, organ/organ, Gordon, same letters, too! O, R, G—there's no D—and God in the middle—oh! I feel sick.

JEAN: Gordon—sold organs?

HERMIA: I thought you were in incoming.

JEAN: I was.

HERMIA: And you didn't know what was in the package?

JEAN: No—I guess I didn't.

HERMIA: That's funny! Well, I'm sorry to ruin your illusions about Gordon. I was never supposed to know—I told my friends he was in waste management. I remember one sad case. Gordon convinced a Brazilian man to give his kidney to a woman in Israel. Gordon paid him five thousand dollars cash. Gordon probably made one hundred thousand dollars in the transaction. He bought me a yellow diamond. (I think they look like something you'd find in a candy machine, but they're very rare.) So the man returned to Brazil, kidney-less. And then his money was stolen from him at the airport in Rio. Can you imagine? He wrote these sad letters to our home. He would draw pictures of his lost kidney. It looked like a broken heart.

JEAN: Oh!

(*The phone rings.* **JEAN** *and* **HERMIA** *look at each other.* **JEAN** *chooses to answer it.*)

Hello—

(*She is cut off. She listens for a while. Film noir music. She hangs up.*)

They said they have a kidney from Brazil. Go to South Africa. To the airport. I'll be wearing a red raincoat. And hung up. I have to go to South Africa.

HERMIA: What?

JEAN: I'll make up for Gordon's mistakes.

HERMIA: Too late, Jean. The kidneys, the corneas, the skin—they're the rings on my fingers and the fixtures in our bathrooms. What's done is done.

JEAN: Someone is *waiting* for a kidney, Hermia! Tell Dwight I'll call him from Johannesburg.

HERMIA: What? Jean! Do you own a gun?

(*But* JEAN *is out the door.*)

Detroit
by Lisa D'Amour

CHARACTERS: **MARY** (mid-30s to early 40s), wife of Ben and Sharon and Kenny's neighbor; **SHARON** (late 20s to mid-30s), a recovering addict, wife of Kenny and new next-door neighbor of Ben and Mary

PLACE: Kenny and Sharon's front porch; the middle of the night

CIRCUMSTANCE: Mary's husband, Ben, has been laid off from his job. Ben plans to start his own business, but is slow to take the initiative.

(*Loud knocking on another door. A knocking and then the sound of* **MARY** *yelling, "Sharon! Sharon, open up! Shaaaaron!" And more knocking.*)

(**MARY** *is in her bathrobe, banging on the front door. She is near tears.*)

(**SHARON** *opens the door in her T-shirt and underwear.*)

SHARON: Mary, what's—

(**MARY** *falls into her arms. She weeps outright for maybe five seconds.*)

Mary, can you just—

(*Another wave of weeping. Eventually* **MARY** *half composes herself. Anytime* **MARY** *curses she says that word kind of under her breath.*)

MARY: It's just I don't know how to help him. I'm at the frayed edge of my wits. He gets to be home all day and I don't get home until 6:45 because of the *fucking* traffic on 694 and he's been home all day and I get home and he's already on his first drink. He *says* it's his first drink anyway. And he's cooked dinner, which is of course very sweet, but then I say something about how his green beans taste different from my green beans, you know, like, "Oh, these taste different," just like that, not saying anything bad, but he drops his fork and I know he's offended and then it starts. And I hate *NASCAR Unmasked and Personal* and he knows I hate it. I mean, he's not a NASCAR kind of guy, he doesn't like NASCAR, he just likes that show, and he turns it on anyway while I'm finishing my dinner, while I'm washing the dishes, and he watches the TV so fucking loud even the commercials and he laughs at commercials, at *dumb-fuck* commercials like the one with the cartoon chicken getting rubbed down with chicken magic.

(**MARY** *imitates the commercial. It is a Latino chicken.*)

"Leeee! It tickles!" I mean, Sharon, it's so *fucking crack-ass* dumb. And so I ask, "How was it today? Did you bring the files to Kinkos?" And he's like, "Oh *shit*, no, I forgot, oh well, I'll do it tomorrow," and I say, "You know you can do it on their website through the file uploader, it's super easy." And he says, "Yes, *yes*, I know," and I say, "Well, you know that book you bought for $65.00 said you've got to be hard on yourself about keeping to a schedule. Because Joe Blow down the street is also probably laid off, and also probably about to set up his dream business where you get to sit home all day and tell other people how to clean up the fucking financial wasteland of their day-to-day existence. And if Joe Blow gets his portfolio together before you do, then Joe Blow gets the clients, not you." And he's says, "Joe Blow can suck my *nut sack*."

(*Pause for a moment, that word is like a bad taste in her mouth.*)

And I say, "Oh, that's a winning attitude." And then that's it—we're fighting and he's all "I'm trying to be proactive," and I'm all "Today sucked, I barely got to eat lunch," and he's all "I'm afraid," and I'm like "Don't say it like that," and he's like "Look, I have to put my beer on the floor! The photo album too!" And I'm like "That coffee table didn't *go* in this *room*—"

SHARON: You can have it / back—

MARY: I don't want it back. I want to live in a tent in the woods. With one pot and one pan. And an old-fashioned aluminum mess kit with its own mesh bag. I want my hair to smell like the smoke from yesterday's fire, when I cooked my fish and my little white potatoes. I want to dry out my underwear on a warm rock. And feel the cold water rushing around my ankles, my feet pressing into the tiny stone bed that holds up the stream. Silver guppies nosing their heads into my calves . . .

(*Quiet for a moment. We hear suburban wind, maybe a car passing on another street. Maybe some teenagers laughing, maybe some kid in the house across the street listening to music in their room.*)

SHARON: Were you a Girl Scout?

MARY: Yes.

SHARON: I thought so.

(MARY *leans over into the bushes—she doesn't get up, she just leans over—and pukes. And pukes. And sits back up.*)

MARY: Oh God, my head. I think I need some water.

SHARON: Mary, have you ever thought about getting some help?

MARY: Some help with what?

SHARON: With your drinking problem.

(**MARY** *looks at* **SHARON** *like she is an alien from another planet.*)

MARY: I thought I could just come to you and talk.

SHARON: You can, you did.

MARY: Because you cried at my house and I thought that was awesome, that you felt comfortable enough to do that, it made me feel like a good host that you felt OK letting go. In that way—

SHARON: I know. You are a good host. But you can be a great host and still have a drinking problem.

(**MARY** *gets loud. Too loud for this neighborhood. She no longer quiets her curse words.*)

MARY: You know what, FUCK YOU.

(*She stands up and stumbles a little.*)

I come over here asking for HELP and what is the FIRST THING YOU FUCKING DO? Accuse me of being a fucking DRUNK? I MEAN, IF THAT IS NOT THE BLACK CALLING THE KETTLE POT. God. My husband is offering the two of you his services FOR FREE. He wouldn't even blink to ask for payment. Wouldn't even BLINK. And look at you. This fucking yard.

(**BEN** *walks up. He is obviously not drunk; he is stone-cold sober, and it takes* **MARY** *a little while to see him.*)

MARY: There's not even a single FERN. You've made no effort.

SHARON: Well, we just moved in—

(*Maybe* **MARY** *grabs on to* **SHARON***?*)

MARY: I was hiding behind our bushes. I snuck out the door to get some air. I JUST NEEDED SOME AIR, I needed to get out of the house. And he wouldn't let me. He kept locking the door on me. And so when the commercial came on, I snuck out the back and climbed over the fence and just squatted there behind the bushes. He called and called. My toes were in the mulch, I was breathing, I was not answering. Because he doesn't like me, nobody likes me, and I just wanted to breathe. And then I thought, Sharon likes me. She cried in my yard.

(**MARY** *pukes over* **SHARON***'s shoulder; she has to kind of brush it off her back and the back of her arm.* **BEN** *catches* **MARY***.* **KENNY** *opens the door, half asleep, in his boxers.* **MARY** *notices it's* **BEN***.*)

GET AWAY FROM ME, GET HIM AWAY!

Inana

by Michele Lowe

CHARACTERS: MENA, Shali's younger sister; SHALI, Yasin's future bride

PLACE: A room in Shali's home

CIRCUMSTANCE: Emad, Shali's father, has arranged for Yasin to wed his daughter, Shali.

(MENA *is peeking through a keyhole.*)

MENA: What do you think?

SHALI: He's thin.

MENA: Thin is good. When they're thin they don't eat a lot. I used to toast almonds for Samir—kilos of them. Now I can't even look at an almond.

SHALI: His shirt is too big.

MENA: When you wash his clothes separate them from yours. He doesn't want your smell on him.

SHALI: He hunches over like he an old man.

MENA: It's probably his neck. Samir has terrible neck-aches. I'm sure that's why he took a second wife. Her hands are big like a man's, but she can't cook or sew. She can't read or write either. That's why if you teach me to read, he'll favor me again. Samir doesn't want a stupid wife. Now we're both dumb and interchangeable. I can cook, she can massage. But I will teach you to read. Yasin's mind if you teach me to read the page.

(SHALI *peeks through the keyhole.*)

SHALI: Did you see his eyes? Very dark, deep-set.

MENA: Looks mean nothing. When you clear the table, bring me his coffee cup so I can read the grounds.

SHALI: He doesn't smile much.

MENA: I like sad men.

(MENA *looks through the keyhole.*)

He looks very sad. I heard his wife died of cancer. You'll give him a child and he'll smile again. Put sage leaves and cardamom pods under your pillow when you make love so you'll have a boy. And whenever you lie with him close your eyes. It makes the time go faster. Most important you must convince him that you think about him every waking hour and nothing else. But, Shali, you can't get married until you teach me to read.

SHALI: What about Baba?

MENA: Baba knows you and Luma read.

SHALI: Yes and he doesn't like it.

MENA: I don't care, I want to learn. I know two more women who want to learn from you.

SHALI: I'm not a teacher.

MENA: If they would pay you.

SHALI: And I'm not a merchant.

MENA: What should I tell them? They're desperate to read.

SHALI: If they come for tea with you tomorrow I have no choice but to invite them in.

MENA: You'll like them. They're smart like you.

SHALI: If they were smart like me I wouldn't have to teach them.

(**MENA** *looks through the keyhole again.*)

MENA: Your man is smiling.

SHALI: No.

MENA: Look for yourself.

(**SHALI** *looks through the keyhole.*)

SHALI: That is not a smile.

MENA: It's a grin.

SHALI: I don't think I like him.

MENA: Baba likes him.

SHALI: He looks morbid.

MENA: Mama says all men are morbid.

(*Beat.*)

SHALI: No, I don't think he's for me.

MENA: Promise me you'll teach me to read before you marry.

SHALI: I don't think I'm going to marry him.

MENA: Promise me.

SHALI: Yes, yes, I'll do it. I promise. Now tell me what they're doing.

(**MENA** *looks through the keyhole.*)

MENA: The men are done. Go clear their cups.

SHALI: I doubt that I will ever like him.

MENA: And bring me the grounds!

Pilgrims Musa and Sheri in the New World
by Yussef El Guindi

CHARACTERS: **SHERI**, an American waitress; **GAMILA**, an Egyptian American in tune with traditional Muslim culture

PLACE: Musa's apartment

CIRCUMSTANCE: Gamila's fiancé, Musa, has been unfaithful while she was in Egypt visiting his parents.

(**SHERI** *lies sprawled on the bed, under the covers. She snores quietly.* **GAMILA** *looks at her. Then* **GAMILA** *notices something on the floor and picks it up. It is* **SHERI**'s *lace underwear. A movement of* **GAMILA**'s *awakens* **SHERI**. **SHERI** *somewhat indecorously wakes up, stretching, scratching. She turns and sees* **GAMILA**. *She lets out a cry.*)

SHERI: Shit! (*She wraps the sheet around herself. Slight beat as she gets her bearings.*) Who—? Who the hell are you?

GAMILA: My name is Gamila. And who are you?

SHERI: How did you get in?

GAMILA: I have a key.

SHERI: A key? Why do you have a key? (*Seeing the suitcase.*) Wait. Okay. Wait. Wait, wait, wait. I have to wake up. Let me just—(*Drinks from a glass of water beside her as she glances at the alarm clock.*) I've been having the weirdest dreams. Where I think I've woken up and someone's in the room. So I just want to make sure . . . (**SHERI** *gets her bearings, looks at* **GAMILA**) You're definitely in the room. Okay. Who are you again?

GAMILA: Gamila

SHERI: And who did you say you were?

GAMILA: I didn't get your name.

SHERI: Sheri.

GAMILA: Hello, Sheri. Are you Abdallah's friend?

SHERI: No. I'm Musa's friend. Do you know Abdallah? We're worried about him. Musa's having a hard time getting hold of him.

GAMILA: He went to Mecca.

SHERI: Nobody knows where he is. Wait. Are you—Musa's sister? He said you might be coming to visit soon.

GAMILA: (*Slight beat.*) Yes . . . I'm his sister.

SHERI: Does he know you're here? He didn't mention you were coming today. Well, of course this would have to be our introduction. The least attractive way to meet a relative, naturally. I'm—(*A laugh.*) feeling just a little bit naked in front of you.

GAMILA: That's because you are.

SHERI: Yeah. Okay. Perhaps I'd, er . . . better get dressed (**GAMILA** *holds out* **SHERI**'s *underwear.*) Thanks. (*From* **GAMILA**'s *look.*) They were on sale.

GAMILA: I imagine they'd have to be. There's not much there to sell. (**SHERI** *will start getting dressed under the bed covers.*)

SHERI: Your brother really should have told me you were coming. He doesn't say much, but this you mention.

GAMILA: I'm a few days early.

SHERI: I would've prepared something.

GAMILA: You live here?

SHERI: No. But I could have got something ready. Will you be staying with Musa?

GAMILA: No. With—someone else. You're his friend?

SHERI: I do usually make friends with the people I . . . Look: I'm really sorry. This is pretty bad meeting you like this. Even for me and I'm no prude; still, you know. First impressions really matter.

GAMILA: Yes, they do.

SHERI: He really should have dropped a hint or something, you know. I'm going to kick his tush for not saying anything. (*She removes the sheet, fully dressed now.*) Okay. Now we can start over. This is how I normally am when I first meet someone: dressed. It's a custom in my country to say hi fully clothed believe it or not. (*Goes over and hugs Gamila.*) I'm so happy to meet you. Now I can get all the family dirt on Musa. *All* the dirt. Don't hold anything back. I want ammo for when we have our first fight. Which is way overdue. Because if nothing else is certain apart from death is that life will find the shit, and the fan that goes with it, and will assemble them both together for you. (*A laugh; noting her lack of response.*) The expression? "When the . . . hits the fan"? Can I get you something to drink? I've taken charge of the kitchen, so now it has actual food stuffs.

Gamila: You *do* live here.

Sheri: I hang out a lot. So I'm contributing.

Gamila: How long have you known Musa?

Sheri: About a month.

Gamila: A month?

Sheri: I'm guessing he didn't mention me.

Gamila: No.

Sheri: Your brother is definitely a work-in-progress. Has lots of good points. But needs to open up a wee bit more. I could sum the actual facts I know about him in a few lines.

Gamila: Tell me. We know so little about his life here.

Sheri: This must look pretty bad to you. My only defense is that we're really happy. Know that your brother is really happy. Like happy for the first time in a long time, he told me. And whatever the religion, I think happiness and love have got to be way up there in God's book, right? You look like you're going to keel over, do you want to sit down?

Gamila: When did you meet exactly?

Sheri: What? Like—what day?

Gamila: Yes.

Sheri: Um. I don't—. I think it was the first . . . Friday of this month. Because the next day we spent most of the day in. Yeah. I think it was about then. (**Gamila** *picks up her suitcases and heads for the door.*) Where're you going?

Gamila: I'm tired. I'll call Musa later. It was nice meeting you.

Sheri: Well, don't go. Rest here. I'll call him up now.

Gamila: No, I'd rather call him myself.

Sheri: We can go to the diner later. I'm supposed to meet him where I work this afternoon. He'd be upset if I didn't try and make you feel at home.

Gamila: I don't think you'll be able to do that.

Sheri: (*Digests what she said.*) What . . . what does that mean?

Gamila: It's not your fault. It was nice meeting you.

Sheri: Because I'm not—what? (**Gamila** *starts exiting.*) Wait, please.

Gamila: There's really nothing more to say.

SHERI: Please don't judge me like this. I don't deserve it. If you're as religious as you seem to be, then I think you could at least give me a chance.

GAMILA: For your information, what I'm wearing doesn't mean I'm a nun. Or a saint. Or even that I have spontaneous warm feelings for everyone I meet. It just means I believe in being modest. Not loud. Not showy. And not—easily available.

SHERI: (*Again, digests what was said.*) You mean—like me? (**GAMILA** *starts to exit again but* **SHERI** *blocks her.*) I'm sorry if I've offended you but you can't just come in and judge me like this.

GAMILA: It's not your fault.

SHERI: Then why are you biting my head off?

GAMILA: I'm not, I'd just like to go.

SHERI: Your brother and I have something wonderful here, please don't just fly in and ruin that.

GAMILA: Can you get out of my way, please?

SHERI: What, you're shocked your brother is having sex? Out of marriage? With a—an American? A non-Muslim? Is that it?

GAMILA: I don't care. I just want to go home.

SHERI: It's not fair if you've made up your mind and you clearly have.

GAMILA: (*Overlapping last couple of words.*) Just get out of my way!

SHERI: No, I won't! (*Then:* **GAMILA**, *surprising even herself, momentarily breaks down and starts crying as she drops her bags. Though she quickly recovers and clamps down on her emotions as she moves away from* **SHERI**.) Shit. Now you have to stay. You can't go like this. I'd feel horrible. Your Musa's sister, for God's sake. I can't have a fight with you. Not after three minutes of meeting you. And then be the cause of you crying.

GAMILA: Don't take satisfaction from this. I'm exhausted, that's all.

SHERI: Satisfaction?—When was war declared? We've just met.—Just come and sit with me, will you? I'll make tea. You drink tea, don't you? I've switched from coffee to sweet tea the way your brother likes. "Shay." I'm even learning some Arabic words.—Just for a few minutes? I have so much I want to tell you. Please.—I'll go heat the water. (**SHERI** *exits into the kitchen.* **GAMILA** *stands where she is for a few seconds looking dazed.* **SHERI** *pops her head out.*) Still here. Good. Won't you sit? We actually have a seating area now where we can have a proper meal. (**GAMILA** *doesn't sit down.*

SHERI *exits back into the kitchen. She reenters with a plate of cookies.*) Musa tells me these date cookies aren't as good as the ones back home. They taste yummy to me. "Kahk" they call it, right? (*She holds out the plate to* GAMILA. GAMILA *takes a cookie but doesn't eat it.* SHERI *moves to the small table and puts the plate down.*) It's not right that Musa didn't tell you about me. Especially if he knew you were coming. And it doesn't make me feel great to know I was being kept a secret. Is the shock discovering he's going out with an American? Or that he's having sex already? I can't imagine the latter, whatever your beliefs are. I mean, he's a guy, right? Guys are the same everywhere.

GAMILA: Yes. So it seems.

SHERI: Did he paint a different picture of his life here? Virtuous? Studying a lot? He said this would be your first visit. But I'm hearing an American accent.

GAMILA: I . . . went to an American school back home. Tell me about Musa then. (*She puts down the kahk.*) It would seem he does have—things he keeps to himself.

SHERI: You want the inside scoop? How your brother is away from you guys?

GAMILA: Yes.

SHERI: Well—it's nothing sinister. It's what you walked into, basically. He's dating me. Drives a taxi. You do know he drives a taxi?

GAMILA: Yes.

SHERI: He talks of going back to school but says the money he makes, most of it, goes back to his family, and that's hard to give up.

GAMILA: He needs to go back to college.

SHERI: That's what I say. He can always fall back on driving later.

GAMILA: What else? I'm sorry if I was unfriendly. I'm upset with Musa, not you. I thought he was more—straightforward. Honest and would tell us.

SHERI: He may've wanted to see if we were serious before sharing the news with his family.

GAMILA: And are you?

SHERI: I think so. No alarm bells have gone off for me, which is a good sign. Everything's felt so normal, and calm. Which is like really rare for me.

GAMILA: (*Slight beat.*) Huh. And living with him has been—?

SHERI: Wonderful. And I know this is the honeymoon phase. And the all-out fights haven't begun. I haven't yet called him an asshole and he has yet to call me a bitch, but. Even the hints of that haven't appeared and I usually pick up on them early on.

GAMILA: What else?

SHERI: (*Perhaps reaches out to touch/squeeze* GAMILA's *hand.*) You and your family did a great job. The streets are crawling with creeps that are like total tools with no inner anything you can connect with. But your brother—even though he doesn't share much about his past he's all about wanting to—I don't know . . . it's probably just those moments at the start of a relationship, where you're discovering little things, but it's like: sometimes I watch him and see this beautiful wrestling inside of him. I so admire people who go for something. I just crossed state lines to start a new life and I give myself credit for that. (*The sound of the kettle boiling is heard.*) I can't imagine what's it's like to travel as far as he has. (**SHERI** *gets up.*) Let me get the tea. The other thing—. Well let me get the tea first.

GAMILA: What other thing?

SHERI: Let me get the tea. (**SHERI** *exits into the kitchen.* **GAMILA** *is left alone for a few seconds. Perhaps she gets up. Or remains seated, emotions gathering.*) (*Offstage.*) The other thing is—selfishly—what it's doing for me. (*Reappears with two glasses of tea and a small bowl of sugar cubes on a tray.*) How it opens up your world, if you let it. I put mint leaves in the tea. Do you mind?

GAMILA: No.

SHERI: Did I put too much?

GAMILA: No.

SHERI: Like actual mint leaves in tea, for instance. How cool is that. And just—finding out there are other ways to look at things. I'm so fed up of the way I look at stuff, you know. The same old world every day. It's so refreshing. And the Qur'an. It's really quite a read. (*Either points to where it is or gets it.*) I've been reading passages and finding out the Prophet was like an immigrant too, right? The migration he had to make, to escape persecution. Which makes him like an unofficial—American. But you know I . . . (*Then:*) I'm sorry, I'm yammering away.

GAMILA: No. Continue. I'd like to know more about the woman my brother has got to know.

SHERI: No, just that, your brother reminds—. He does remind me of the sheer—chutzpah that must have carried my great grandparents to come here. And then I start thinking that—when I'm watching Musa, that, yeah: I can go for something too, be something different if I choose, you know. I see so many of my customers pissed off and grumbling all the time. It's like they've forgotten that dream. The sheer wonder that drove their distant relatives to take the risks they did. And at the end of the day, it's all about that, right? Going for something. Daring yourself.

GAMILA: Sheri.

SHERI: (*Continuing.*) And love of course. The biggest dare of all. Which I'd become such a coward about.

GAMILA: Sheri. I need to tell you something.

(*A thud above them is heard. Heavy footfalls, then a door slamming.* **WOMAN'S VOICE:** *Kiss my ass! You can kiss my ass, you piece of shit.*)

SHERI: Get a divorce already! You're beyond counseling! Jesus Christ. You know about them? Did Musa tell you?

GAMILA: Yes. Sheri—

SHERI: They need to divorce or find somewhere else to sort their crap out.

GAMILA: I have to tell you something. I haven't been completely frank with you.

(*The bedside alarm goes off.*)

SHERI: Hold that thought. (**SHERI** *gets up to turn it off.*) I have the night shift. Just so you don't think I'm lazy or anything.

GAMILA: Sheri. Please listen. Musa isn't—he isn't my . . . he isn't my brother. I'm sorry I haven't been honest with you. But finding you here was a—shock to me, to say the least. I needed to find out what was going on. I like to be straightforward myself, so I apologize for that. Musa is my—well, he's my fiancé. We've been engaged for the past ten months. I've just returned from visiting his family in Cairo. I was raised in this country, not too far from here. Went to the local high school. Musa omitted more than just a few important . . . facts.

SHERI: (*Slight beat.*) You know . . . I know I may be like the bull in the China shop here. Not the most graceful thing to walk into your family's life. Clearly religion is a big deal, I'm getting the impression, but I really—

GAMILA: No—

SHERI: —respect it.

GAMILA: I'm his fiancé, for real.

SHERI: If you're trying to push me away.

GAMILA: This is not about that. (**GAMILA** *goes to get something from her bag.*)

SHERI: And I'm not *that* much older than him if that's the issue. And shouldn't I meet the rest of the family before getting dismissed? And by the way, wasn't the Prophet's wife like fifteen years older than him?

GAMILA: (*Searching in her bag.*) I'm his fiancée. I'm not making this up.

SHERI: I don't come across well in first impressions, I know that. But I know your brother. He wants this to work, long term. I brought up marriage the other day and he smiled.

GAMILA: He smiled because he's gaming you. Here. (*She hands* **SHERI** *one of the photographs retrieved from the bag.*) I don't think that's the shared look of a brother and sister. (*Hands* **SHERI** *the second photograph.*) Nor that one. The Arabic in the back says, "Thank you for coming into my life. With you, I have a future now." That's his signature.

(*Slight beat. The alarm goes off again.* **SHERI** *stares at the photograph.* **GAMILA** *goes over and turns the alarm bell off.*)

I'm sorry I led you on like that. I'm sorry Musa led us both on. It's why I wanted to know when you two first got together. He brought you back here two days after dropping me off at the airport. So much for fidelity. I don't blame you, you didn't know. And I'm not sure I . . . I even blame Musa. I guess he was . . . Knowing how he talked of America. No offense to you but I think he was just . . . wanting to dip his toe in. So to speak. (**SHERI** *tosses the photographs and exits into the kitchen.* **GAMILA** *picks up the photographs.*) Again. I'm sorry you had to find out like this.

SHERI: (*Offstage.*) Yah . . . (*Reenters with a beer. She opens it.*) You know . . . I only once ever experienced anal sex. And I can't say I took to it. So it's kinda strange to me I'm having flashbacks to that particular moment right now. Maybe because I don't know who I feel more reamed by. Did you enjoy that? Was that fun playing me like that?

GAMILA: None of this is fun.

SHERI: Really.

GAMILA: And I'm not sure I have to be that sorry.

SHERI: You don't?

GAMILA: As I said, while I'm not blaming you—

SHERI: (*Interrupting.*) How very big of you.

GAMILA: (*Continuing.*) I did still find you here.

SHERI: I think we should return to the part where he dropped you off at the airport. Because that's where he left you and started off with me.

GAMILA: You still like him after this?

SHERI: That's my business. If I dump him, it will be me who dumps him and not because of you springing this crap on me.

GAMILA: Nonetheless, these are the facts.

SHERI: No, really, how fun was that? Getting all that information out of me.

GAMILA: I needed to know how serious this was.

SHERI: I don't even remember what I said. Let's see, you handed me my underwear. And then I spent the rest of the time trying to be sweet and welcoming.

GAMILA: I'm sorry.

SHERI: No you're not.

GAMILA: He is my fiancé. I've just returned from talking about wedding arrangements with his family. He's not some boyfriend like he is for you.

SHERI: Listen, bitch. And I think we've broken enough ice to be on a first name basis. Why don't you get your bags and fly out to talk some more with his family.

GAMILA: Sheri, instead of drawing this out and making this more painful for yourself—

SHERI: Get out!

GAMILA: He's not going to stay with you. He was just using you. He was *getting off.*

SHERI: (SHERI *picks up the suitcases, opens the front door, and throws them out.*) You want me to throw you out as well?

GAMILA: (*Slight beat.*) I used to always wonder about girls like you in high school—when I first came—I couldn't understand how some girls could just throw themselves at boys. Be that easy. With no respect for themselves. People look at me and think I'm the weak one for wearing this. When I used to look at girls like you and think what a waste. How weak, and pathetic. To get used like that. Do you think Musa thinks of you as anything else? I felt threatened by you for a second, but—you're just the woman he went to bed with. Whether I can forgive him for that,

I don't know. I do know, to save you time and before you really get hurt, that knowing Musa he's *not* going to go any further with you, whatever he said. You were just keeping him company while I was away.

(*Slight beat.* SHERI *looks like she might reply. Instead, she puts down the beer, grabs her handbag, and exits. Beat. Above her,* GAMILA *hears several thuds and a door slamming.*)

Time Stands Still
by Donald Margulies

CHARACTERS: **MANDY**, an event planner (mid-20s); **SARAH**, a photojournalist who covers wars and global strife (late 30s–early 40s)

PLACE: James and Sarah's loft in NYC

CIRCUMSTANCE: Sarah was severely hurt by a roadside bomb in Iraq.

EDITOR'S NOTE: Slash marks (/) indicate where lines should overlap.

(**MANDY** *and* **SARAH** *sit in awkward silence.*)

MANDY: You guys seem to have such a great marriage.

SARAH: Oh, we're not married.

MANDY: You're not? / I thought . . .

SARAH: No, we've been together for eight years, but we never actually bothered to make it legal.

MANDY: Oh. Wow. I thought . . .

SARAH: No. Too busy saving the world.

MANDY: I don't know how you go to these places. *War* zones.

SARAH: Not as hard as you might think. War was my parents' house all over again; just on a different scale.

(*Pause.*)

MANDY: It must be so intense. I mean, how you can even concentrate with all that going on?

SARAH: It's so automatic, I don't even think about it. When I look through that little rectangle . . . time stops. It just . . . all the noise around me . . . everything cuts out. And all I see . . . is the picture.

MANDY: Your pictures are beautiful.

SARAH: Thank you.

MANDY: I don't mean "beautiful," I mean . . . / *You* know . . .

SARAH: You can call them beautiful . . . I think they're beautiful. Then again, I'm their mother.

(*Pause.*)

MANDY: Um. Listen, I, uh . . . I know how much you and Richard mean / to each other . . .

SARAH: Mandy, you don't / have to . . .

MANDY: I know; Richard told me. (*A beat.*)

SARAH: That was twenty years ago.

MANDY: Yeah, but you stayed *friends*. That's wonderful. And I come along and it's like: "Who is *she*? Oh, she must be Richard's midlife crisis."

SARAH: No . . .

MANDY: Well, I'm not. Okay? Whatever it was that brought us together, we're together. For real. This is not a passing "thing." I *love* Richard. He is a very good man.

SARAH: Yes, he is.

MANDY: Probably the nicest man I've ever known. He's smart, and kind, and caring. And I love his voice; I love the way he *sounds*. So he's a lot older than me. So what? It's not like I go around thinking, "Oh my God, he's like three years younger than my dad!" 'Cause I don't; I don't think about it. The only thing that matters—to *me*, anyway—is he takes care of me. He makes me feel safe. And one day, when he's old, and demented? I'll take care of *him*. (*A beat.*) Look. I know I have a lot to learn.

SARAH: Mandy . . .

MANDY: I know that. I'm totally *provincial*. My world is like *this* big. (*Makes a small globe with her hands.*) And yours is like . . . (*She enlarges her imaginary globe.*)

SARAH: Right now my world is as big as from here to the bathroom. I've got to get this leg working like a leg again. (**SARAH** *stands and walks around.*)

MANDY: You are so brave.

SARAH: Oh, please. Don't call me brave.

MANDY: You are. How many people could do what you do?

SARAH: I know what bravery looks like and, believe me, this is not bravery. This is dumb luck. An occupational hazard.

MANDY: What happened? I mean, Richard told me a little . . . You don't have to / talk about it . . .

SARAH: Roadside bomb. I got thrown I don't know how many feet into the air . . . One of my cameras turned up like forty yards away.

MANDY: Oh, wow.

SARAH: Headful of shrapnel, banged up this leg pretty good. Medivac'ed to Germany. Kept in a coma for like two weeks till the swelling went down . . .

MANDY: It was great Jamie was there—I mean, James.

SARAH: Jamie was *here*. He'd come home. He flew over after.

MANDY: Oh. I thought he was with you.

SARAH: (*Shakes her head, then*—) Something happened. He . . . needed to get home.

MANDY: Sorry about your friend.

SARAH: (*Distracted.*) Hm?

MANDY: Didn't you have a friend? You were with?

SARAH: Yeah. My fixer.

MANDY: Your what?

SARAH: Fixer. That's what we call interpreters over there: Fixers. Guides. Go-betweens. They make contacts, talk to the locals, set up interviews. They take care of everything for us. Everything. We're lost without them.

MANDY: He was right next to you? (SARAH *nods.*) That must've been horrible.

SARAH: Actually, I don't remember. All I know is, there he was . . . next me . . . (*Pause.*) And I never saw him again.

MANDY: Wow. (*Long pause.*)

SARAH: He was an engineering student before it all went to hell. Who taught himself American English by reading *A Farewell to Arms* over and over again. Carried it with him wherever he went. That and the Koran. (*A beat.*) He had a wife. Who was killed. And two little girls. Also killed. About a year into the war. A mortar attack on their apartment building while he was at school. (*A beat.*) He was a lovely, lovely man. Funny! And he *loved* America. Loved it. Everything about it. Television.

(*Pause.* SARAH's *mind is elsewhere.*)

MANDY: What was his name?

(*Pause.* SARAH *looks at* MANDY.)

SARAH: His name was Tariq.

Part 4
Multiple-Character Scenes

A Twist of Water
Written by Caitlin Parrish
Story by Caitlin Montanye Parrish & Erica Weiss

CHARACTERS: **NOAH**, white, homosexual schoolteacher, adopted Jira; **TIA**, Jira's birth mother, African American; **JIRA**, African American teenager

CIRCUMSTANCE: Noah's partner and Jira's other dad by adoption died in an auto accident over a year ago. Jira is meeting her birth mother, Tia, for the first time.

(*TIA enters and waits. NOAH enters. They stare at each other for a moment. NOAH goes to TIA and extends his hand.*)

NOAH: Noah Calder.

TIA: Tia Young.

(*They shake hands. NOAH stares at TIA.*)

Do I look like her?

NOAH: (*Pointing at a section of TIA's face.*) Here.

TIA: Where is she?

NOAH: She needs a second. She's coming. I just didn't want you to think we'd bailed.

TIA: Is there anything I should know? Or be ready to hear?

NOAH: I don't know. She hasn't, uh . . . I don't know what she wants to ask. She wants to know more about you, and herself. So just be ready to talk about yourself.

TIA: There's not much to say.

NOAH: God, you were just a baby, weren't you?

TIA: It was a while ago, yeah.

NOAH: Does she have any brothers or sisters?

TIA: I have a boy.

NOAH: Wow. How old?

TIA: Seven.

NOAH: What's his name?

TIA: Benny.

(*Almost automatically* TIA *takes out her cell phone and shows* NOAH *a picture.*)

NOAH: That is a grin.

(**NOAH** *takes out his cell phone and shows* TIA *a picture.*)

TIA: Oh my God, she's my mother.

NOAH: Are you all right?

TIA: No? I don't know.

NOAH: Is there anything I can tell you?

TIA: Is she a sad kid?

NOAH: No. She gets angry first.

TIA: Okay. Okay, I can take angry. Is she a scared kid? Does she get scared?

NOAH: At the funniest things. Bridges. Hates going over bridges. She used to curl beneath the backseat in the car.

TIA: Is she a happy kid?

NOAH: Not this year.

TIA: The . . . the sudden death?

NOAH: Yes.

TIA: She's young to have to do that.

NOAH: Yes.

TIA: Losing a daddy is hard for a girl.

NOAH: It was a car accident. We got there in time for Jira to say good-bye to him.

TIA: That's something.

NOAH: That's how I try to think of it.

TIA: Did anyone tell you how long we have the room?

NOAH: The lady at the desk said as long as we're out by five.

TIA: It's after three-thirty.

NOAH: We came from school. I'll go check on her.

(**NOAH** *leaves.* TIA *stares after him. Several long moments.* NOAH *enters. And then, after a second,* JIRA, *with a backpack.* JIRA *and* TIA *stare at each other. Suddenly* TIA *rushes to* JIRA *and hugs her as tight as possible.* JIRA, *too surprised to hug back, drops her backpack.* NOAH *watches.* TIA *proceeds to lose her shit.*)

TIA: (*Wails.*) I'm so sorry! Oh, God, I'm sorry!

JIRA: Don't say that.

(JIRA *hugs* TIA *back.*)

TIA: I've carried so much darkness in my heart over this.

JIRA: Me too!

TIA: I was just a kid. My momma wouldn't let me keep you. They wouldn't let me. I'm sorry.

JIRA: Don't say sorry.

TIA: Oh my God, I love you so much.

JIRA: I love you, too.

(*The women continue to hold each other.* NOAH *can't take it. He makes to leave. But he does not go.* TIA *lets go, exhausted.*)

TIA: I need to sit in a chair.

NOAH: Okay. It's okay. Come sit.

(NOAH *helps them. They collapse into chairs.* TIA *and* JIRA *cannot stop looking at each other.* NOAH *retreats to a corner.*)

TIA: You look like the pictures of my mother when she was married.

JIRA: Is that good?

TIA: Oh, God, yeah! She looked beautiful. She was twenty. She could be your older sister.

(JIRA *wipes her eyes and tries to calm.*)

JIRA: Oh my God, this is so weird.

TIA: Yeah. Yeah.

JIRA: I have so many . . . I wrote down questions. Where's my . . . ?

(NOAH *grabs the backpack and brings it to her.*)

Thank you.

NOAH: (*Quietly.*) You're welcome.

(JIRA *opens it and pulls out a legal pad.*)

JIRA: Okay.

(*She straightens her glasses, and tries to calm her voice.*)

One. What were your primary reasons for placing me and do you regret it?

(TIA *is a bit taken a back.*)

Tia: Wow. This sounds like a job interview in hell.

Jira: I'll do another one.

Tia: No! It's okay! Just joking. Uh . . . I was young. Very.

Jira: Yeah, I wouldn't want a kid right now. I get that.

Tia: Wanting wasn't a part of it. That couldn't be a reason.

Jira: I saw . . . you wrote down that you couldn't get an abortion . . .

Tia: I didn't mean that. That was never something I was gonna do. No, I . . . I didn't really have a choice with my mom and dad, but I would think sometimes about ways to get us away. They weren't ever gonna work, but I thought of that so many times when I was pregnant. But you look . . . you look okay.

Jira: Yeah. I'm okay.

Tia: Good. (*To* **Noah**.) Thank you.

Jira: You met my dad, right?

Tia: Yeah. Hi.

Noah: Hi

Tia: She's so beautiful.

Noah: I know.

Tia: (*Smiling.*) You missed out on my hips, you skinny bitch.

Jira: Got an ass, though.

Tia: Look at you.

(**Tia** *gets quiet and inward for a minute.*)

Jira: Are you okay?

(**Tia** *puts her hand to her head as if it hurts.*)

Tia: Yeah, I'm good. Just need a second.

Jira: Should I get someone?

Tia: No. Just. It's a lot.

(**Tia** *keeps her head in her hand.* **Jira** *places her fingers on either of* **Tia**'s *temples.*)

Jira: Hold still.

(**Jira** *holds her fingers there lightly, slowly making small circles.* **Tia** *looks up at* **Jira**.)

Tia: What're you doing?

JIRA: It's for headaches.

TIA: Thank you. (*To* **NOAH.**) She gets rid of headaches?

NOAH: Apparently.

TIA: (**TIA** *takes* **JIRA**'s *hands in hers. To* **JIRA.**) I didn't meet him when I picked parents. I met the doctor.

JIRA: Richard.

TIA: He's the one who died?

JIRA: Yeah.

TIA: He was really nice to me. Made it clear he appreciated what I was doing. Didn't make me feel bad. It was a little easier after meeting him. He was a good dad?

(**JIRA** *nods.*)

You've had a bad year; right?

(**JIRA** *nods again.*)

My daddy died a few years ago. He was . . . he never really liked me. Having boys was a big deal for him and he never got one. I was the baby, his last chance, you know, and I came out me, so . . . so we got off to a bad start. He got really sick, and my mama and my husband and I took care of him—

JIRA: You're married?

TIA: Nine years. Scotty.

JIRA: Is your mom alive?

TIA: Oh, she's never gonna die. End of the world'll come, it'll be her and some cockroaches left over and she'll start cleanin' . . . but my dad. He didn't tell me he was grateful for the help, if he was. I don't know. But I miss him every day. Your daddy's your daddy. Only man that raised you. At least you got two.

JIRA: No mom.

TIA: You didn't want the mom I was gonna be at sixteen. You're doing okay.

JIRA: I'm . . . I'm really tired. I stay up a lot. Trying to . . . I hate not knowing what I should do. It feels like getting to school and remembering that you didn't do a big project. And . . . and I really wish Richard was here, because he was always like, "Okay. Problem. Here's how we fix it. Do this, do this, do this." And if there are steps, then it's not scary.

TIA: Not everything has steps, though.

JIRA: So, maybe not right away, but could we keep talking and meeting and then maybe I could come visit? Please? Mom?

TIA: Oh, I don't . . . No.

JIRA: No?

(**TIA** *turns to* **NOAH.**)

TIA: We started too fast. That was my fault. I just saw her and . . . I didn't expect to cry—

JIRA: Please?

TIA: Jira, listen . . .

JIRA: I'm not mad at you. I promise I'm not. You'd know if I was mad.

TIA: I can tell.

JIRA: So can I? Not, like, today or anything.

TIA: Jira, no one knows. I never told anyone. I mean, my parents knew. But I never told my husband. I didn't tell him I was coming here. I haven't lied to him in ten years, but I didn't tell him. I didn't know how this would go, you know? I didn't know if today was going to be me sitting and listening to you tell me how I'd messed up, which would have been okay. I was ready for that. I didn't know I was . . . I don't usually cry. I'm sorry if that . . . you've just got to understand. You've been buried for me for a long time. It will be a while until you're a real person in my mind.

JIRA: But we're right here. We can talk and hug.

TIA: (*To* **NOAH.**) Are you—?

JIRA: Don't ask him. Okay? He didn't want me to meet you. This was my— this was what *I* did.

TIA: He wrote to me first—

JIRA: Legal stuff. This is between us.

TIA: (*To* **NOAH.**) Are you okay with this?

JIRA: Stop asking him! You're my mom.

TIA: No . . . no. (*Pause.*) It's not your fault. You didn't do anything wrong. I swear. But I lost you. I blamed you. And *I* survived you. We're here. We can talk. But I've already mourned you. You're not . . . you don't understand, because it just hasn't been long enough yet. But you get better. I hadn't thought about you in a few years when I got the letters. I hadn't thought about you. I came here . . . I came here to see you and talk to you and know you were okay. You know what I've been picturing all this time? Pigtails, and a purple dress, dancing by yourself in a corner at maybe nine years old. Is that you? I'm not what you imagined either, right? You're not un-adopted because we said "I love you." Just 'cause it's true doesn't mean we know each other. I'm not your mom.

(Tia *shows* Jira *a picture.*)

I'm Benny's mom.

(Jira *stares at the picture.*)

Jira: He looks happy.

Tia: (*Pause.*) I need some water. I'm gonna get some water.

(Tia *exits.*)

Jira: Don't say anything. Please? (*Pause.*) No one wants me.

Noah: Jira. You have no idea how badly I wanted you. Or how happy Dad and I were when we finally met you and got to take you home. We wanted a little girl. We so desperately wanted *you.* And the day they put you in our hands . . . you were so breakable. You were the size of a book, and we could each hold you in one hand. We fought over who got to hold you. Dad was working nights at the hospital when you were small, so I got you to myself after dinner, and you'd fall asleep every night on my chest. I could feel your little heart against me. And I swear to God my pulse would always line up with yours. It still does.

(Noah *takes* Jira's *hand.*)

Baby. If you ache, I ache.

Jira: . . . Dad.

(Jira *collapses into her father's arms.* Noah *holds her tightly.*)

Compulsion
by Rinne Groff

CHARACTERS: MR. SILVER (45), a successful novelist and early advocate of Anne Frank's diary; MISS MERMIN (23), recently promoted editor at Doubleday publishing company; MR. HARRIS (40s), in charge of subsidiary rights at Doubleday

PLACE: The office of Doubleday publishing house in New York City, 1950s

CIRCUMSTANCE: Mr. Silver believes he has an understanding with Otto Frank that he is the man to see Anne Frank's story come to life for the stage.

> (MISS MERMIN *reads* MR. SILVER*'s review from the inside flap of the latest edition of Anne's diary.*)

MERMIN: "One forgets the double significance of this document in experiencing it as an intimate whole, for one feels the presence of this child-becoming-woman as warmly as though she was snuggled on a nearby sofa."

SILVER: Sounds nice. Makes me want to buy a copy. (*And then—*) Is that layout final?

MERMIN: Already at the printer. With your words right there on the inside flap.

> (*He looks at the book.*)

SILVER: Why not my name?

MERMIN: They hardly ever put names.

SILVER: I put Albert Einstein's name.

MERMIN: He wasn't writing for *The New York Times Book Review*, and if he was, be honest: you would have put that instead.

SILVER: I would have put both. They took out the part about Anne's voice becoming the voice of six million vanished Jewish souls.

MERMIN: I recommended that they print the whole review on the flap, but the advertising department said they didn't want readers to think they were in for something depressing.

SILVER: Morons. How many printings now?

MERMIN: We're starting on the fourth, thanks to your review. Forty-five thousand copies already sold. Anne's book will be on shelves for . . . Oh, I can't even think it.

(**MR. HARRIS** *enters and shakes* **SILVER**'*s hand.*)

HARRIS: What a pleasure. I'm a huge fan.

SILVER: Thanks. Good to see you again.

MERMIN: This is Mr. Harris.

SILVER: Mr . . . ?

HARRIS: Louis Harris.

SILVER: Oh. I thought you were . . . (*Beat.*) Aren't you the guy who . . . ?

MERMIN: Mr. Harris is in charge of the subsidiary rights department.

SILVER: Rights? Oh, right. I don't have anything definitive to report on that front. I was focusing all my attention on the review. But I have several very good leads, and now that the book is selling so well . . .

HARRIS: He doesn't know?

SILVER: Know what?

HARRIS: (*To* **MERMIN.**) Too busy bragging about your promotion to fill him in on the matters at hand?

SILVER: Promotion? Congratulations.

HARRIS: You write a review and she gets a promotion. How's that for quid pro quo?

SILVER: I'm certain Miss Mermin is worthy.

MERMIN: Very kind. No, Mr. Harris is referring to the interest in the dramatic rights to the diary. I forget who knows what, everything's moving so fast. I have a list of potential producers. I almost have a waiting list.

HARRIS: All the top people: theater, film, radio. We'll even sell radio.

SILVER: Well, let's have a look at this list.

HARRIS: We already have. We've narrowed it considerably.

SILVER: Without me?

HARRIS: Uh, yes.

SILVER: Not to be pushy, but Mr. Frank authorized me to be his representative in the sale of the theatrical rights.

HARRIS: Mr. Frank led us to believe that you didn't feel comfortable accepting the full agent fee.

SILVER: I never wanted an agent's fee at all.

HARRIS: We were so glad to hear that. Because these are complicated matters and, with all due respect, ones in which you have no expertise.

MERMIN: But we're eager to work very closely with you.

SILVER: "Closely"? What does "closely" mean?

HARRIS: You get five percent of whatever deal we negotiate with the producers, and Doubleday gets five. Fifty-fifty. It's more than generous, beyond the terms we typically offer, even to a qualified agent.

MERMIN: It's a great deal.

SILVER: Even at half of the fee, might it seem, well, unseemly? I shouldn't accept agent money if I'm going to turn around and write the stage adaptation like Mr. Frank asked me to.

HARRIS: Mr. Frank asked you to write the stage adaptation? When was this?

SILVER: Always.

HARRIS: Always as in since the beginning of time?

SILVER: I know for a fact that there was a letter to your offices in which Otto Frank requested that I be involved in the writing "in order to guarantee idea of book." That's what he wrote.

MERMIN: It was a cable. I'll make sure you see it on your desk today.

SILVER: Even beyond the cable, Mr. Frank and I have an understanding from Paris.

HARRIS: This isn't about the French language rights. That's a completely separate bailiwick.

SILVER: No, in Paris when I first met him and told him that his daughter's book could make a wonderful play. That beginning. He couldn't see it. I had to convince him. I left that meeting with his blessing to make it happen. The first step was the book publication in English, which I secured.

HARRIS: Which *you* secured? We have a man in Europe who signed a contract with Frank.

SILVER: Through your assistance.

HARRIS: Assistance? We published the book.

SILVER: And what about the review? My goddamn review is what made her diary a hit, or else you were looking at a shitty 3,000 copies tops.

(*Silence.*)

That's not what I meant. Anne's book. Anne.

HARRIS: Indeed. Because that's an insult to a young Jewess who wrote a heck of a diary.

SILVER: Mr. Harris, I would lay down my life to serve this book and all that it represents to the Jewish people. I would sacrifice everything and ask for nothing in return. But my review, come on . . . Tell him.

MERMIN: Mr. Silver's review helped the diary very much.

SILVER: A bestseller. Those don't come along every day. Believe me, I know.

MERMIN: Why don't we look at some of the people on the list? Together. We all know that Mr. Frank is eager for us to arrive at consensus.

SILVER: Looking at the list is what I proposed from the beginning. (*After a nod from* **MR. HARRIS,** **MERMIN** *hands the list to* **SILVER.**) All these names are . . . ?

MERMIN: That's only the theater people, or if they're film people, they've expressed an interest in producing the stage version as well.

SILVER: Well, this is tremendous. Sorry if I got a little agitated. Any one of these names would be . . . tremendous. But let me ask you something, Mr. Harris: don't you think the producer should be Jewish?

HARRIS: Jewish?

MERMIN: How would you even know for sure, just based on the name?

HARRIS: Names can be deceiving. I met a "Harris" once who turned out to be a Jew. That was embarrassing.

MERMIN: I think the particular background of the producer shouldn't matter so very much. It's not like he's the adaptor, or the director.

HARRIS: You don't have to worry about the director being Jewish. They all are.

MERMIN: We're not searching for a director right now. Our only goal is to advise Otto, Mr. Frank, who confesses to know nothing of any of these producers.

SILVER: Mr. Frank has already seen this list?

MERMIN: The list is changing every day. But you know what? This reminds me of that slight disagreement you had with Mr. Frank as to the Jewish sphere, I think he called it. How that aspect is more in the background for him.

SILVER: Yes, that's the background. That it's a Jewish story. He disagrees about that?

MERMIN: He was quite clear, as you recall, that he didn't want a Jewish person writing the introduction.

SILVER: Turning the diary into a play means making choices. That's the writer's job, but the producer will have opinions. It's our duty to Mr. Frank and his daughter to select someone whose mind, whose heart is in the right place.

MERMIN: Every single person rallying to be involved in this project *loves* the project. They believe in it. Every one.

SILVER: But *what* do they love about the project? What do they believe?

MERMIN: I wish there was a way that we didn't have to concern ourselves with the religion of the producer.

HARRIS: Amen. That kind of discrimination is not what Doubleday wants to be known for.

SILVER: I agree completely. But some of these people—even some of the Jews quite frankly, so you shouldn't think I'm prejudiced—some of these people are anti-Zionist.

MERMIN: Anne herself wasn't a Zionist.

SILVER: She has a crush on a boy who attends meetings. Her sister talked about Palestine, that she wanted to move there.

MERMIN: But Anne didn't.

SILVER: But she clearly wasn't *anti*-Zionist. She clearly wasn't a communist.

HARRIS: Are you saying some of these people are communists?

MERMIN: Are you saying that's a reason we should strike them from the list? We should blacklist?

SILVER: No. I have nothing against the communists. On the contrary. If you read my book about the steel strike, you know that. But what if these Congressional hearings spread beyond the movie business and into the theater world? I would just hate for any political concerns to jeopardize the fate of Anne's play.

HARRIS: Are we talking about Zionists or communists now?

MERMIN: We're not talking about anything; we're whispering.

HARRIS: If we're whispering, I'd just as soon not have to whisper. That's not what Doubleday wants to be known for.

(*Beat.*)

MERMIN: It is my opinion that the best producer for this proposed adaptation is Cheryl Crawford.

SILVER: From the Group Theater?

MERMIN: They're not communist. They've been painted with that brush in conversations like these.

SILVER: I wasn't implying anything about their politics. Miss Mermin, I went to Spain to fight the fascists. Ask Hemingway. If he's too drunk, ask Martha Gellhorn. She was there. I'm no redbaiter.

MERMIN: Maybe I'm getting agitated, too.

HARRIS: Miss Crawford is that female producer who's a . . . ? She's not married.

MERMIN: Neither am I, Mr. Harris.

HARRIS: Yet. And you know what I mean.

SILVER: I heard that, too, but it shouldn't be an issue.

MERMIN: I should think not. In the theater?

HARRIS: She can raise the money?

MERMIN: Cheryl Crawford? She produced *Brigadoon*.

HARRIS: So?

MERMIN: So, yes.

SILVER: I'll go with Miss Mermin. She seems to know the field.

HARRIS: We can pursue it. Now, Mr. Silver, should we be in touch with Floria Lasky about any papers that need to be drawn up?

SILVER: If that's necessary.

HARRIS: It's always best to cross all our T's. Whether or not it's the five percent. But I do hope you'll reconsider. For your sake. Not ours. We'd be happy to take one hundred percent of everything.

(*Laughs as if the previous was a joke.*)

Miss Mermin will help you with your coat.

(**HARRIS** *exits.* **MISS MERMIN** *gets his coat.*)

SILVER: Thank you, Miss Mermin.

MERMIN: Just doing my job.

Silver: How'd you get to be so gracious?

Mermin: Practice.

Silver: I could learn a thing from you. My wife tells me I put people off with my . . . enthusiasm. But she's French. You know how the French are.

Mermin: Well, I'm not French. You don't have to worry about enthusiasm with me.

Silver: Can I ask you one more thing?

Mermin: Fire away.

Silver: It's about Crawford's relationship with Lillian Hellman.

Mermin: Lily isn't lesbian, too, if that's what you're asking.

Silver: Quite the opposite from what I hear.

Mermin: What a gossip.

Silver: No, I ask because . . . I admire much of Hellman's writing a great deal. But what none of us want is for some so-called famous playwright, who has never championed the Jewish cause, quite the opposite again in the case of Lillian Hellman. And I worry that she would insinuate herself because she's chummy with the producer, and I could get left out in the cold.

Mermin: If you have a solid deal with Otto, Lily can't change that just because Cheryl comes on board.

Silver: You do know everybody, don't you? First name basis.

Mermin: I don't really know you yet.

Silver: I'm pretty simple.

Mermin: Now, I know that's a lie.

Silver: So you do know me.

Mermin: I'm starting to.

Detroit
by Lisa D'Amour

CHARACTERS: **BEN**, recently laid off from his job; **MARY**, Ben's wife (both late 30 to early 40s); **KENNY**, a recovering addict fresh out of rehab; **SHARON**, a recovering addict (both late 20s to early 30s)

PLACE: Ben and Mary's backyard

CIRCUMSTANCE: Ben and Mary have welcomed their new neighbors, Sharon and Kenny, who have moved in to the empty house next door. They have become fast friends.

(*BEN, KENNY, and MARY are dancing their asses off on BEN and MARY's porch. BEN is dancing on a chair with his broken leg. KENNY is maybe fake-humping the grill. MARY is spinning in circles. They are all beerwasted. Which is different from bourbon-wasted. Bourbon makes you mean and switches on your regret.*)

BEN: Yay-eah, yay-eah, yay-eah, yay-eah, yay-eah.

MARY: I'm a sexy mothafuckah on yo roof.

I'm a sexy mothafuckah on yo back porch

I'm a sexy mothafuckah in yo kitchen

I'm a sexy mothafuckah on yo lawn.

BEN: Yay-eah, yay-eah

Yay-eah-yay-eah-yay-eah.

KENNY: (*Wailing, high-pitched R & B style.*)

I'm your lover I'm your daddy I'm your car tire I'm your devil I'm your sexy

I'm your burger I'm your boyfriend

I'm your superstar!

BEN: (*Wailing too.*) I'm your superstar!

MARY: Hey, Ben, do this! Do this! Ben, do this!

(*MARY does some kind of dance move she wants BEN to do. BEN does it. KENNY comes up behind MARY and dirty-dances with her a little.*)

MARY: Wait, everybody, do this! Do it!

(*She does a dance move. They don't do it.*)

DO IT!

(*The two guys do it, they are all in a line.*)

We're on that show! You know that show with the dancers.

BEN: Yay-eah, yay-eah, yay-eah-yay-eah-yay-eah.

KENNY: I was on that show when I was sixteen!

MARY: Really!

KENNY: No. Sometimes I just say shit.

BEN: Look, I'm doing the one-legged twist.

(**KENNY** *cracks up.* **MARY** *twists with* **BEN.** **KENNY** *cracks up more.*)

KENNY: That is some funny shit.

(**KENNY** *starts doing some weird vaguely John Travolta-esque humping of the air, almost like he is swinging his dick around. Or maybe using barbecue tongs as his dick?*)

MARY: Kenny!

BEN: (*Kind of cracking up but kind of like "what?"*) Holy shit!

(**KENNY** *wails and grinds.*)

KENNY: I'm a superstar!

MARY AND BEN: I'm a superstar.

(**SHARON** *enters with two bowls—one filled with water and one filled with some other kind of food. She puts them on the floor and looks at them.*)

KENNY: What are you doing?

SHARON: I'm feeding my dog. I have a dog, remember? I'm feeding it.

KENNY: Oh, that is fucking funny.

(**KENNY** *gets two beers out of the cooler.*)

MARY: Oh right, your dog! You love your dog!

BEN: Ha-ha, that is fucking funny.

SHARON: Now I'm walking my dog.

(**SHARON** *fake walks her dog, it is on a leash and she kind of dances while she does it. The others crack up*).

KENNY: Walk that dog.

(**SHARON** *walks the dog sexier. The other take up fake leashes and walk their dogs, dancing while they do so.*)

MARY: Oh no, my dog just pooped! Look at me!

(*She pretends to pick up the dog shit with a fake bag and throws the bag away. They all hoot and holler and cheer while she does so. SHARON steps up on to the table and walks her dog up there. KENNY hands her a beer and she gulps it down.*)

MARY: Are you allowed to have that?

(**SHARON** *keeps dancing.*)

SHARON: Yeah, sure, it's just beer.

KENNY: Her problem was really freebasing heroin anyway.

SHARON: Kenny!

MARY: That was a joke, right?

BEN: Yay-eah, yay-eah, yay-eah, yay-eah, yay-eah.

SHARON: Yay-eah, yay-eah, yay-eah, yay-eah, yay-eah.

(**KENNY** *gets up on the table and starts dancing with* **SHARON**. **BEN** *and* **MARY** *walk their dogs.*)

MARY: Oh my God, I just got the greatest idea!

SHARON: What?

MARY: We should all fake-walk our dogs over to the lady-in-the-pink-jogging-suit's house! We should fake-walk our dogs over there and have them take a fake crap on their lawn! And we'll be like whoooooo-hoooooo!

BEN: Let's do it!

SHARON: Oh my God, that's hilarious.

(**MARY, BEN,** *and* **SHARON** *start to go.* **KENNY** *starts herding them back: he is a seasoned partier and he knows that crazy shit could bring cops and spoil everything.*)

KENNY: No, no, no, we're going to stay back here.

MARY: Come on!

KENNY: Come on, let's keep the party here. No, no, come on.

MARY: Party pooper!

(**SHARON** *cracks up.*)

SHARON: Get it? Party pooper!

(**MARY** *cracks up.* **MARY** *and* **SHARON** *fake-poop or fake-fart on* **KENNY**.)

KENNY: Alright, bitches!

(**KENNY** *picks both ladies up and spins them around. The ladies squeal. He puts them down and the three of them dirty-dance for a few seconds.* **BEN** *sits on the patio table with his feet on a chair.*)

SHARON: Come on, Ben!

BEN: Just a second, I'm resting.

MARY: No! No resting! No resting! No resting, resting, resting, resting!

(*It becomes a chant.* **BEN** *kind of dances in his seat.* **MARY** *couple-dances with* **SHARON**.)

MARY: Oh my God, I really needed this! Some downtime!

BEN: It feels good just to release!

(*The patio table breaks and* **BEN** *falls to the ground. A moment, they look, just music, then* **BEN** *jumps up.*)

I'm okay!

(*They all chant and dance. Maybe do a little "He's okay!" chant.* **BEN** *dances with everyone.* **SHARON** *acts like she is holding a giant cup.*)

SHARON: Guess what this is!

(*Everybody says, "What!?"*)

SHARON: It's a giant cup of party juice and I'm drinking it down!

(*Everyone hoots and hollers as* **SHARON** *drinks.* **MARY** *pretends to be holding something over her head.*)

MARY: Guess what this is!

(*Everybody says, "What!?"*)

MARY: It's a big bowl of get down and I'm pouring it all over you!

(*They all hoot, holler, and get down as* **MARY** *pours the fake juice.* **KENNY** *pretends to be holding something over his arm, like a purse.*)

KENNY: Guess what this is!

(*Everybody says, "What!?"*)

KENNY: It's my handbasket and we're all going to hell in it!

(*Everybody hoots and hollers "Going to hell! Going to hell!"* **SHARON** *starts dirty-dancing with* **BEN**. *Pretty quickly they start to make out. Pretty quickly it is pretty hot.* **MARY** *and* **KENNY** *are still dancing and saying "Going to Hell!" Then* **MARY** *sees* **SHARON** *and* **BEN** *and stops dead in her tracks. She reaches out for* **KENNY**'*s arm, who is still dancing.*)

MARY: Kenny, what's happening. What is that?

KENNY: Oh, it's nothing, nothing, hold on.

(**KENNY** *dances over and dances* **SHARON** *away from* **BEN**. *He dances with* **SHARON** *and whispers in her ear.* **SHARON** *kind of giggles and says, "You're right, you're* *right," only to* **Kenny**. **Ben** *is shell-shocked for a minute and then starts dancing again.* **Mary** *is shell-shocked for a minute longer and starts dancing again.* **Kenny** *is dancing with* **Sharon**, *and when* **Mary** *isn't looking* **Sharon** *looks to* **Ben** *and mouths the words "Sorry, I'm sorry" to him.* **Ben** *smiles at her and kind of shrugs his shoulders and laughs back.* **Kenny** *and* **Sharon** *start making out.* **Ben** *and* **Mary** *get a little uncomfortable and sort of half-dance.* **Kenny** *grabs* **Sharon's** *ass in this major way, like his finger is sliding down the back of her ass crack on top of her pants over and down between her legs.* **Sharon** *kind of rides his leg.* **Mary** *freaks a little.*)

Mary: Okay, okay, okay, okay! I think we are stopping! I think it is time for us to be stopping!

(**Sharon** *breaks away from* **Kenny**.)

Sharon: No, no, no, no stopping! No stopping!

Mary: Weird things are happening!

Sharon: No, no, *things* are happening. Can't you see?

Ben: It's OK, Mary, don't worry.

Mary: I'm going to call the police.

Kenny: No, you're not.

Mary: I mean, somebody—somebody is going to call the police.

Ben: It's our house. We're on our lawn.

Sharon: This is nothing compared to what's going down on Solar Power Lane right now.

Mary: Yes, but they do it quietly.

Sharon: (*Yelling.*) AND WE DO IT LOUD! Whoooo!

(**Kenny** *turns the music up a bit.*)

Kenny: Just keep dancing, Mary, it gets the endorphins going. We learned this in rehab. It can take the place of drugs. But you have to keep moving.

(**Mary** *keeps moving: half-dancing, half-exercising.*)

Sharon: It's beautiful! You're beautiful, Mary.

(**Sharon** *kisses* **Mary** *deeply.* **Mary** *lets her. The guys watch.* **Sharon** *lets go.*)

Mary: Did that really happen?

Sharon: Of course it did! Things can happen. You can just *do* them. You have to just do them. If you don't, then the world just stays the same.

(*Music. Music.* **MARY** *busts a chair on the cement patio. Music. Music. Is Ben going to be mad?*)

BEN: Whooooooo-hoooooo!

(*Another mad round of dancing. On chairs, with each other. Nothing real sexual, just mad dancing. At some point* **BEN** *breaks another chair.*)

BEN: I hate these fucking chairs! Who wants a chair that you can break with one hand?

MARY: They were on clearance from Patio Depot.

BEN: Fuck Patio Depot!

(*They cheer and dance.* **SHARON** *starts piling the wood from the chairs into a pile.* **KENNY** *downs another beer.* **MARY** *starts a chant.*)

MARY: I'm feeling, I'm feeling, I'm feeling, I'm feeling.

(**KENNY** *joins her.*)

KENNY AND MARY: I'm feeling, I'm feeling, I'm feeling, I'm feeling.

KENNY: Take it, Mary!

MARY: I'm feeling electricity, electricity running through my arms and legs—

KENNY: Yeah!

MARY: It's in my blood, the electricity is in my blood!

SHARON: That's good!

KENNY: I'm feeling, I'm feeling, I'm feeling—

MARY: Yes, Kenny?

KENNY: I'm feeling like my whole body is filled up with some kind of sweet air, strawberry air, and strawberry shortcake air—

MARY: Whooo!

KENNY: And it's making me feel like I can do fucking anything!

MARY: Waaaaaahhhhh!

KENNY: Look at me!

BEN: I'm feeling, I'm feeling—

(*Kenny joins him.–*)

KENNY AND BEN: I'm feeling, I'm feeling, I'm feeling.

BEN: I'm feeling like telling the truth!

Kenny: Yeah!

Mary: Tell it! Tell it! Tell it, tell it, tell it!

(**Sharon** *breaks another chair and keeps piling wood.*)

Ben: Should I?

Mary: Tell it, baby, tell it!

Mary and Kenny: Tell it, baby, tell it!

Sharon: We're here for you! We'll catch you! It's a truth fall, a trust fall!

(*Does* **Sharon** *get* **Ben** *to stand on a chair?*)

Ben: I'm feeling it!

Mary: Say it!

Ben: (*Still in party chant mode.*) Alright! I have no website! I said, there ain't no website! I have no website, I have no business cards, I have no plan, I got nothing! Nothing, nothing, nothing!

Kenny: Yea-ah, yeah-ah, yeah-ah, yeah-ah, yeah-ah!

Mary: What?

(**Kenny** *is dancing around.*)

Ben: After seven whole weeks. I've got nothing! Nothing to show! Nothing to show, show, show!

Mary: What did your computer crash or something?

Ben: No. I just. I think I don't want to, Mary.

Mary: You don't want to?

Ben: I mean, I've got a domain name. A domain name that I own. On the Internet. But I don't think I want to run a financial planning business.

Mary: Well, what do you want to do?

Kenny: Ben's got nothing! Ben's got nothing!

(**Sharon** *joins in.* **Mary** *and* **Ben** *are still, kind of looking at each other.*)

Kenny and Sharon: Ben's got nothing! Ben's got nothing! Ben's got nothing!

Mary: No!

Sharon and Kenny: Ben's got nothing!

Mary: NOOO!

(**Mary** *kind of runs at* **Ben** *to hit him.* **Sharon** *and* **Kenny** *catch her.*)

SHARON: No, no, no, Mary. It's a beautiful thing, Mary! Do you know what just happened? Do you realize what just happened? A beautiful thing has happened! Ben just admitted he's at zero. And guess what, Mary. When you are at zero anything can happen. It's like total possibility.

BEN: Yeah, Mary.

SHARON: He's like a tennis player with his knees bent, poised to jump in any direction. It's a beautiful thing, Mary.

BEN: Yeah, Mary.

MARY: But what are we going to do?

SHARON: (*A moment. Then—*) We are going to start a fire.

BEN: Huh?

KENNY: Really?

SHARON: Yeah, just like we used to do in Plano.

KENNY: Yeah, but that was Texas.

SHARON: Yes, but it's such a beautiful thing.

KENNY: True dat.

SHARON: It's a ritual, a healing ritual for Mary and Ben. Their clearance patio furniture will go up into the air, like a flower petal on the wind. And then you will be at zero, together.

MARY: Um.

(**SHARON** *couple-dances with* **MARY**.)

SHARON: We're going to do this, Mary. It's going to happen right here before your eyes. And it is going to open up a space.

MARY: What kind of space?

SHARON: You are living inside a tiny spectrum, Mary.

(*She shows* **MARY** *with her fingers—like pinching her forefinger to her thumb.*)

Like this small. And do you know how big the spectrum really is, Mary? Do you know?

MARY: I don't know.

SHARON: Light it, Kenny.

(**KENNY** *lights a match. Somehow, the pile of wood instantly catches fire. A roaring fire. They are all mesmerized.*)

MARY: A campfire!

BEN: Woah. Isn't that kind of big?

MARY: You're taking me camping!

SHARON: Yes, Mary. Yes.

(KENNY *maybe dances around the fire a bit.*)

MARY: I can feel the heat. And the wind. Going into my eyes. I can feel my eyeballs and my inner ear, my inner ears. And I feel a splitting feeling, like maybe in my bones down here, the bones that make up my hips, I feel a splitting feeling. Ben? Ben? Where are you?

(MARY *goes to* BEN.)

BEN: The funny thing is, I always wanted to be British, but I never really told anyone.

MARY: My forehead separating from my skull.

BEN: When I was ten I would watch *Masterpiece Theater* and read Agatha Christie, and when I would go to McDonalds I would order iced tea, because I thought that is what a British person would do. And there was a whole year, when I was eight, when I ate all my sandwiches with the crusts off. Until one time I got beat up for doing that and so I stopped. I think I've felt British from the moment I first opened my eyes.

(SHARON *goes to* BEN *and* MARY. *At some point, both couples stand together before the fire, maybe even in a kind of group hug. This is a shared experience.*)

MARY: I think I am feeling another skin just below my real skin. It's been there the whole time.

BEN: I rolled up my pants just above my ankle for a time. "For a time." That sounds kind of British. Falling asleep wondering what a crumpet was.

SHARON: That's so sweet. Mary, are you hearing this?

MARY: Yes.

BEN: And the funny thing, Mary, is there is a website out there called Brit-Land and it is designed especially for non-Brits who want to be British. And I have an identity on that website. A British identity. It all plays out in real time.

SHARON AND KENNY: Tell us, tell us . . .

BEN: My name is Ian. I'm a prep school teacher. I teach history. I like to bike. I have a cat. I am engaged to be married. I drink a pint of ale each afternoon. Right now I am asleep, because I like to get up early to go for my jog and a cuppa tea before heading to campus. Right now I am asleep in my flat.

(*The fire is getting pretty big.*)

MARY: Huh?

BEN: Right now I am asleep in my flat. With my girlfriend, Julia. I spend more time there than I do on my website, Mary. I spend quite a bit of time in Brit-Land.

SHARON: That's amazing!

KENNY: Anybody got marshmallows?

SHARON: So much is happening right now!

MARY: Yes, but is the table supposed to be on fire too? Is that really happening?

(*They look into the kitchen.*)

KENNY: Uh . . .

BEN: Oh shit, look at the curtains!

MARY: Somebody call the . . . oh shit, my phone is inside.

SHARON: This could be good! This could be amazing!

(**SHARON** *and* **KENNY** *dance.*)

MARY: Ben, let's go next door. Quick, let's go next door!

(**MARY** *helps* **BEN** *off the porch.*)

Edith Can Shoot Things and Hit Them
by A. Rey Pamatmat

CHARACTERS: EDITH, Filipino American (12); KENNY, Filipino American (16); BENJI, Kenny's classmate and friend (16)

PLACE: An ice cream parlor

CIRCUMSTANCE: Edith and Kenny's mother is dead and their father leaves them at their home without adult supervision. Edith shoots and wounds her soon-to-be stepmother, who shows up unannounced late one night. Meanwhile, Kenny and Benji have been developing an amorous relationship.

(KENNY, EDITH, *and* BENJI *sit around a table in an ice cream parlor. They eat ice cream cups in silence—rocky road, butter pecan, and strawberry cheesecake, respectively. They look very, very tired.*)

EDITH: Can you have butter pecan ice cream without the ice cream?

KENNY: Yeah. They're called wet nuts.

EDITH: Wet nuts? That doesn't sound all that good.

BENJI: I love wet nuts.

KENNY: Even now, that's all you can think about.

BENJI: Especially now.

EDITH: What is?

KENNY: What is what?

EDITH: All he can think about.

BENJI: Wet nuts.

KENNY: Stop it.

BENJI: Even dry nuts would be nice.

EDITH: You mean dry roasted?

BENJI: Hey, Kenny, let's get our nuts.

(KENNY *slams down his ice cream and walks away, exiting the parlor.* EDITH *and* BENJI *each eat a spoonful.*)

EDITH: I wouldn't have shot her if I knew who she was.

BENJI: He's mad at me, not you.

EDITH: He's mad at me, and you're standing in the way. If he stood up to things, I wouldn't have to. And then I wouldn't mess things up. If he had his way, we'd just be quiet and alone on that farm. Till we died. Surrounded by hay and grass and nothing.

BENJI: He's trying. To take care of you.

EDITH: I can take care of myself.

BENJI: Ed, you shot your future stepmother. She went to the hospital to get a pellet removed from her shoulder.

EDITH: She should have backed away. And she's basically a stranger. He should have called us and told us she was coming.

BENJI: He said he tried, but the phone was unplugged.

EDITH: And anyway, I didn't mean it; I was protecting you.

BENJI: Except you didn't shoot—she wasn't even my—

EDITH: I thought I was protecting you, okay? You should be thankful. That's what I'd do for you. Kenny would just slither away, like he did just now.

BENJI: I don't really want you to shoot people for me. Not even my mom.

EDITH: Why? You want to shoot her yourself?

BENJI: No.

EDITH: What if she were going to shoot you?

BENJI: She would never do that. She's my mom.

EDITH: She's sitting at home right now with no idea whether you're eating, whether there's a roof over your head, whether you're even alive. You think someone capable of that could never shoot you, just because she gave birth to you?

BENJI: Stop it.

EDITH: Even if she loves you, her love doesn't mean anything. When it matters, it doesn't mean a thing.

(**KENNY** *reenters.* **EDITH** *and* **BENJI** *clam up.* **KENNY** *walks deliberately to the table and sits. Without a word, he starts eating his ice cream again.* **EDITH** *stares angrily at* **BENJI** *as she rapidly shovels the rest of her ice cream into her mouth. When she finishes, she turns to* **KENNY.**)

I'm cold. I left my coat in the car.

(**KENNY** *hands her the keys.* **EDITH** *exits.*)

BENJI: I'm sorry. I was trying to make you laugh.

KENNY: No, it's . . . I'm sorry. It's hard to laugh right now.

BENJI: Okay, so what should we do next?

KENNY: I don't know. I wasn't thinking. She shot Chloe and I switched into automatic. I thought, while he brings Chloe to the hospital, get Edith in the car and out of there as fast as possible. But that . . . that was all. It's just . . . the way he screamed at her. And the way she screamed back. And the rifle, still in her hands. I was like, "She's going to shoot him. Ed'll shoot him, too." Which is ridiculous.

BENJI: I can see why you would have thought that.

KENNY: But now, we've been sleeping in the car for two days, we can't keep skipping school, and we only have money for a week, at most. And I don't . . . it's like I got us in even deeper trouble than we were. I'm such a . . . GOD—WHAT A FUCKING LOSER. I'm such a fucking idiot.

BENJI: You're not an—

KENNY: We don't have anywhere to live. I don't make any money. I can't take care of us. Of her. I don't know how. I look like I've got it together, but Ed's right: I'm a robot who learned a program. If this, then that. But I'm not programmed for this. We're trapped in that house, and now that I got us out, I don't know what to do or where to go.

(*A beat.*)

BENJI: You know the first thing Ed said to me?

KENNY: What?

BENJI: She walked right up to me and went, "I can shoot things. I can hit stuff."

KENNY: Well, she wasn't lying.

BENJI: Totally. I could never shoot someone.

KENNY: I'm glad. I don't want you to shoot anyone.

BENJI: And, like, when you're planning what groceries to get so you can make dinner and lunch and all the food for the week? I can't do that. I couldn't take Ed to school and extracurriculars and still get straight A's in pre-calc and chem.

KENNY: I got a B in chem.

BENJI: I couldn't do half the stuff you can do. My mom tells me what to wear, and when kids used to be, like, "Your mom dresses you. Loser!" I didn't know why that was an insult, because I didn't really know that other people could do stuff. The only food I can make is a bowl of cereal. I still have my learner's permit. My mom does everything for me. Did.

KENNY: Do you miss her?

BENJI: No. Not . . . not really.

KENNY: Then why are you telling me this?

BENJI: Because you're not a loser. You and Edith. You're all alone in that house and sometimes it's creepy and sometimes you're running out of money, but you can take care of yourselves. I would just be helpless. Or scared.

KENNY: But I am. I'm really scared, Benji. What have I gotten us into? Fine. Edith can shoot things and hit them. But she shouldn't have to shoot things. And I'm not a robot. I should be allowed to be scared sometimes instead of always fixing things. I just want to sit and be scared and for things to be okay.

(BENJI brushes his fingers against KENNY's hand.)

BENJI: Okay.

(BENJI slips his hand under the table. KENNY does, too, so they can hold hands.)

KENNY: What if people see?

BENJI: Who cares? I don't have anyone I care about anymore. Except you. So don't look at anyone but me. Just be scared for a minute. Okay? Be scared. And then we'll figure out what to do. And I'll help. I can help. You won't have to do it by yourself.

KENNY: Okay. *(Ten seconds. KENNY really does look terrified. BENJI squeezes his hand, and after a moment the fear starts to fade.)* SHE SHOT HER.

(They both start to laugh, uncontrollably.)

BENJI: Edith shot your stepmother.

KENNY: Potential stepmother. Or, I mean, formerly potential stepmother. I can't imagine she'll want anything to do with us now.

BENJI: Why, because she walked into the house and got shot in the shoulder with a bb?

KENNY: And the part where she walked in on my boyfriend and I in our undies.

BENJI: Maybe that'll be a plus in the whole "Should I be a stepmother?" debate. Con: stepdaughter with air rifle. Pro: stepson who looks good in undies.

KENNY: That's just . . . *ew. (A beat.)* I should take you home.

BENJI: What?

KENNY: To your dad. You should go home, Benji. It's our mess.

BENJI: I don't want to. I'm going to help. You'll see.

(**EDITH** *enters, wearing her coat, looking utterly defeated. She's been crying.*)

EDITH: He's standing at the car. He says you have one chance to walk out on your own, bring me with you, and drive back home. He says if you don't, he'll tell the police that you kidnapped me and stole the car. He said Benji's mom wants to tell the police that we kidnapped Benji.

(*Silence.*)

KENNY: We're trapped.

(**KENNY** *stands up.*)

EDITH: Don't do it, Kenny, please. Let's sneak out the back or something. Don't. (**KENNY** *heads for the door.*) Don't, Kenny. PLEASE. PLEASE!

KENNY: We're going back. If the police get involved and catch us, they could take you away from me.

EDITH: They won't catch us. Let's run. Let's fly away.

KENNY: Edith, we're kids. We're just kids.

(**KENNY** *takes* **EDITH**'s *hand.* **EDITH** *reaches out to* **BENJI**, *who takes her other hand. All three look petrified as they exit the ice cream parlor.*)

End Days
by Deborah Zoe Laufer

CHARACTERS: **SYLVIA**, Rachel's mother (40s); **ARTHUR**, Rachel's father (40s); **RACHEL** a nihilistic Goth; **NELSON**, the Steins' new neighbor, dresses like Elvis (both 16)

PLACE: The kitchen of the Steins; September 2003

CIRCUMSTANCE: After 9/11 the Steins fled NYC, Sylvia has renounced Judaism and converted to an Evangelical Christian. She believes the Rapture is coming soon.

RACHEL: So . . . now you're a prophet.

SYLVIA: It's not important how I know. I just know.

RACHEL: Have you told anyone else about this?

SYLVIA: Just a few people.

RACHEL: Who?

SYLVIA: I told Reverend Peter and the congregation.

RACHEL: Okay.

SYLVIA: And I put an ad in the *Penny Saver*.

RACHEL: Was your name on it?

SYLVIA: Of course not.

RACHEL: Okay.

SYLVIA: And I handed out flyers in front of Shoprite today.

RACHEL: Oh my God, Mom! What did they say?

SYLVIA: The Rapture is coming this Wednesday. Repent and be saved.

RACHEL: Oh my God. I'll never be able to leave the house again.

SYLVIA: I'm trying to save as many people as I can. I'm praying to do good in the world. Will you wait with me Wednesday?

RACHEL: I have a social studies quiz Wednesday.

SYLVIA: It's not going to matter, honey. None of this is going to matter.

RACHEL: But when you're wrong, I'll have to make it up Thursday during study hall, which means I won't be able to audit physics, which I'm going to do now, by the way.

SYLVIA: There won't be any Thursday. The Rapture will have started, and there will be chaos on earth and we'll be gone.

ARTHUR: I just bought milk. Will it keep while we're gone?

SYLVIA: We won't need milk where we're going.

RACHEL: You bought milk?

ARTHUR: I went grocery shopping today.

(**RACHEL** *goes to the refrigerator and opens the door.*)

RACHEL: Oh my God. It's full! There's lunch meat. Cheese! Apples! Oranges! Yogurt! Wow. Thanks, Dad!

(*She goes to him and gives him a hug. For the first time in a long time. He's very moved.*)

ARTHUR: You make a list, Rach. Every day you make a list. And I'll go back and get whatever you want.

(*To* **SYLVIA.**) You too, honey.

SYLVIA: We'll be gone Wednesday. We won't want for anything.

RACHEL: Is there bread?

ARTHUR: Check the bread box.

(*She does. Jumping up and down like a little kid.*)

RACHEL: Rye! Yay! I'm going to make a ham and cheese sandwich! There's mustard. Yay! Does anyone else want a sandwich?

ARTHUR: I could use half.

RACHEL: I'll split one with you. Baloney! Wow! This is so excellent. Mom, you want one?

SYLVIA: No, hon. Will you stay with me?

RACHEL: Won't Jesus be able to find me at school?

SYLVIA: I need to have you with me. I need to know that we're all going. Together. That we're all going.

(*There's a knock on the door.*)

NELSON: Mr. S.? (**NELSON** *enters.*) Hey! Everybody!

RACHEL: There's food! You want a sandwich?

NELSON: Food?

RACHEL: My dad went shopping.

NELSON: Mr. S.! By yourself?

ARTHUR: I made three trips.

NELSON: That is so awesome!

RACHEL: You want a sandwich?

NELSON: Sure. Can I help?

RACHEL: Spread the mustard.

SYLVIA: Will you stay with me, Arthur?

ARTHUR: Yes, Sylvia.

RACHEL: Pickles! For the list.

ARTHUR: Got it!

SYLVIA: Rachel? Will you stay?

NELSON: Where are we staying?

RACHEL: You didn't get the memo?

NELSON: What?

RACHEL: Jesus told my mom . . .

SYLVIA: Nobody *told* me, honey. He didn't *tell* me.

RACHEL: The Rapture is coming Wednesday.

NELSON: We have a history of U.S. government quiz Wednesday.

SYLVIA: There's not going to be any history. There's not going to be any U.S. There's not going to be any government. I know this is hard for all of you to accept, but all our earthly needs will vanish.

NELSON: What's going to happen exactly?

SYLVIA: Well, first the dead forgiven will rise.

RACHEL: From their graves?

NELSON: What was that movie about? Where the dead people rise up from their graves?

SYLVIA: Their *souls.*

RACHEL: *Night of the Living Dead.* Ughhh.

SYLVIA: Their *souls* will rise. And then Jesus will come with a shout, with the voice of the archangel and the trumpet of God, and the living will rise to the clouds to meet the Lord in the air.

NELSON: Cool. Count me in, Mrs. S.

Rachel: We have school.

Nelson: But we have school every day. This seems like a once-in-a-lifetime event. What time does it all start?

Sylvia: We'll begin our vigil at midnight on Tuesday.

Nelson: Should I bring anything?

Rachel: That's it? You're in? She says the world is ending and you start packing your bags?

Nelson: Do we need to pack?

Rachel: What are you going to tell your stepparents? Won't they think it's weird if you leave the house at midnight?

Nelson: They're still kind of in that honeymoon phase. So . . . they don't keep all that good track. Should I bring something? I make a really nice dip with onion soup mix and water chestnuts.

Arthur: I'll pick up some chips. Maybe a veggie platter.

Sylvia: We're going to be praying. And repenting.

Nelson: Definitely.

Arthur: And I'll make everybody waffles for breakfast.

Sylvia: We're going to be reading the Bible.

Arthur: Nelson, I'll finally get to teach you gin. Or, wait! There are four of us! We could play hearts.

Sylvia: No cards, Arthur. What is wrong with you today?

Arthur: (*Over this.*) Your mother used to be a killer hearts player. Remember, hon? Our third year at NYU? We called her the Shark.

Rachel: Really?

Arthur: We used to wager copying fees at the student center, and your mother and I . . .

Sylvia: We're not going to have time to play games, Arthur.

Arthur: But it's the whole day, right? We'll all be here a long time together.

Nelson: Unless Jesus comes like, right after midnight.

Arthur: It'll be great. Nelson, bring your guitar.

Sylvia: This isn't a party! This is your last chance to repent. To be saved. And when he comes, you won't need to play games. You'll be free. You'll feel joyful and loved.

ARTHUR: I do feel loved.

(*He goes to put his arms around her. She shrinks away from him, involuntarily, repulsed. There is a quiet moment when everyone takes this in.*)

SYLVIA: Rachel? Will you stay?

RACHEL: Why?

SYLVIA: Haven't I explained this?

RACHEL: No. Why do you want me? Why do you want Dad? It doesn't seem like you can stand the sight of us here. Why do you want us there?

SYLVIA: Of course I want you here.

RACHEL: You want our souls. The rest of us you could do without.

SYLVIA: That's not true.

RACHEL: What happens when Jesus doesn't come?

SYLVIA: He's going to come.

RACHEL: But what if he doesn't?

SYLVIA: I have complete faith in him.

NELSON: Stay, Rachel.

RACHEL: You think Jesus is going to come for us?

NELSON: I don't know. But we already know what happens if we go to school. Now we'll find out what happens if we don't.

RACHEL: We'll be marked absent. That's what happens.

ARTHUR: I'll make Reuben sandwiches for lunch.

RACHEL: This is wrong, Dad. You know it's all crazy.

ARTHUR: We'll all be together. All four of us. For twenty-four hours. We'll be a family.

RACHEL: And then what?

NELSON: Stay, Rachel.

RACHEL: Mom. If he doesn't come—will you give it all up?

ARTHUR: Rachel. Don't do that to your mother.

RACHEL: But if she's so sure . . . once there's proof that she's wrong . . .

NELSON: Rabbi Baumbach says faith doesn't need proof. If there's proof it isn't faith.

ARTHUR: That's very smart. He sounds very smart.

RACHEL: What are you talking about? You're an atheist.

ARTHUR: I was observant at one point in my life.

RACHEL: You were? What happened?

ARTHUR: I got busy. Working. Making money. Starting a family.

RACHEL: You gave it up for her.

ARTHUR: No.

RACHEL: You did. She wanted you to stop, and you caved.

ARTHUR: Other things became important. I made choices.

RACHEL: It always had to be her way.

SYLVIA: Rachel. If you'll stay Wednesday, if you'll really repent . . .

RACHEL: Yeah?

SYLVIA: In your heart . . .

RACHEL: Yeah?

SYLVIA: If Jesus doesn't come by midnight, I'll stop. All of it.

ARTHUR: You don't have to say that, Sylvia.

SYLVIA: I know he'll come. Please wait with me, Rachel. Having you off at school when it all happens—I just won't be able to stand it. It'll be that day all over again. All the chaos and panic and I won't know if you're all right. Please.

(*Pause.*)

RACHEL: (*A breath.*) Swiss Cheese? On the Reuben?

ARTHUR: Of course. And pastrami. And sauerkraut.

RACHEL: I'll stay.

Legacy of Light
by Karen Zacarías

CHARACTERS: **Millie**, a potential surrogate (20); **Peter**, Olivia's husband; **Olivia**, a scientist (both early 40s)

PLACE: Peter and Olivia's house

CIRCUMSTANCE: Peter and Olivia are unable to conceive a child and need a surrogate.

Millie: Hi. I'm Millie.

Peter: Thank you for meeting with us. I'm Peter.

Olivia: I'm Olivia. I like your hat.

Millie: I made it.

Olivia: It's stellar.

Millie: You're the astrophysicist.

Olivia: Most people assume Peter is the scientist.

Millie: I don't understand what you do. But I think it must be amazingly amazing.

Olivia: I used to study dark matter. But I got tired of trying to know the unknowable. Now, I study the formation of planets.

Millie: The formation of planets. Wow!

Peter: Olivia is a tenured scientist at the Department of Terrestrial Magnetism at the Isaac Newton Institute. The first and only woman to have a tenured senior science position there.

Millie: And you are the teacher?

Peter: Yes, I teach elementary school. You work at the library.

Millie: I like books.

Peter: I do too.

Millie: But I'm not a librarian. You need a degree in library sciences to be a librarian. I'm still un-degreed.

Peter: So what do they call you at work?

Millie: Millie, the book stacker. So you want to have a baby.

OLIVIA: You're direct. I like that.

PETER: Yes. We want to have a baby.

OLIVIA: We always assumed a baby would come. But we got so busy.

PETER: Olivia's work is very demanding.

OLIVIA: Stars can be that way sometimes. And Peter . . . well, helping to build a charter school . . . raising money . . . doing educational research. It's also a demanding job.

PETER: Fulfilling.

OLIVIA: Yes, fulfilling. We love our work. But suddenly I was almost forty.

PETER: How did we get to forty so fast?

OLIVIA: I feel young.

PETER: You look young.

OLIVIA: Thanks. But a body doesn't lie. We tried to get pregnant. And nothing happened.

PETER: We got tested.

OLIVIA: It turned out Peter had a low sperm count.

PETER: Not a low sperm count . . . a lower than average . . .

OLIVIA: Sorry, a lower than average sperm count. But that wasn't the problem. The problem was me.

PETER: It wasn't you. It was the cancer.

OLIVIA: Late-stage ovarian cancer.

MILLIE: Oh dear.

PETER: It was terrible.

OLIVIA: I think it was almost worse for you than for me. Peter took very good care of me.

PETER: I was worried sick. I screamed. I cried. I prayed.

OLIVIA: I just focused.

PETER: You have to be focused to survive late-stage ovarian cancer.

MILLIE: Focused . . . and very lucky.

OLIVIA: I've been in remission for a year.

PETER: And she, we want to start where we stopped.

OLIVIA: Although clearly, I cannot be part of it. (*Pause.*)

MILLIE: But I can. (*Beat.*) Anyway, here are the medical forms you requested. And the background check from the police station. I was hoping you would call. So I prepared.

OLIVIA: Your essay was beautiful.

MILLIE: Thank you. Anyway, I brought some things from my scrapbook. So you can get to know me and my family a little. To help you with your choice.

PETER: This is great.

MILLIE: This is my brother, Lewis. He is twenty-three, and two years older than me. He has a degree in computer science. He started a little IT company out of our mother's house.

OLIVIA: He is very handsome!

MILLIE: And he has no idea. Here is a book report I wrote in fifth grade. I thought you might both like it.

PETER: A book report on Jack London's *To Build a Fire* by Emilia Montenaro.

MILLIE: Everyone calls me Mille, except my mom.

PETER: "It is dumb to build a fire under a branch of ice. Everyone knows that fire is heat, light, oxygen, and carbon monoxide. And ice is crystallized water sensitive to heat. Everyone except the stupid cold hunter. The end."

OLIVIA: A nice English-science mix.

MILLIE: And this is a picture of my dad. He was a pilot; he flew off with a stewardess when I was three.

OLIVIA: Montenaro. He doesn't look Italian.

MILLIE: Montenaro is my mom's family name. And this is my mom.

OLIVIA: She's beautiful, like you.

MILLIE: Thank you.

PETER: She's so young.

MILLIE: Forty-four.

OLIVIA: What does she do?

MILLIE: She died a year ago.

OLIVIA: Oh, I'm sorry.

MILLIE: She was caught in a storm and hit by lightning.

OLIVIA: That's horrible.

MILLIE: It turns out that lightning is the natural force that kills the most people per year in the U.S.

PETER: I didn't know that.

OLIVIA: Our telescope gets hit by lightning hundreds of times a year.

MILLIE: Lewis was living at home with her when this all happened and I left school to help him with everything. We inherited the house and all that comes with that.

PETER: You are going to go back to school, aren't you?

MILLIE: Yes! (*Beat.*) But not back to college. I want to go to another school.

PETER: Another school?

MILLIE: There's a fashion design school . . . in Paris.

PETER: Paris!

MILLIE: They take ten students a year . . . and . . .

OLIVIA: You are one of them.

MILLIE: Imagine . . . me designing hats in Paris!

OLIVIA: Sounds like happiness.

PETER: And that's why you want to do this?

MILLIE: I've been thinking about this for a long time. I could help you, I could help myself, I could have your baby. I'm not ready to be a mother . . . but I am curious about being pregnant. I mean . . . a nine-month investment could change the world . . . for all of us. Life is short. I want to do something that matters.

OLIVIA: I like you.

MILLIE: I like you too.

OLIVIA: If we decide to move ahead with the plan, then we must establish that you are entering this agreement of your own free will for a total fee of twenty-eight thousand dollars.

PETER: And as the biological mother to this child, the state of New Jersey recognizes your absolute right to refuse to give up the baby at birth.

MILLIE: But I would be having this baby for you.

OLIVIA: Millie, do you think you could turn me into a mother?

MILLIE: No, but your baby will turn you into a mother. And I will help you have your baby. (*Olivia sighs.*) I am interviewing five other couples. But I want you to be the parents.

PETER AND OLIVIA: You do?

MILLIE: I know I don't fit the perfect profile of a "preferred surrogate mother." I'm not married. I don't have kids. I don't have a full college education.

OLIVIA: Yes.

MILLIE: I've suffered the loss of my mother.

PETER: Yes.

MILLIE: But I'm smart.

OLIVIA: Yes.

MILLIE: And I'm healthy.

PETER: Yes.

MILLIE: And you like me.

PETER AND OLIVIA: Yes.

PETER: We still have six interviews set up.

OLIVIA: What shall we do?

MILLIE: It's a big decision. Whoever you choose, her egg will become half of your child. You have to be meticulous . . . and rational . . . and careful. So interview all the preferred fertile women you want. And then: choose me.

On the Spectrum
by Ken LaZebnik

CHARACTERS: **Elisabeth**, Mac's single mother (early 50s); **Iris**, is autistic; **Mac**, has Asperger's syndrome—passing as "typical" after years of mainstreaming and therapy (both early 20s)

PLACE: Elisabeth and Mac's place

CIRCUMSTANCE: After negotiating a business deal online, Mac and Iris met in person and fell in love. Iris still owes Mac money for his work.

Elisabeth: Hello.

Iris: (*Hurrying in, not making eye contact.*) Hi.

> (**Iris** *gets inside and stops. She rocks back and forth. When she speaks, it is with some difficulty.*)

Elisabeth: Is Mac with you?

Iris: No.

Elisabeth: Oh God. It's so late. I thought maybe he was with you.

Iris: Are you his mother?

Elisabeth: Yes. I'm Elisabeth. Not biological. But believe me, I am his mother. (*A beat.*) Do you know where Mac is?

Iris: No.

Elisabeth: Oh God.

Iris: Mac hates your yak bells.

Elisabeth: I'm going to sell them. Did you talk to Mac tonight?

Iris: Yes.

Elisabeth: What did he say?

Iris: He was mad.

Elisabeth: He wanted his money, didn't he?

Iris: Yes.

Elisabeth: We need to talk, Iris.

Iris: It's not easy.

ELISABETH: Talking can be very hard. It's hard for a lot of people. Mac told me you use a computer to talk. Would it be easier to use your computer now?

IRIS: I wanted to live in the world.

ELISABETH: Mac has put in a lot of work on your website.

(**IRIS** *holds out the mason jar stuffed with change, cutting her off.*)

IRIS: I brought three hundred twenty-two dollars.

(*She hands* **ELISABETH** *the jar.*)

ELISABETH: That's a lot of money for a mason jar.

IRIS: Yeah.

ELISABETH: I . . . I appreciate this, Iris. But you still owe him a lot.

IRIS: I don't know what to do. My mother won't give me any money.

ELISABETH: Your mother manages your money?

IRIS: It's in her name. She says my $34,000 is for college. I don't know what to do, Elisabeth.

(**ELISABETH**'s *face softens with* **IRIS**'s *sudden vulnerability.*)

ELISABETH: It sounds like you're in a jam.

IRIS: I'm in a jam. If I don't pay him he won't come back. I love him.

ELISABETH: Oh. (*A beat.*) He's an easy guy to love. I love him, too.

(*A pause.*)

IRIS: And Mac loves me.

(*A pause.*)

ELISABETH: I . . . You haven't known each other very long.

IRIS: He does love me.

ELISABETH: For so many years, Iris, I have hoped that Mac would find someone to love.

IRIS: So you're happy.

ELISABETH: I . . . I just don't know if you're reading into whatever has gone on—you haven't known each other, I mean, how many times have you actually seen him?

(**IRIS** *holds up two fingers.*)

Twice. That's . . . that's not many times to see someone and say that he loves you.

IRIS: You hoped that Mac would find a typical girl.

ELISABETH: No, the truth is I am happy if Mac is happy. I just don't know what his feelings are.

IRIS: I'm autistic. Mac is autistic. We understand each other more than you ever will.

ELISABETH: I'm his mother. Don't try to tell me I don't understand him.

IRIS: You want him to be normal.

ELISABETH: He is my son. I love him more than you will ever know or understand.

IRIS: If you could give Mac a pill to take away his autism, would you?

ELISABETH: I spent twenty years taking him to therapists and years of floor time playing with him and making social story books and holding him when he cried and feeding him special foods and running with him and going to endless IEP conferences and paying endless bills and ruining my career because I couldn't take jobs out of town and I had to pick him up from OT and take him to the next therapy and I have fought for his life with blood sweat and tears every day and night for twenty years and when you've spent twenty fucking years sacrificing your life for someone else then you get the right to ask me that fucking question.

(*Silence. The door opens slowly. It's* **MAC.** *He looks around. He a little unsteady on his feet.* **ELISABETH** *gathers herself. Assaulted by* **ELISABETH**'s *outburst,* **IRIS** *starts rocking rapidly and remains silent.*)

ELISABETH: I was so worried, Mac—

MAC: You were yelling. Why were you yelling?

ELISABETH: It was—it doesn't matter.

MAC: (*To* **IRIS.**) Why are you here?

ELISABETH: She's just leaving, Mac. Iris, it's time for you to leave.

(**IRIS** *continues to rock, unable to speak.*)

MAC: (*To* **IRIS.**) No, don't. Don't go. You came all the way here by yourself? (**IRIS** *nods affirmatively.*) On the subway? (**IRIS** *nods again.*) She came all the way here and you were yelling at her.

ELISABETH: She said things to me . . . thing that aren't true. I was upset. I had a right to be upset.

MAC: You shouldn't have yelled at her.

ELISABETH: She came in here, Mac, and she said some horrible things to me.

MAC: The emotion police say you shouldn't yell. It's not right to yell. What did she say that was so horrible?

ELISABETH: She said . . . that I wish you were normal. That I'm not happy you are on the spectrum.

MAC: I'm not thrilled about it either. But it's who I am. This is me—on the spectrum, Asperger's, theory-of-mindchallenged, executive-function-screwed-up, autistic me. And I'm just fine with it. We are who we are. We're all on some kind of spectrum. The spectrum of humanity. I'm just a little bit further to one side than most people. I was just telling the bartender that.

ELISABETH: Bartender?

MAC: At the White Horse. I needed a drink. I'm an adult. I got a drink. You know what? Now I'm on the spectrum of drunkenness.

ELISABETH: Mac—

MAC: That was a joke. Don't you know when I'm joking?

ELISABETH: I'm sorry.

MAC: (*To* **IRIS**.) I thought the world was supposed to come to you.

(**IRIS**, *still rocking, finally speaks.*)

IRIS: I'm here now. I can change.

MAC: Life changes everyone. We are all in transition.

ELISABETH: Mac . . . You seem . . . hyped up.

MAC: Hyped up? Yes, I'm hyped up. You know why?

(*He turns to* **IRIS**.)

Because I spent a night drinking at a bar thinking I'm going to lose my house but I met Iris and I don't have any money but Iris likes me and at least we'll have *The New Yorker* although what if there's no address to deliver it to but Iris put on a red steampunk gown just for me and now I've come home and here is Iris and somehow things will work out because I am in love.

(**IRIS** *stops rocking.*)

I love you, Iris.

(**IRIS** *runs to him and hugs him fiercely.*)

MAC: (*To* **ELISABETH**.) Are you okay?

(*A beat.* **ELISABETH** *looks at them.*)

ELISABETH: I would not have known how to ask God for what I got . . .
Iris . . . I have learned to love things I never thought I would in my life.
Mac has brought most of them to me. A cappella singing. Sound waves.
The Greek gods. I would like to love everything Mac loves.

IRIS: Okay. Are you still going to . . .

ELISABETH: (*With renewed energy.*) I am selling my yak bells.

MAC: Finally!

ELISABETH: And they will bring in money, and we will figure it out. We
people of the spectrum are tough, you know. We'll figure it out.

(**IRIS** *and* **MAC** *kiss.*)

Perfect Mendacity
by Jason Wells

CHARACTERS: **WALTER**, a microbiologist and defense contractor, White American (50s); **SAMIRA**, Walter's Moroccan wife (30s to 40s); **ROGER**, Walter's colleague, white African American (50s)

PLACE: Walter and Samira's home

CIRCUMSTANCE: Walter is being investigated by his employers over an incriminating memo that was leaked to the media.

EDITOR'S NOTE: Slash marks (/) indicate where lines are to overlap.

WALTER: So, are you too good for me now, is that it?

SAMIRA: I'm *worried* for you. I have that much sense. I'm worried for when they ask you if you dislike black people, or just the ones you helped *kill*?!

WALTER: They're not going to *ask* that! And I don't dislike black people, anyway. *You* do. For God's sake, you said they were animals.

SAMIRA: And what did *you* say?

WALTER: I said you were *wrong*.

SAMIRA: No, you didn't. You said I went too *far*. Which is different. And then you married me.

WALTER: Because I was in love with you.

SAMIRA: You were in love with someone who said black people were animals.

WALTER: Because I knew you were just an ignorant girl from North Africa who was just repeating things she heard around her.

SAMIRA: But even though I was so ignorant, you never tried to change my mind.

WALTER: Why? What difference did it make? I knew you were smart enough not to say it at *parties*.

SAMIRA: You never noticed when I changed.

WALTER: I noticed. And it's *fine*. But was I supposed to embarrass you with it? "Hey, I've noticed you're not such a racist anymore"? "Since you've been watching *Oprah*"?

Samira: What if it was *Oprah*? So what? Is that supposed to make me silly? Because it was *Oprah*, and not . . . Mandela, or someone? And I knew about Rhodesia from Day One because you *bragged* about it! And you may have been a boy when it happened, but you were a man when you bragged to me about it, because that was only ten years ago!

Walter: I was not bragging, and I / have never brought it up . . .

Samira: You *were* bragging. I know you. In that way where / "I can't say so much, because it's all very secret . . ."

Walter: I was not bragging, and I have . . . No. I was not bragging, and I haven't brought it up since.

Samira: Because you got a new job, and you knew they thought it would look bad, if people would find out! So you never mentioned it again, even to me, because that's how you make things go away! That's how you're going to pass this lie test—by making it all go away! The stupid Africans and the stupid memo and your stupid wife who watches *Oprah*! I'll tell you what your red picture should be: It should be me being *FUCKED* by black Africans who have the ANTHRAX!

(*A knock at the door.*)

Walter: Oh shit. Please, Samira. I'm begging you.

(*He opens the door, revealing* **Roger Stanhope** *in the hallway.*)

/ Rog—

Roger: Who's fucking *who*, now?

Walter: Oh—*God*. She was just— Come in, will you?

(**Roger** *enters.*)

Don't say "fucking" in the hallway.

Roger: Oh. Sorry. Just.

Walter: She was . . . making . . . / helping me with something.

Roger: Sure. I know. Sorry. Hi, Samira. But why don't you get a *house*, like everyone else? Then we can say fucking this, and / fucking that . . .

Walter: Yeah, she was—we were discussing something.

Roger: Apparently.

Walter: No. Ha.

Roger: I'm just teasing you. But why not buy a house? It's the bloody suburbs. Do you have a gambling problem?

WALTER: No. We have enough room. We . . .

ROGER: Can I have a Coke or something? I'm parched.

WALTER: Sure, sure. Honey? No. I'll get it. Coke, or 7-Up, or . . . ?

ROGER: Coke, please.

WALTER: We have beer.

ROGER: No. Coke, thanks. How are you, Samira?

SAMIRA: I'm fine.

ROGER: Bea was just saying how long it's been since we've had you to dinner.

SAMIRA: It's nice of her to think of us.

ROGER: When she's remodeled the kitchen, she'll want to show it off.

SAMIRA: That will be nice.

ROGER: Good. You know—I'm glad you're here. It occurs to me there's something I wanted to ask you.

SAMIRA: Oh?

ROGER: Yes. I was just wondering: Did you leak that confidential memo to Amnesty International? By any chance?

WALTER: *What*? Roger. *What* the *hell*?

ROGER: Come on, Walter. I'm just asking. Let's just ask the question.

SAMIRA: I don't know what you mean.

WALTER: (*To* ROGER.) See? What is wrong with you?

ROGER: (*To* SAMIRA.) You know the memo I mean, though.

SAMIRA: The one that was on the Internet, I suppose.

WALTER: (*To* ROGER.) Why would you do that?

ROGER: I had to ask.

WALTER: Why? Why did you have to ask?

ROGER: I'm asking everyone.

WALTER: You're asking *everyone*. In hopes of what? That someone will say, "Oh yes, that was me. Why do you ask?"

ROGER: You never know.

WALTER: That was ridiculous, Roger. Here's your Coke.

ROGER: Thank you.

WALTER: Is that why you wanted to come over here? / To ask her that?

ROGER: No, no, no. And yes. Yes and no. I *did* want to discuss our reaction to the . . . Our PR strategy, if you will, in light of the—*whatever*. *Yes*. I needed to ask her.

WALTER: I don't understand this.

ROGER: I'm just being vigilant.

SAMIRA: If I had done it, do you think I would just betray my husband to you, just like that?

ROGER: Mm. Possibly?

SAMIRA: I'm going out.

ROGER: Oh, no, no. Please don't be offended.

SAMIRA: I'm not at all offended. I'm just going out.

WALTER: Where are you going?

SAMIRA: To Jennifer's. Where's my phone?

WALTER: I thought you were tired.

SAMIRA: I'm awake now. I feel like going out.

ROGER: I can't help feeling I've made you angry.

SAMIRA: Certainly not. You were right to ask. I'm happy to say that I would never, ever do such a thing.

WALTER: If you're just mad at Roger, he's . . . goddamnit, he's leaving.

ROGER: I've just started my Coke.

SAMIRA: He can stay, Walter. I'm going out.

WALTER: I, I, I, I don't know *why* he would just ask you that.

ROGER: You're making much too big a deal of it. Let's relax.

SAMIRA: Yes, dear. Please. You both have a lot to talk about. And none of it concerns me. In any way.

ROGER: Samira, it was so nice to see you again. We *will* have you to dinner. It's been too long.

SAMIRA: That sounds wonderful. And I'm so sorry you had to hear me yelling at my husband earlier.

WALTER: / Honey . . .

ROGER: "Yelling" at him? Surely not. If so, I'm sure he deserved it.

Samira: Yes. It was about the two of you killing all those people in Rhodesia.

Roger: Ahmm . . .

Samira: Now, where did I put my . . . ? Ah.

Roger: Shit. Well, that won't do.

> (*He raises his shirt to reveal a small recording device.*)

> Talk amongst yourselves, while I sort this out.

> (*He switches it off, and erases the recording.*)

> We can't just go back a few seconds; they'll hear the edit. We'll have to start the whole thing over.

Walter: What is that?

Roger: It's a recorder, obviously. The problem is, if I cut it off just before Samira's . . . controversial *allegation*, they'll wonder why. They're very paranoid, right now, and they know we're friends.

Walter: Roger.

Roger: I can't bring them a five-minute recording, can I? Oh, close your mouth, will you? And I can't bring them something all chopped up. We've got to just go again.

> (**Walter** *looks stunned.*)

> *Walter.*

Walter: Roger. What . . . ?

Roger: Walter. We're *friends*. If anyone had said anything incriminating, I would have called it off.

Walter: You're *recording* this?

Roger: They didn't give me much of a choice. I mean, what would you have had me say? "No"? "That seems *wrong* to me, a bit"? The point is, I'm bringing you in on it.

Walter: Because she said that . . . thing.

Roger: What do you mean?

Walter: You're only telling us about it because she said something you didn't want on the tape.

Roger: Oh, oh, oh. Yes. Well. I didn't want to tell you *ahead* of time. The conversation wouldn't have been natural. I mean, you're not *actors*, either of you. But obviously, we should have gone that route.

Samira: Why would Chenoweth care if you killed some people in Rhodesia?

Walter: Samira.

Roger: Walter and I are part of the public face of the company. You see?

Samira: Yes. He's mentioned that.

Roger: Chenoweth can tolerate some rough types in the mix, of course— that's sort of the idea. But if they discovered that Walter and I had a history of, *race relations*, well, they might think of that as too much of a . . . vulnerability.

Samira: Because you might lose your . . .

Roger: Right.

Samira: Your government contracts.

Roger: Precisely.

Walter: You're recording our conversations for Chenoweth?

Roger: Good God, *yes*. As I've explained.

Walter: Is that even legal?

Roger: No.

Walter: You *asked* her if she leaked the memo!

Roger: Of course. / I knew she . . .

Walter: That thing was running.

Roger: Yes. Because I knew she would deny it. Of course.

Walter: You came in here wearing a *wire*.

Roger: You're choosing to completely misunderstand the circumstances, simply because of / the sensational . . .

Walter: You're wearing a *wire*.

Roger: . . . The sensational nature of someone . . .

Walter: Because you're / wearing a . . .

Roger: Yes. Because of someone revealing a . . .

Walter: Wearing a *wire*.

Roger: . . . Revealing a recording device, in your . . .

Walter: Get out of here.

ROGER: Wait, now. I'm trying to explain to you. I'm in a lot of trouble right now. We all are. I couldn't say no. But I knew, Walter, I knew you'd both make it clear, unequivocal denial. Which is perfect for everyone. I'm doing you a huge favor right now. Look, I could have skittered out of here, you know, skittered off, and you'd be none the wiser. But what have I done? I've *revealed* to you the ruse. So that we can . . .

WALTER: Roger . . .

ROGER: So that we can use it to our advantage. But I can't go back with nothing. We have to make a new recording.

SAMIRA: Can I hear what I sounded like?

ROGER: I'm sorry, dear. I've already erased it.

SAMIRA: Oh.

ROGER: But we'll make a new one.

SAMIRA: No, thank you. I'm not an actress, as you say. I would probably forget my lines and confess.

WALTER: Ha. She's kidding.

ROGER: Why would you confess to something you didn't do?

SAMIRA: Exactly.

ROGER: Exactly what?

SAMIRA: Exactly as Walter says. I'm kidding.

ROGER: You know I love you, Samira, but you absolutely cannot tell a joke.

SAMIRA: In French, I'm funny. In Arabic, I'm hilarious.

ROGER: Would you like to confess in Arabic? I speak a little.

WALTER: No. Shut up. I don't like the tone of this.

ROGER: The recorder's off. Look.

WALTER: I don't care. She didn't do it, and you know it.

ROGER: Of course.

WALTER: Yes. And that's it.

ROGER: Right. But I still have to bring back a recording.

WALTER: Tell them we weren't home.

ROGER: Well . . .

WALTER: What's wrong with that?

ROGER: Why not get it over with? It has to happen sometime. It'll be good practice.

WALTER: For what?

ROGER: For your polygraph, for one thing.

WALTER: Why would I need to practice for my polygraph?

ROGER: Walter.

WALTER: What?

ROGER: For what *she* said.

WALTER: About what?

ROGER: Rhodesia. It'll come up.

WALTER: How can it come up?

ROGER: In a million ways. "Have you lied about your past?" "Have you lied to your employers?"

WALTER: Those would be *comparison* questions. I'm *supposed* to lie about those.

ROGER: I don't think they care what the questions are *called*. They're still embarrassing.

WALTER: They have to go over the questions ahead of time.

ROGER: Really?

WALTER: Yes.

ROGER: Um . . . You know that you're specifically prohibited from doing research on polygraphs. It's okay with me, of course, but . . .

WALTER: So why mention it?

ROGER: To caution you against, you know, sharing your research. As you're doing with me.

WALTER: Oh.

ROGER: Yes, but I'm honored. In fact, I'm encouraging you to, to do whatever. Just pass it, right? But pass it all. All the embarrassing questions. Do you see?

WALTER: I'm trying.

ROGER: You know what the Russians told Aldrich Ames, when he was facing the polygraph?

WALTER: What.

ROGER: "Just relax." That's it. That's all they said. And you know what?

WALTER: He passed.

ROGER: That's right.

SAMIRA: Who's Aldrich Ames?

ROGER: Oh, he sold some things to the bad guys. Now let's make this recording, and I'll be out of your way.

SAMIRA: I don't want to make a recording.

ROGER: You want to help Walter, don't you? Be a sport. Just say what you said before, and you can excuse yourself, or whatever. Okay?

SAMIRA: Is this what you want, Walter?

WALTER: Yeah, actually. This might be a good thing.

SAMIRA: Fine. Turn the thing on.

ROGER: We have to do the whole bit, or they'll be suspicious. I'll go out and knock.

WALTER: Okay.

(**ROGER** *exits, still holding his drink.*)

SAMIRA: Where should I be?

WALTER: Wherever. I don't think it matters.

(**ROGER** *knocks,* **WALTER** *immediately opens the door.*)

WALTER: Oh, hi, / Roger.

ROGER: Whoa. Well, well, hi, Walter, / you must have . . .

WALTER: Come in.

ROGER: You must have been right at the door. / Thank you.

WALTER: Hm?

ROGER: You must have—Hi, Samir—(*Dropping character.*) You can't be right at the door.

WALTER: Oh.

ROGER: You have to wait / a second or two.

WALTER: Sorry.

ROGER: Let's go again. (*Exits.*)

WALTER: Sorry.

(*Closes door. Pause.* **ROGER** *knocks.* **WALTER** *waits, then opens door.*)

ROGER: Oh. Hi, Roger.

WALTER: Well, hello.

ROGER: Come in.

WALTER: Thank you. Hello, Samira.

SAMIRA: Hello.

(**ROGER** *quite audibly tilts crushed ice into his mouth, with:*)

WALTER: Do you want something to drink?

(**ROGER** *spits out the ice.*)

ROGER: Shit. We've blown the take.

WALTER: Huh?

SAMIRA: This is too hard.

ROGER: No, no. We're just working out the kinks. Take four.

(*Puts down the glass. Exits. Pause.*)

SAMIRA: Maybe he left for good this time.

(*Knock. Pause.* **WALTER** *opens door.*)

WALTER: Oh, hi, Roger.

ROGER: Well, hello.

WALTER: Come in.

ROGER: Thank you. Hello, Samira

SAMIRA: Hello.

ROGER: And how have you been?

SAMIRA: Fine.

WALTER: I'll get you a drink.

ROGER: Oh. Thank you. I'm parched. You two should get a house.

SAMIRA: We don't have children.

ROGER: Ah.

SAMIRA: I want to adopt.

ROGER: Oh. How nice. And how does Walter feel about that?

WALTER: It might be a good idea. She could use more help around the house.

ROGER: Ah. How, sort of, *Dickensian*.

SAMIRA: (*Abruptly.*) Why have you come here?

ROGER: Oh. To . . . Well, I need to speak to Walter about some issues that have been / raised at . . .

WALTER: Your drink.

ROGER: Oh. A *Coke*. It's as if you read my mind.

WALTER: Right. I mean, um, is that okay?

ROGER: It's fine, thanks. But now, you might as well know, Samira, since you ask: We're good friends, right? You would never lie to me about something . . . about something very serious.

SAMIRA: No. What is it?

ROGER: Well, now, I hope you won't be offended, but I have to ask you about this memo.

SAMIRA: What memo?

ROGER: Well. The one that was recently leaked to the media.

SAMIRA: Oh?

WALTER: (*Tensely.*) You know about the memo.

SAMIRA: No, I don't.

WALTER: (*Glaring lasers into her.*) *Samira*. You know about this memo. Everyone is *talking* about it. It was *released*. To the *media*.

SAMIRA: (*Up to speed.*) Yes. I would know about it from the media.

ROGER: Yes. So. My question is, did you happen to see it *before* it . . . it . . . went *out*.

SAMIRA: What did it say?

WALTER: Well, honey, you wouldn't have seen *any* memo, from my work, would you? I wouldn't— Look, Roger, I hope you're not suggesting that I would ever, *ever* bring home anything from work that I would put in the way of my wife or anyone else, for God's sake. I mean, come *on*. What are you accusing me of?

ROGER: I'm sorry, pal, / I just felt I had to . . .

WALTER: And my *wife*. What do you think we are? How could you even *ask* an idiotic question like that?

ROGER: / Well, I . . .

WALTER: You should be *ashamed* of yourself. You know me better than that.

ROGER: I just had to ask. I'm sorry.

WALTER: I think you should leave now

ROGER: Yes.

(*He starts to go.*)

SAMIRA: What did it say, though?

ROGER: / Huh?

WALTER: Honey . . .

SAMIRA: This memo. I don't really follow these things. But some Nigerians. They were found dead, recently? Is that right?

WALTER: It's ridiculous.

(*He gestures for* **ROGER** *to leave.* **ROGER** *ignores him.*)

ROGER: Some criminals were found dead, yes.

SAMIRA: Protesters. Yes?

ROGER: Vandals. Our lab in Nigeria was vandalized, and then these locals showed up dead, and some idiot, / some . . .

SAMIRA: Shot in the back of their heads.

ROGER: Yes. Shot in the back of their heads.

SAMIRA: And left in a ditch. Yes?

ROGER: Yea. Left in a ditch.

SAMIRA: And "some idiot"—?

ROGER: Yes. This . . . ha! . . . this Human Resources *cretin*, this *imbecile*, actually took it upon himself to recommend a, what do you call it, a psychological *review* of the boys who are *alleged* to have done it.

SAMIRA: Post-traumatic . . .

ROGER: Yes! Post-traumatic stress disorder! For security personnel! And then, good God: He cc'd it to every science department! For its scientific interest! (*Laughs, then stops.*) Which doesn't mean we did it.

SAMIRA: It doesn't?

ROGER: Of course not. It just means he's an idiot with an e-mail account and his head up his ass all day.

SAMIRA: But it sure looks bad.

ROGER: Don't worry, Samira. We'll be all right.

SAMIRA: Will Walter be all right?

ROGER: / Of course.

WALTER: Honey, it's fine. It isn't relevant. Should we . . .

(*Gestures "turn it off" to* **ROGER**, *who returns an "it's okay" wave.*)

SAMIRA: It isn't relevant?

WALTER: To this conversation.

ROGER: Or at all. Even if the allegation were true, which it isn't, it wouldn't even be against the law.

SAMIRA: Really?

WALTER: (*"On topic."*) The point is, we had nothing to do with that memo, and that's it.

ROGER: (*To* **SAMIRA**.) We're independent contractors, in a foreign land. U.S. laws do not apply to us, and if our hosts have a problem with us, they'll ask us to leave. Which they haven't.

SAMIRA: Because they need the money.

ROGER: We're not responsible for the problems they've created for themselves. It's like the bloody Wild West down there.

WALTER: But we had nothing to do with the memo being leaked, and that's . . . / that's the thing.

ROGER: They're creating their own hell down there. What can we do?

WALTER: Exactly. So that's it.

SAMIRA: I remember a story I heard once.

WALTER: Honey, he needs to go.

(*Gives her a broad "wrap it up" gesture, which she ignores.*)

SAMIRA: There was this king, in this kingdom, and he had this huge catapult. This enormous catapult that he was very proud of.

ROGER: This would have been a long time ago.

SAMIRA: Yes. And when a citizen was unhappy, and would complain, the king would say, "You should go to another country," and then he would put the person in the catapult and *fling* him over the trees into the next country.

ROGER: I imagine that put an end to the whining.

SAMIRA: But no, it didn't. People kept complaining, and the king kept shooting them in the catapult to the next country. Day after day, month after month, many people.

ROGER: Hm.

SAMIRA: Then, finally, one day, some people came from the other country to see the king. And they said, "You must stop this. How can you kill all these people?" And the king said, "*Kill* them? You mean haven't you been *catching* them?"

(*Pause.*)

ROGER: As I said, darling, you cannot tell a joke.

SAMIRA: It wasn't funny?

WALTER: So, anyway. *There*. We didn't do it. You should go now, Roger.

ROGER: Of course. Thanks for the beverage. Sorry to have bothered you. See you at the office. (*He gives them a wink and a thumbs-up, and exits. Pause.*)

SAMIRA: How did I do?

Water by the Spoonful
by Quiara Alegría Hudes

CHARACTERS: ODESSA, aka Haikumom, founder of a Narcotics Anonymous chat room; JOHN, aka Fountainhead, a computer programmer; ELLIOT, Odessa's son, an Iraqi war vet; YAZMIN, Odessa's niece and Elliott's cousin

PLACE: A diner

CIRCUMSTANCE: Odessa and John meet in person for the first time after chatting online. With an impending funeral, Odessa's family is trying to raise funds to cover the costs.

(ODESSA *and* JOHN, *aka Fountainhead, sit in a booth.*)

ODESSA: To lapsed Catholics. (*They clink coffee mugs.*) And you thought we had nothing in common.

JOHN: When did you become interested in Buddhism?

ODESSA: My older brother used to terrorize me during mass. He would point to a statue, tell me about the evil spirit hiding behind it. Fangs, claws. I thought Saint Lazarus was gonna come to life and suck my eyes out. Buddhism? Not scary. If there's spirits, they're hiding inside you.

JOHN: Aren't those the scariest kind?

ODESSA: So, how many days do you have? It should be two now.

JOHN: I put my son's picture on my cell phone, so if I get the urge, I can just look at him instead.

ODESSA: How many days?

JOHN: (*Small talk.*) I love Puerto Rico. On my honeymoon we stayed at that hotel in Old San Juan, the old convent. (ODESSA *shrugs.*) And that Spanish fort at the top of the city? El Morro?

ODESSA: I've always been meaning to make it there.

JOHN: There are these keyholes where the canons used to fit, and the view of the waves through them, you can practically see the Spanish armada approaching.

ODESSA: I mean, one of these days I've gotta make it to PR.

JOHN: Oh. I just figured . . .

ODESSA: The Jersey Shore. Atlantic City. The Philadelphia airport. Oh, I've been places.

JOHN: On an actual plane?

ODESSA: I only fly first class, and I'm still saving for that ticket.

(**ODESSA**'s *cell phone rings.*)

JOHN: You're a popular lady.

ODESSA: (*Into her phone, her demeanor completely changing.*) What? I told you, the diner on Spring Garden and Third. I'm busy, come in an hour. One hour. Now stop calling me and asking fucking directions. (*She hangs up.*)

JOHN: Says the one who censors.

ODESSA: My sister died.

JOHN: Right. You sure you're okay?

ODESSA: She's dead, ain't nothing left to do. People act like the world is going to fall apart.

JOHN: You write very Zen messages. And yet.

ODESSA: My family knows every button to push.

JOHN: My condolences. (*Pause.*) You don't strike me as a computer nerd. I used to employ an entire floor of them.

ODESSA: You should've seen me at first, pecking with two fingers. Now I'm like an octopus with ten little tentacles. In my neck of the woods, staying clean is like trying to tap-dance on a minefield. The website fills the hours. So how are we gonna fill yours, huh? When was the last time you picked up a javelin?

JOHN: Senior year of high school.

ODESSA: (*Hands him a sheet of paper.*) There's a sober softball league. Fairmount Park, games on Sundays. Sober bowling on Thursdays.

JOHN: I lied in my first post. I've been smoking crack for two years. I've tried quitting hundreds of times. Day two? Please, I'm in the seven hundredth day of hell.

ODESSA: You got it out of your system. Most people lie at one time or another on the site. The good news is, two years in, there's still time. (*Hands him another sheet of paper.*) Talbot Recovery Center in Atlanta. It's designed for professionals with addictions. Paradise Recovery in Hawaii. They actually check your income before admitting you. Just for the wealthy. This place in Jersey, it's right over the bridge, they have an outpatient program for professionals like you.

JOHN: I'm tenacious. I'm driven. I love my parents.

ODESSA: Pitchforks against tanks.

JOHN: I relish in paying my taxes.

ODESSA: And you could be dead tomorrow. (*Pause.*) Is your dealer male or female?

JOHN: I had a few. Flushed their numbers down the toilet like you suggested.

ODESSA: Your original connection. The one who got you hooked.

JOHN: Female.

ODESSA: Did you have sex with her?

JOHN: You don't beat around the bush, do you?

ODESSA: I'll take that as a yes. (*No answer.*) Do you prefer sex when you're high to sex when you're sober?

JOHN: I've never really analyzed it.

ODESSA: It can be a dangerous cocktail. Some men get off on smoking and fucking.

JOHN: All men get off on fucking.

ODESSA: Are you scared your wife will find out you're addicted to crack? Or are you scared she'll find out what came of your wedding vows?

JOHN: I should go.

ODESSA: We just ordered.

JOHN: I promised my son. There's a science fair tomorrow. Something about dioramas and crazy glue.

ODESSA: Don't talk about them. Get sober for them.

JOHN: Fuck you.

ODESSA: Leave me three bucks for your coffee 'cuz I ain't got it.

(*He pulls out three dollars. She throws the money back at him.*)

You picked up the phone and called me.

JOHN: (*He sits down again.*) I don't know how to do this. I've never done this before.

ODESSA: I have and it usually doesn't end up so good. One in twenty, maybe, hang around. Most people just don't write one day and then thirty days and then you're wondering . . . And sometimes you get the answer. 'Cuz their wife looks on their computer and sees the website and logs on and writes, "I found him facedown in the snow."

JOHN: How many day ones did you have?

ODESSA: Seven years' worth.

JOHN: Do you still crave?

ODESSA: On the good days, only every hour. Would you rather be honest with your wife, or would you rather end up like me? (*Pause.*) That wasn't rhetorical.

JOHN: You're not exactly what I wanted to be when I grew up.

ODESSA: Truth. Now we're talking.

(**ELLIOT** *and* **YAZ** *enter.*)

YAZ: There she is.

(**ELLIOT** *and* **YAZ** *sit down in the booth.*)

ELLIOT: You were supposed to meet us at the flower place.

YAZ: The deposit was due at nine.

ODESSA: My alarm clock didn't go off.

ELLIOT: Were you up on that chat room all night?

ODESSA: (*Ignoring him.*) Can I get a refill, please?

ELLIOT: Where's the money?

ODESSA: I told you I don't have any money.

ELLIOT: And you think I do? I been paying for Mami Ginny's meds for six months straight—

ODESSA: Well, get it from Yaz's mom.

YAZ: My mom put in for the headstone. She got an expensive one.

ODESSA: Headstone? She's getting cremated.

YAZ: She still needs a proper Catholic piece of granite. Right beside Abuela, right beside your dad and sister and brother.

ELLIOT: And daughter.

YAZ: Everyone agreed.

ODESSA: No one asked my opinion.

ELLIOT: Everyone who showed up to the family meeting.

Odessa: I wasn't invited.

Yaz: I texted you twice.

Odessa: I was out of minutes.

Elliot: We just spoke on the phone.

Odessa: Whachu want me to do, Elliot, if I say I ain't got no fucking money, I ain't got no money.

John: Hi, I'm John, nice to meet you.

Yaz: Yazmin.

Elliot: You one of Mom's rehab buddies?

John: We know each other from work.

Elliot: You scrub toilets?

Odessa: (*To* **John**.) I'm a practitioner of the custodial arts.

Elliot: Is she your sponsor?

John: (*To* **Odessa**.) I thought this was going to be a private meeting.

Elliot: I'm her son.

John: (*To* **Odessa**.) You must have been young.

Elliot: But I was raised by my aunt Ginny and that particular aunt just died. (*To* **Odessa**.) So now, you got three hours to find some money to pay for one basket of flowers in the funeral of the woman who changed my Pampers.

Yaz: We're all supposed to be helping out.

Odessa: You both know I run out of minutes all the time. No one could be bothered to drive by and tell me face to face?

Elliot: Because you always bothered to drive by and say hello to Mami Ginny when you knew she was sick? Because you bothered to hit me up one time this week and say, "Elliot, I'm sorry your mom died."

Odessa: You still got one mom alive.

Elliot: Really? You want to go there?

Yaz: The flower place needs the money today.

Odessa: She was my sister and you are my son, too.

Yaz: Guys. Two hundred dollars by end of business day.

Odessa: That's my rent.

ELLIOT: Then fifty.

ODESSA: I just spent fifty getting my phone back on.

ELLIOT: Ten dollars. For the woman who raised *your* son! Do we hear ten dollars? Going once!

ODESSA: I spent my last ten at the post office.

ELLIOT: Going twice!

(**JOHN** *goes into his wallet.*)

JOHN: Here's fifty.

(*They all look at him like he's crazy. He pulls out some more money.*)

JOHN: Two hundred?

(**ELLIOT** *pushes the money back to* **JOHN** *with one pointer finger, like the bills might be contaminated.*)

ELLIOT: No offense, I don't take money from users.

JOHN: I'm not . . . I think that was my cue.

ODESSA: Sit down. My son was just going.

ELLIOT: Did world's best mom here tell you about her daughter?

ODESSA: I'm about to throw this coffee in your fucking face.

YAZ: Come on, Elliot, I'll pay for the flowers.

(**ELLIOT** *doesn't get up.*)

ELLIOT: I looked at that chat room once. The woman I saw there? She's literally not the same person I know. (*To* **JOHN.**) Did she tell you how she became such a saint?

JOHN: We all have skeletons.

ELLIOT: Yeah, well, she's an archaeological dig. Did she tell you about her daughter?

ODESSA: (*Suddenly resigned.*) Go ahead, I ain't got no secrets.

YAZ: (*Getting up.*) Excuse me.

ELLIOT: Sit here and listen, Yaz. You were born with a silver spoon and you need to know how it was for me.

YAZ: I said I'd pay for the goddamn flowers so LET'S GO. NOW!

ELLIOT: My sister and I had the stomach flu, right? For a whole day we couldn't keep nothing down.

ODESSA: Three days. . . . You were vomiting three days straight.

ELLIOT: Medicine, juice, anything we ate, it would come right back up. Your coworker here took us to Children's Hospital.

ODESSA: Jefferson.

ELLIOT: It was wall-to-wall packed. Every kid in Philly had this bug. ER's were turning kids away. They gave us a flyer about stomach flu and sent us home. Bright blue paper. Little cartoon diagrams. It said give your kids a spoonful of water every five minutes.

ODESSA: A teaspoon.

ELLIOT: A small enough amount that they can keep it down. Five minutes. Spoon. Five minutes. Spoon. I remember thinking, wow, this is it. Family time. Quality time. Just the three of us. Because it was gentle, the way you said, "Open up." I opened my mouth, you put that little spoon of water into my mouth. That little bit of relief. And then I watched you do the same thing with my little sister. And I remember being like, "Wow, I love you, Mom. My moms is alright." Five minutes. Spoon. Five minutes. Spoon. But you couldn't stick to something simple like that. You couldn't sit still like that. You had to have your thing. That's where I stop remembering.

ODESSA: I left.

ELLIOT: A Department of Human Services report. That's my memory. Six hours later a neighbor kicks in the door. Me and my sister are lying in a pile of laundry. My shorts was all messed up. And what I really don't remember is my sister. Quote. Female infant, approximately two years, Pamper and tear ducts dry, likely cause of death, dehydration. 'Cuz when you dehydrate you can't form a single tear.

JOHN: (*To* **ELLIOT**.) I'm very sorry . . . (*He puts some money on the table.*) For the coffee. (*Exits.*)

ELLIOT: That's some friend you got there.

(*Pause.*)

YAZ: Mary Lou. We can at least say her name out loud. Mary Lou. Mary Lou. (*To* **ODESSA**.) One time you came to babysit me, you brought Elliot and Mary Lou—she was still in Pampers—and Mary Lou had this soda from 7-Eleven. She didn't want to give me a sip. You yelled at her so bad, you totally cursed her out and I said, "You're not supposed to yell at people like that!" And you said, "No, Yaz, let her cry. She's gotta learn that ya'll are cousins, ya'll are flesh and blood, and we share everything. You hear me, Yaz? In this family we share *everything*." You walked out of the room, came back from the kitchen with four straws in your hand, sat us down on the floor in a circle, pointed to me, and said, "You first." I sipped. "Elliot's turn." He sipped. "Mary Lou's turn." She sipped. Then you sipped. You made us do like that, taking turns, going around the circle, till the cup was empty.

(**ODESSA** *hands* **ELLIOT** *a key.*)

ODESSA: The pawn shop closes at five. Go into my house. Take my computer. Pawn it. However much you get, put towards a few flowers, okay?

(**ODESSA** *exits.*)

Part 5

Male Monologues

9 Circles
by Bill Cain

CHARACTERS: Reeves, an Army private

PLACE: A female shrink's office, Iraq

CIRCUMSTANCE: Reeves recently witnessed the death of his sergeant.

Reeves: If I were laying here on your floor bleeding from the head, *how long* would you feel bad for me? (*No response.*) Because—out there—they put a bullet in me—they'd celebrate for a month. A year. Fuck. Forever. They kill me, they get to go to God, directly to God, do not stop at any checkpoints. When those construction workers got killed—they hung their body parts from the bridge and they danced their asses off for days. Now you want to talk about sympathy—I've got all kinds of sympathy for that because that is *exactly* how I feel about them. We want each other dead. Now you—you've got all the sympathy in the world for a dying sergeant—fuck—ANYBODY CAN FEEL SYMPATHY FOR THE GOOD GUY. He doesn't *need* your sympathy. He's got a wife and a kid for that. But that guy who shot him—I want to fucking kill him over and over. That's what goes on in my head and you've got no sympathy for that. "Don't tell me that. You're on your own with that and you know what that means? You've got no sympathy for the one thing that *needs* it here and I don't want to make him an excuse. I think I've *always* wanted to kill everybody. Him dying just makes me think I'm finally going to do it.

Becky's New Car
by Steven Deitz

CHARACTER: STEVE, Becky's co-worker, widowed (50)

PLACE: Becky's cubicle at a car dealership

CIRCUMSTANCE: Steve has trouble accepting his wife's accidental death.

STEVE: You don't know, Becky . . . you and Joe, you're *set*, you're *locked in*, you'll have each other forever . . . but some of the rest of us—

(BECKY: *I know . . . I'm sorry.*)

(*Overlapping*)—I want to get past this stuff. I really do. I'm sick of talking about it, and you must be *really* sick of hearing it—(BECKY's *desk phone rings,* STEVE *lifts and hangs up the receiver in one motion and never stops talking.*)—but it's like yesterday: I'm getting a coffee, and this little boy and his mom are in line behind me, and they have this puppy. So I'm minding my own business, and I hear the mom say to her son: "Why don't you go show the puppy to that sad man over there—maybe the puppy will cheer him up!"—and I am really trying to ignore this, but now the puppy is sniffing at my boots and the little kid is saying: "Hi, mister, you look sad— do you want to pet my puppy?" And what I *thought*—what I didn't *say*, even though I wanted to—what I *thought* was: "You bet I do, sonny boy—I want to pet your little puppy—and then I want to take him for a nice walk, a little hike in the mountains with you right by his side—and as we approach the rugged vista, which is our destination, I want to let go of his leash for just a *second*, just an *instant*, right when the path beneath his little paws starts to give way—and I want you to watch your puppy's desperate eyes as he tries to grab at that ground—but his little paws touch nothing at all, nothing but *air*, nothing but you and your screams, and you might as well *scream your heart out*, sonny boy, because THERE IS NOTHING YOU CAN DO for that puppy of yours who is falling into a dark abyss that will NEVER EVER GIVE HIM BACK."

(*Pause.*)

(BECKY: *At least you only thought it.*)

I only thought I thought it. Turns out I *said it.*

(BECKY: *Oh my God . . .*)

It was ugly. The kid cried till he threw up. His mom poured a Frappuccino on me.

Edith Can Shot Things
and Hit Them
by A. Rey Pamatmat

CHARACTER: BENJI, Kenny's friend (16 years old)

PLACE: Kenny and Edith's home

CIRCUMSTANCE: An amorous relationship is blossoming between Benji and Kenny. Benji's mother does not approve of the relationship.

BENJI: I made a mixtape.

(*To* KENNY.)

For you. Some songs that made me think of you.

(KENNY: *Oh. Thanks.*)

I put it in my schoolbag. And I wrote a note to give you with it. To pass to you in Pre Calc tomorrow.

(KENNY: *And she found it.*)

I'm doing my chores—washing dinner dishes. I go in my room when I'm done, and she's sitting there holding the tape and the note. Her face is all twisted. Disgusted. And then she yells for my dad and brother, and when they come in, she shoves the note at me and goes: "Read it. Aloud. To your father." And I read. And she shakes and cries. And my brother swears. And my dad just stands there. I get to the end and I hear this . . . this crack sound. And she snapped it in half. Your tape.

(BENJI *goes to his bag and pulls out the ruined cassette and the note.*)

I snatched it from her. I don't know why. It's useless now. She tried to take the note, too, but I held on to it, because I had to give it to you. And then things are so messed up. She tells my brother to take me outside. And he just picks me up and she yells and yells as he takes me out front and throws me out of the house. He actually threw me off the porch. And they go back in, and I don't know what to do, so I just sit there on the front lawn too scared to go back in. And I hear more yelling, until eventually my dad comes out with a bunch of my stuff. He puts me in the car and says he'll talk to her, and if that doesn't work maybe his sister can take care of me for a little while, but is there somewhere I can stay right now? I'm sorry I told him to call you. I don't mean to—

(**KENNY:** *Don't be sorry.*)

My dad goes, "I'm going to make sure Mom talks to you tomorrow." But I don't want to talk to her. I don't want to go home, to . . . with her. I want her to leave me alone.

(**EDITH:** *Read the note.*)

(**BENJI:** *Huh?.*)

(**EDITH:** *Just do it. Kenny's here now. Read it to him.*)

I don't—

(**KENNY:** *It's okay, you don't. Ed . . .*)

(**EDITH:** *Just read it. It's right there. Just read it.*)

(**BENJI,** *still a bit stunned; starts to read the note.*)

(*Reading.*) "Dear Kenny, I don't know if you like all these songs, but they're mostly about not knowing how someone feels. So I really relate to them a lot, because sometimes I wonder what we're doing. If you relate, too, then I just want to tell you that you don't have to wonder about how I feel. You should have faith in me, and I hope, hope, hope that you want me to have faith in you. I can't dress stuff up with words like you do. Mostly, what I think or feel just comes out, so here it is. You make me feel really good. I'm happy when we're together. It's hard to concentrate on pre-calc homework, because you're in that class with me, and college and differential equations just can't compete. I hope you feel the same way. I have a feeling you do. Even if you don't, I hope you at least like the tape. Love, Benji"

End Days
by Deborah Zoe Laufer

CHARACTER: **ARTHUR**, Rachel's father and Sylvia's wife, hasn't changed out of his pajamas since 9/11 (40s)

PLACE: The Steins' den; late September 2003

CIRCUMSTANCE: Arthur worked in the World Trade Center and was the only survivor from his company. He and his family fled to the suburbs after 9/11.

ARTHUR: I feel like I am saved.

(**SYLVIA:** *You're not.*)

I feel like I'm waking up. All these years. I know I kind of checked out. You needed me and . . . I wasn't there. For a long time. I know. It's crazy, but I forgot why I was here. Even before the attacks, even before that. I'd forgotten. What I really cared about. But I remember now.

(**RACHEL** and **NELSON** *have stopped their Reuben preparations to listen.* **ARTHUR** *searches for the right words.*)

I don't have faith like you have, Sylvia. I'm concrete. You know that. I like proof. I like facts. Even when I used to go to temple, it was never about faith or God. It was about my father, my grandfather. There was only one time in my life I had real faith. It was when I fell in love with you. When we got married—we didn't even know each other that well—but I knew. I knew that whatever happened I could take it. We could take it. If we were together. That I wanted to face whatever happened with you. I know I let you down, Sylvia. Please forgive me. Please take me back.

(**SYLVIA:** *I'm going to lose you again.*)

But could we be together now? Whatever time I have left with you? Even if it's only a few more hours. Could we just give up on me for eternity—I'm a lost cause for eternity. But could I be with you now?

(*She looks at him. A rush of memories comes back. She goes to him. He wraps his arms around her.*)

Thank you. This could last me. I love you, honey.

Great Falls
by Lee Blessing

CHARACTER: Monkey Man, a prizewinning writer and Bitch's ex-stepdad

PLACE: A hotel room

CIRCUMSTANCE: Monkey Man has taken Bitch on a road trip. Bitch is showering in bathroom.

Monkey Man: Divorce is no reason to lock people out of your life. Divorce is . . . normal, and natural, and more people do it than don't. So . . . so why compound the damage? Why take sides, or pretend that one partner or the other is an ogre or . . . a villain of some sort, when the truth is *always* that it's *both* people's fault?

(*Nodding, as though someone is responding.*)

I know, I know. I did bad things. I did very unthinking and heartless things that came out of what was really—what was it? What was it really? It was *really* . . . arrested development, that's what it was. Emotionally, I was still a child. I was incapable of anything like real introspection, or real growth, or real . . . fidelity. But you know the worst thing I did? I can say this, now that we're being honest. Now that we're here, face to face. The worst thing wasn't going outside the marriage, it was . . . it was telling her. Because you can never do that. You can never think a thing like that will ever do any good—not the least, tiniest little grain of good. Because we're all weak. We're all . . . we're subject to it. She told me, your mother told me, when we were in the middle of breaking up, when we—

(*Looking at the bathroom door, then resuming.*)

—were in the middle of that entire mess of shit *and anger* and . . . shame . . . that she flirted with it. She was romanced by someone. Well, romanced—he was trying to . . . fuck her, and he was a friend of ours, a very charming and handsome . . . What? No, I'm not going to say who it was. The point is, the *much larger* point—and this is when I realized it by the way, when it became *clear* to me—is that fidelity is not what people demand from each other in marriage. What we demand . . . No, no—hear me out. What we *demand* is not to be humiliated. Which ninety-nine percent of the time means not to be told.

"Honey, I almost slept with that guy. We were sitting, talking on the couch in his apartment. He was so attentive, he really seemed to care. And we'd had some wine—" No. No! "We made out for a while. It was just kissing, but then—" *No!* We don't do this. We demand from each other not to do this. Because it's humiliating to sit in a conversation and be told that the person you give yourself to gives himself to . . . someone else—under any circumstance. And the point is, I know that *now*.

(*The shower turns off. He stares at the bathroom door, then continues, softer.*)

Because . . . and this is what it really is. Under everything. The essence of it. Unless you're having your spouse tailed twenty-four seven by the world's best detective agency, you can *never know for certain* if they've stayed faithful every minute of every day. But what you can know is if they've told you. That you can know. And the reason your mother and I divorced—I think anyway, this is definitely my interpretation—is that I told her. But I didn't have the affairs because I wanted out of the marriage. And I didn't tell her because I wanted out of the marriage. Honestly, that was never—at least until the very end, maybe—that was *never* the reason. I didn't want these revelations to end things. I wanted them to . . . change her. That she would hear these things, and they would wake something up in her. That she'd realize that I didn't enjoy these . . . *activities*, that I was in pain. Every day. I was in pain every day with her, and these . . . lapses, adventures—I don't know what to call them—were a kind of relief that instantly palled. Lost its appeal, became ugly and pointless, instantly, because I didn't love them.

Our Enemies:
Lively Scenes of Love and Combat
by Yussef El Guindi

CHARACTER: HANI, Egyptian American, first-generation American

PLACE: Egypt

CIRCUMSTANCE: Hani is visiting his extended family in Egypt for the first time.

HANI: Where do I start this . . . I don't know what's in the air here—apart from way too much pollution. And we're not in the mountains, so it's not the altitude. But that smiling I was talking about? It hasn't stopped. I'm like—on this permanent high. So: what do I do the very next day after I arrive? I go to the pyramids, of course. Tourist freak that I am. Early, on account of jet lag. Family members were just getting up. Lotta kissing and "kula sana wa inta tayib." God, you weren't kidding. Our family is *really* extended. Relatives in from the village here to celebrate the feast. They all want to take a look at the American weirdo that's related to them. They wanted to come with me, worried I'd get lost. But I wanted to do this on my own, without anyone to—protect me. You know. I wanted the real thing. So I took the bus—the bus! (*A laugh.*) Every day must be like they're trying to break the Guinness book of records or something. I don't know how people take it, because sardines does not describe it. And with the bus rattling and shaking, it felt like we were in a blender. Sardines in a blender with all the natural oils and funk people put out. And I have to tell you—it was a *blast*. I *loved* it. I was, like, smiling. People were grumbling and full of that early morning snit of having to go to jobs they hate. And I'm, like, *yeah*. It's humid as heck, I have no room to move, I'm in a strange country, and I was, like, rocking and rolling. (*Slight beat, then:*) Actually . . . it's really weird when I think about it. Because . . . like—back home—when I'm on the bus—or train, it's so . . . it's different, right? Even in rush hour. And maybe I was just excited at being here and had that wide-eyed thing going on, and it's really the same back home, but it was like . . . everyone on this bus felt so—I don't know . . . solid. Connected. Like they knew each other. I mean, they didn't, of course. But back home . . . it feels like everyone's on a different bus, if you know what I mean, even while riding the same bus. Which makes for all these "who the hell are you" vibes, you know. Like there're no guarantees about anything when you meet someone. Which is normal . . . I guess. I'm not explaining this right. Let me get back to you on this. I'm just saying, for a complete foreigner—I didn't feel any of that . . . And that was, like, a very quiet, amazing thing. Like there was zero friction. For a bus packed with some pissed-off people. And maybe that's what you were talking about. Which I didn't get because it's like normal life to me back home. To always look at others, and have others look at you, like you're . . . from different planets. . . . Damn, twenty-four hours and I'm a philosopher. That's what total exhaustion and being pumped will do to you. Anyway. Got to the pyramids. They're impressive. Big. But I think I got such a high from just being around people that I wasn't into anything made of bricks, you know. So I got back home and what do you know, they try and play a trick on your American son. As soon as I walk in they hand me a knife. Walk me into the kitchen and say I have to kill the sheep—Aeid El Kabeer. Right? Commemorating God giving Abraham a sheep to sacrifice instead of his son. An honor, they say. Given only to guests. And I'm like: you have got to be kidding me. And the sheep's looking at me like: you have got to be kidding me. What was wrong with the son? Change the story. And I'm just standing there, freaking out. And they're going, do it, do it, come on; you American tough guy, no? And just when I start to really freak out, your nephew Kareem blows their cover and laughs. . . . I'm going to have to watch myself with these guys. Our family has some serious jokers. (*Slight beat.*) Puppy . . . ! I know. I know you told me to drop this. But you didn't mention if you'd called Munir yet. And I—I don't want to keep on about it, but I have to tell you . . . the whole flight over . . . I couldn't stop thinking about what happened. . . . About what *didn't* happen. What I should have done instead of just standing there like a fool, letting him get away like that. I should have—I should have done something. I should have been more of a son, for starters. Grown a pair of you know what then and there. I'm . . . I'm sorry I didn't do anything. From this distance, surrounded by family, I realize just how unprotected you are, living in the States. Please let me know if you've called him, will you? So I can enjoy the rest of my stay here . . . Okay. Gotta go. Love . . . your son.

Perfect Mendacity
by Jason Wells

CHARACTER: ROGER, Walter's colleague, white African American (50s)

PLACE: A laboratory office

ROGER: Do you remember that night in Johannesburg, when you had that little get-together at your place to signal the end of a good run? But I had to work, so I showed up a bit late? Here's what happened to me on the way there: I'm driving up that road toward your house, and I'm on that long, empty part between the back of that supermarket and the back of that warehouse? You know where I mean?

(WALTER: *Yes.*)

I'm driving along that stretch, and up ahead, this black woman is crossing the road. She's looking at me as I'm approaching, but she's not breaking her stride in the least. There's no intersection, no crosswalk, no stop sign, so of course I expect her to wait as to pass, but as I continue to bear down on her, I realize she has absolutely no intention of doing so. At the last second, I actually have to swerve to avoid hitting her. And as I go by, do you know what this woman does? This sixty-ish Bantu woman in a Dashiki? Do you know what she does? She gives me the *finger*. Not the devil's eye, not the horns, not the fist or the open palm or any of the other domestic and international gestures available to her, but the good old, American finger. America's export to the world, apparently. And I was outraged. I mean, I had the right of *way*. So before I even knew what I was doing I slammed on the brakes, and I look in the rearview, and she's just standing in the road back there, looking at me. No shame at all. So now I'm angry, and I think, "This'll get her attention," and I get my nine mil out of the glove compartment, and I step out into the road with it, and I aim it at her. Just one hand, like a cowboy, you know? And you know what she does? She gives me the *finger*. So I fire the pistol. I'm fifteen yards away, you understand, and I'm firing with one hand, in the *dark*, no chance of hitting her, no chance at *all*, and I'm not even trying to, of course, but you know what? I got her right in the head. I think. I *think* in the head, I never actually found out. All I know is, she went straight down, *straight* down, like one of those demolished buildings, into a position too, um . . . *tortured* for a living person to endure. I was surprised by what I'd done, of course, and I looked around, and there was no one. I was alone. So I got back in my car, and I continued to the party, and I was quiet at first, you might recall, but very quickly I came to grips with a very simple fact: Nobody gives a shit. Nobody gives one shit. Shouldn't that fill you with a sense of . . . freedom?

Song of Extinction
by E. M. Lewis

CHARACTER: KHIM, a Cambodian biology teacher

PLACE: A classroom

CIRCUMSTANCE: Khim is helping his student from failing his class. The lesson: extinction.

KHIM: I know something about extinction. Yes.

(*After a moment,* MAX *goes over to his viola case, and kneels down on the floor beside it.*)

I do not know why you have a difficult year this year. (*Beat.*) Fifteen, yes? You are fifteen? Yeah.

(MAX *opens the viola case and stares down into it.* KHIM *walks slowly over and looks over* MAX's *shoulder into the case. Nods. Props one hip on the edge of* MAX's *desk.*)

When I am fifteen, Khmer Rouge rise in Cambodia and take over the whole country. Communism. Red Cambodia. My countrymen take up guns and knives against our own people. (*Beat.*) You do not know this, maybe, because Mr. Kerr, who teaches history of the world, does not go past the Second World War. Too complicated after that. You do not know this because . . . why is it important outside country of Cambodia? Why is it important forty years later? (*Beat; increasingly to himself, more than to* MAX.) But this is my own lesson in extinction. In my country, which is not Wisconsin, one-fifth of the population was killed by the red Communists. Khmer Rouge. Maybe two million people. Estimations vary. Murdered, some for being intellectuals, or members of government, or for no reason. Forced from their homes and cities. Made to work the land with no food. (*Beat.*) I remember my sister, ten years old, very sick, lying down on the cold red earth, and we left her there, because they made us leave her there, even though I said I would carry her. Even though I tried to carry her. She reached out her hand, but she did not cry. (*Beat.*) Our dead were scattered across those fields. Their *besach*—spirits—follow us wherever we go, asking if we will feed them, asking if we will burn their bones so they may rest. But there is no rest.

Strike-Slip
by Naomi Iizuka

CHARACTER: **DAN**, Caucasian, married, a seismic analyst and associate professor at Caltech (late 30s)

PLACE: Lecture hall at a university

CIRCUMSTANCE: Dan, intending to meet his male lover, walked into a store to find a man recently shot.

DAN: It starts miles below the surface. There's a fault between two rock planes and the movement of these rock planes causes a friction or a strain that grows over time until the pressure becomes so great there's finally a rupture. The sudden release creates seismic waves that radiate outwards, creating a string of smaller seismic disturbances in an interlocking network of related fault lines. Most major faults on the North American continent are what we call strike-slip faults, which refers to the way in which parallel rock planes slide past each other in a horizontal, or sideways, motion. Though scientists have tried to track the movements leading up to a major seismic event, there are often no clear patterns. The challenge we face is to construct a paradigm for events that do not appear to conform to any discernible model of cause and effect, and that happen without any kind of advanced warning. We have in the past relied on what we thought to be indicators in the landscape: topographical anomalies visible to the human eye or sound waves caused by vibrations inside the earth. We have tried to extrapolate from past seismic events looking for recurring patterns, but what we have found in recent years is that we are dealing with faults we never even took into account, faults we thought were dormant, faults we never even knew existed. And so we're left trying to make sense of phenomena which defy our customary models of quantification and analysis. We're left with a series of variables that come together in violent, seemingly random, and discontinuous ways across fault lines we have, it seems, radically and fatally misunderstood. This is the challenge we now face. And we think it's a question for science, but perhaps it's more a question for philosophers. Perhaps it's more a question of how we live our lives in the face of uncertainty, how we understand our relationship to a larger and indifferent universe in which we play the smallest part.

(*The sound of a bell tower on campus ringing the hour.*)

All right, we're out of time. The problems are posted, small groups meet Friday. I'll see you all on Monday.

Superior Donuts
by Tracy Letts

CHARACTER: ARTHUR, Polish American, owns donut shop (58)

PLACE: Superior Donuts shop; Uptown, Chicago

CIRCUMSTANCE: Vandals have broken into the donut shop Arthur's Polish immigrant father started.

ARTHUR: Dad dropped dead. Right here, right where I'm standing. May Day, 1970. Three days before the National Guard murdered four kids at Kent State University. Wonder what the old man would have said about that.

What did you do?

Couldn't come to the funeral. Mom sent photos. Including a snap of two guys from the FBI. Just looking around. Looking around at my father's funeral. That seems weird, they'd send someone just for me. But they did.

What did you do, where did you go?

Further away. Split Toronto, headed up to the Great Slave Lake, outside Yellowknife, in the Northwest Territory.

What did you do?

Cut timber and read a lot of books. Until President Carter invited me home.

What did you do?

Caught a cab at Midway, had the driver take me directly to the cemetery. Stared at the old man's headstone there in St. Adalbert's. Remembered the last word he ever said to me: coward.

Coward.

The Crowd You're in With
by Rebecca Gilman

CHARACTER: DWIGHT (30-ish), a friend of the hosts and a waiter

PLACE: A backyard of a two-flat on the North Side of Chicago; early evening on the 4th of July, 2007

CIRCUMSTANCE: Three married couples have gathered for a barbecue. One couple is expecting, one trying to conceive, and the other chosen to not raise children.

DWIGHT: Here's what I don't like about people with kids—

(**DAN:** *What the fuck?*)

Since we've opened up the subject. (*To* **KAREN** *and* **TOM.**) I'm a waiter, right? The people with the kids come in, and it's one of two things. Either they bring a whole refrigerator's worth of food with them, in these little Tupperware containers, or they don't bring anything. Both suck equally. If they bring in the food, it's, like, they hand you a Tupperware full of some sort of mush and they ask you to take it back to the kitchen and put it in the microwave for thirty-six seconds, like you have nothing else to do and, like, there's a fucking microwave in the kitchen, which there isn't. So you take it back and you throw it under a warming lamp, for, like, two minutes, then you bring it back and they stick their finger in the mush and they ask you, "Could you warm it up for eleven more seconds? And while they wait, they open Tupperware number two, which *always* has Cheerios in it. Always, always. Fucking *Cheerios*. Which the kids—they don't eat the Cheerios. They *throw* the Cheerios. They spread the Cheerios like seed, like they're seeding the restaurant with little Cheerio trees. These people leave their tables, and it's like a goddamn cereal . . . PB and J . . . booger . . . *tsunami* hit.

(**DWIGHT** *breathes.*)

But if they don't bring the food, it's fucking torture the other way. "Could the kitchen make, like, a bowl of plain pasta, with no sauce of any kind on it?" "Could he get a cheese pizza? But could you scrape the cheese off before you bring it out?" "Do you have, like, any kind of melon or fresh fruit in the kitchen? Could you just bring us a little bowl of cut-up fruit? Oh. That's a lot of fruit. Is that the only size bowl you have?" "Was this—did you make a cheese pizza? Because you have to make a cheese pizza and scrape off the cheese. If you didn't put the cheese on at first, then it's just a sauce pizza, and he won't eat it. He won't eat that." (*Beat.*) Eat this, asshole.

(**DWIGHT** *grabs his crotch.*)

(**WINDSONG:** *God.*)

Here's an idea: Next time, go to Applebee's. There's a menu there, for kids. It's called a "kids' menu." Chicken fingers. Wieners in sauce. It's on the fucking menu. Along with a word search and a crazy maze. Here are your crayons. Go wild.

The History of Invulnerability
by David Bar Katz

CHARACTER: BENJAMIN, a middle-aged Jewish man

PLACE: Auschwitz, Birkenau; WWII

CIRCUMSTANCE: Benjamin fantasizes about taking action to break out of the death camp.

(JOEL: *They just go in there, Benjamin, they just go in there like sheep. . . .*)

BENJAMIN: Don't use that word! Listen to me, Joel, it's only because when they arrive here they can't accept the truth of this place. They don't want to believe it, so they go in there hoping they're really showers. That's not weakness. To walk in there and not believe, even as they hear the guards up on the roof with the pellets, even as they breathe that gas . . . don't let anyone tell you that's weakness. Anyone can suspect, anyone can hate, anyone can think the worst. Some of the greatest minds in Europe have died thirty feet from where we're standing now. Do you think they were fooled by those cheap fake shower heads? By Nazi guards telling them to tie their shoes together so they can find them when they're done showering? Do you know how much strength it takes not to believe what your eyes are telling you? To not believe what men can do? I don't have such strength. To believe man can do what they do here? To conceive of this horror is to be able to do it. God bless them for not accepting what's all around them! God bless them for not believing the truth. We all cling to our own fantasies, Joel.

(BENJAMIN *continues working on the bombs.*)

And all I can do is the same thing that those Jews in the showers do, and you do and that Saul does.

(JOEL: *And what's that, Benjamin?*)

(BENJAMIN *looks up at the boy.*)

Pray that my fantasy is the right one.

Victoria Musica
by Michele Lowe

CHARACTER: JEREMY, a music writer/critic

PLACE: Jeremy's home

CIRCUMSTANCE: Jeremy suspects and has been spreading rumors that the recordings of a world-famous cellist are frauds.

(He is listening to the Debussy CD on the stereo.)

JEREMY: I listened to it every morning and every night and a hundred times in between. It was one piece of music; it could've been the only piece of music. . . . I breathed it. Spoke it. Needed it. And then one day it was gone. I felt it right away. She'd probably gotten some cosmic sense of what I was doing . . . asking too many questions, making trouble for her . . . and she disappeared. What kind of man crusades against someone he loves? Someone so treasured . . . admired. Who the hell was I? She'd given music to people. I can't play an instrument, I can't move people the way she . . . it would take me forty years to be able to . . . she was so gifted. . . . She didn't ask to get sick, she didn't ask to fucking die; suffocating at fifty-six, my God, fifty-six years old and dead.

What had I done?

Water by the Spoonful
by Quiara Alegría Hudes

CHARACTER: FOUNTAINHEAD, aka John, a computer programmer and entrepreneur

PLACE: A Narcotics Anonymous chat room

CIRCUMSTANCE: Fountainhead is new to the chat room, a place for addicts to connect.

FOUNTAINHEAD: I've, uh, wow, hello there, everyone. Delete, delete. Good afternoon. Evening. Delete.

(*Deep breath.*)

Things I am taking:

—My life into my own hands

—My gorgeous, deserving wife out for our seventh anniversary

Me: Mildly athletic, but work twice as hard. Won state for javelin two years straight. Ran a half marathon last fall. Animated arguer. Two medals for undergrad debate. MBA from Wharton. Beautiful wife, two sons. Built a programming company from the ground up, featured in the *New York Times* Circuits section, sold it at its peak, bought a yellow Porsche, got a day job to keep myself honest. Salary was 300K, company was run by morons, got laid off, handsome severance, which left me swimming in cash and free time.

Me & crack: long story short, I was at a conference with our CFO and two programmers and a not-unattractive lady in HR. They snorted, invited me to join. A few weeks later that little rock waltzed right into my hand. I've been using off and on since. One eight ball every Saturday, strict rations, portion control. Though the last three or four weeks, it's less like getting high and more like trying to build a time machine. Anything to get back the romance of that virgin smoke.

Last weekend I let myself buy more than my predetermined allotment—I buy in small quantity, because as with my food, I eat what's on my plate. Anyway, I ran over a curb, damaged the underside of my Porsche. Now it's in the shop and I'm driving a rental Mustang. So, not rock bottom but a rental Ford is as close to rock bottom as I'd like to get. Fast-forward to tonight. I'm watching my wife's eyelids fall and telling myself, "You are on punishment, poppa. Daddy's on time out. Do not get out of bed, do not tiptoe down those stairs, do not go down to that basement, do not sit beside that foosball table, do not smoke, and please do not crawl on the carpet looking for one last hit in the fibers."

(*Pause.*)

In kindergarten my son tested into G&T. Gifted and talented. You meet with the school, they tailor the program to the kid. Math, reading, art, whatever the parent chooses. I said, "Teach my son how to learn." How to use a library. How to find original source material, read a map, track down the experts so he becomes an expert. Which gets me to—

You: the experts. It's the first day of school and I'm knocking at your classroom door. I got my number-two pencils, I'll sit in the front row, pay attention, and do my homework. No lesson is too basic. Teach me every technique. Any tip so that Saturday doesn't become every day. Any actions that keep you in the driver seat. Healthy habits and rational thoughts to blot out that voice in the back of my head.

Today, I quit. My wife cannot know, she'd get suspicious if I were at meetings all the time. There can be no medical records, so therapy is out. At least it's not heroin, I'm not facing a physical war. It's a psychological battle and I'm armed with two weapons: willpower and the experts. I'm taking my wife out tomorrow for our seventh anniversary and little does she know that when we clink glasses, I'll be toasting to Day One.

Part 6
Female Monologues

A Twist of Water
Written by Caitlin Parrish
Story by Caitlin Montanye Parrish & Erica Weiss

CHARACTER: JIRA, African American teenager

CIRCUMSTANCE: JIRA's father by adoption died in an auto accident. She is currently being raised by her other father by adoption, Noah. Jira was given up for adoption after birth and has never known her birth mother.

JIRA: Dear Mom . . .

(JIRA *doesn't like the sound of it. She takes a moment.*)

Dear . . . To whom it may concern. You had a baby girl awhile ago. I'm seventeen now. I sent this to the agency. Don't worry. I don't know your name or where you live, or anything. I'm sorry if hearing from me ruins your day 'cause I don't mean for that to be the case. I would just like to know a little about where I come from and who I might have been if things had been different. I'm not mad. I don't really know how to say anything or what to say, so I looked up sample cover letters, well, actually, I did it a while ago when I was doing some college application prep, I like doing things early, and I found one called "Sample Cover Letter Requesting a Meeting," and I've changed it to make sense 'cause it seemed like a good jumping-off point. It might seem too formal but I don't know what you do or don't like so formal seems inoffensive so here goes. Dear Ms. Birth Mother. For the past seventeen-plus years I have considered you, and your decision to bring me into the world is not one I resent, nor is it one for which I believe you should be reproached. Although I'm not sure that I would make your choice if I were in a similar situation, not that I know the details. Also, this is not to say that I would keep an unwanted daughter if I found out I was pregnant, because I think I would favor a medical abortion, but again, I can't be sure as I do not even have a boyfriend. But I lean towards abortion. I don't know what that says. Here are a few facts about me. I'm a junior in high school. I'm on the honor roll. I like science and math the most, especially biology and geometry. I think that's because those are the subjects that have more solid facts than theories. You can build a building with geometry. You can diagnose someone with biology. It's practical. I like that side of things, which I believe means that I'm a left-brained person. I also like baseball. A lot. It's okay if you don't.

However, if you'd call yourself indifferent or uninformed I would highly recommend the Chicago Cubs. You will have to trust me on this, as the research does not bear out my opinion. I'm reading over this and it sounds like how my dad used to talk. I have another dad, but he talks differently and likes the Chicago White Sox. I would like an opportunity to visit with you to get your insight on what the people I come from are like, and, maybe, why I am the way I am. I have no desire to disturb you. I have spring break in April. If this would be a viable time to meet, if you're so inclined, please let me know at your earliest convenience. I look forward to hearing from you. Sincerely, Jira Calder Brennan. P.S. If you decide you wouldn't like to meet me I'd appreciate it if you could send a list of hereditary conditions or things I should look out for. Thank you.

Becky's New Car
by Steven Dietz

CHARACTER: **GINGER**, Walter's neighbor (50s)

PLACE: The terrace of Walter's estate; night

GINGER: The boats are gone. The artwork is gone. The horses.

(**WALTER:** *Even the horses?*)

No way to keep them. Or the place at the lake. Or the season tickets.

(**WALTER:** *You gave up the season tickets?*)

Along with the cars and most of my jewelry.

(**WALTER:** *I had no idea.*)

It finally caught up with us—the Timber Baron's kids. We all assumed that the money none of us made would never run out—then the investments went bad, the trust funds got emptied, and the bills came due.

(**WALTER:** *I'm so sorry—*)

No—please—the last thing we deserve is sympathy. The fact is: after a hundred years of being pampered and deferred to, *none of us know how to do a fucking thing.* We've never worked. Never had jobs. We have no tangible skills. Oh, sure, we know how to stay *busy*—we're all the time telling each other how *busy* we are—but if we had to walk out the door tomorrow and do something practical, something *useful*—something other than dressing up, attending a function, and eating with the proper fork: we wouldn't have a *clue.*

(**WALTER:** *Ginger—*)

If our great-grandpa—the Timber Baron—came back and saw what *soft little spoiled ninnies* we've become, he'd kick our ass to hell and back. And here I am: the woman who kept putting off getting married—putting it off till the last minute and *beyond*—and I could do that, you see, because I always had this safety net. I had my *money.* And I knew that even when my looks were long gone, I'd still have my inheritance . . . and at least there'd be someone who would want that . . . even if he didn't really want *me.*

Dead Man's Cell Phone
by Sarah Ruhl

CHARACTERS: MRS. GOTTLIEB, Gordon's mother

PLACE: A church

CIRCUMSTANCE: Gordon passed away at a café.

MRS. GOTTLIEB: I'm not sure what to say. There is, thank God, a vaulted ceiling here. I am relieved to find that there is stained glass and the sensation of height. Even though I am not a religious woman, I am glad there are still churches. Thank God there are still people who build churches for the rest of us so that when someone dies—or gets married— we have a place to—I could not put all of this—(*She thinks the word "grief."*)—in a low-ceilinged room—no—it requires height.

(*A cell phone rings in the back of the church. JEAN turns to look.*)

Could someone please turn their fucking cell phone off. There are only one or two sacred places left in the world today. Where there is no ringing. The theater, the church, and the toilet. But some people actually answer their phones in the shitter these days. Some people really do so. How many of you do? Raise your hand if you've answered your cell phone while you were quietly urinating. Yes, I thought so. My God.

Where was I? A reading from Charles Dickens's *Tale of Two Cities*. A wonderful fact to reflect upon, that every human creature is constituted to be that profound secret and mystery to every other. . . . No more can I turn the leaves of this dear book . . . that the book should shut . . . forever . . . when I had read but a page. . . . My friend is dead, my neighbor is dead, my love, the darling of my soul—

(*JEAN's cell phone rings. She fumbles for it and shuts it off. MRS. GOTTLIEB looks up and sees the audience.*)

Well.

Look at this great big sea of people wearing dark colors. It used to be you saw someone wearing black and you knew their beloved had died. Now everyone wears black all the time. We are in a state of perpetual mourning. But for what?

Where was I? Gordon.

Well. I've forgotten my point. Let's have a hymn. Father?

(*A hymn. Preferably "You'll Never Walk Alone." The singing begins.* JEAN's *cell phone rings.* JEAN *sneaks out, covering the phone.*)

You'll never walk alone. That's right. Because you'll always have a machine in your pants that might ring. Oh, Gordon.

(**MRS. GOTTLIEB** *sings.*)

Detroit
by Lisa D'Amour

CHARACTERS: SHARON, a recovering addict, wife of Kenny and new next-door neighbor of Ben and Mary

PLACE: Sharon and Kenny's backyard

CIRCUMSTANCE: Sharon and Kenny are hosting a party with new neighbors.

SHARON: Kenny, you are not going to believe this. I am fucking losing it—do you see me—I am losing it! It was the pink jogging suit lady. At our door! Only she wasn't wearing a pink jogging suit, she was wearing shorts and a blue T-shirt. And she came over to ask us politely—sort of—politely if we could keep our dog from shitting on her lawn.

(**KENNY:** *We don't have a dog.*)

SHARON: WE DON'T HAVE A DOG. Exactly. And so I said to her, politely, I said, "We don't have a dog," and she said, "Yes, you do have a dog and it is quite fond of taking craps on my lawn." "Quite fond." Like slicing a razor blade across my face "quite fond." And I said, "Lady, do you want to come in my house? We've got NOTHING in our house, especially a DOG. Especially we do not have a DOG." And she said, "Listen, Missy." FUCKING MISSY! "Listen, Missy. I've lived in this neighborhood for six years, and I jog every morning. This dog appeared out of nowhere and started crapping on my lawn. I'm not asking you to get rid of it, I'm just asking you to clean up his crap." And I practically started crying—look at me, I'm crying now—and I said, "Ma'am, people have accused me of many things before but they have never accused me of having a dog, you need to investigate further, you need to knock on other doors"—And she said—her voice changed and she said, "Look, if it craps on my lawn one more time I am calling the police," and I said, "Are you kidding? The police are going to fucking LAUGH IN YOUR FACE if you call them about some dogshit." And she said, "AHA! So you DO have a DOG!" And I said, "No, no, no, no, no fucking NO, there is no dog here, lady!" And she just shook her head and kind of kicked our plant and said, "Ha, I thought it was fake," and turned around. I mean, FUCK. KENNY. FUCK. This is like FUCKED UP.

Detroit
by Lisa D'Amour

CHARACTER: **SHARON** (late 20s to mid-30s), a recovering addict, wife of Kenny and new next-door neighbor of Ben and Mary

PLACE: The back porch of Mary and Ben's place; late night

CIRCUMSTANCE: New neighbors Mary and Sharon became fast friends and plan to go on a camping trip to get away from it all. Sharon recently has fallen off the wagon with her addiction.

SHARON: I think nature is really going to help. Mary, every day really is a new day. But, Mary, I open my eyes every morning and all I want is a pipe to smoke. It's like there's a fire burning in the center of my head, Mary, and the pipe is the water that will put it out. And I say this at our meetings, and they are all very supportive but the fire only goes down a little bit. Every day, all day. And in the middle of this burning I am supposed to envision my life, Mary. I'm supposed to set goals and maybe take night classes that will expand my horizons. And I guess that works, Mary, I guess so. But to be honest, I feel like the real opportunities are the ones that fall into your lap. Like winning the lottery or someone's rich uncle needing a personal assistant. That almost happened to me once, Mary. And everything would have been different.

Mary, I fell off the wagon for a day. I called in sick and walked down to the gas station and bought a stash from the kid with the skateboard. And I got high right there, Mary, in the parking lot by the Dumpster. And I walked home, and nobody fucking walks here, so I stuck out like a sore thumb, and I got lost a little, so I wound up walking around the neighborhood—which looks soooooooo beautiful when you're high, especially when you let the street signs really sink in—and this guy in a pickup truck gave me a ride home—by that time I had accidentally walked out of one of my shoes and didn't realize it, Mary. So anyway we were talking in his truck outside my house and he finally said, "Are you high?" And I said, "Yes, I am," and he told me about all the ways he parties—he does ecstasy, he eats mushrooms, and every now and then but not too often he shoots heroin. But he's careful because he doesn't want to get hooked on it. Oh, and sometimes he takes ludes and sometimes he does whip-its just to remind himself of high school. All like three streets away from here, on Solar Power Lane. And I said, "What do you do for a living?" And he said: "I'm an electrician. I do house calls." And I said, "How do you afford all that stash?" And he wouldn't tell me. And I said, "Do you want to be an electrician forever?" And he said what he really wanted to do was be a marine biologist and we were just getting into this amazing conversation about the many varieties of sharks—the guy was rubbing my feet—when Kenny came home.

Kenny knew immediately what I had done. He was nice to the guy, considering. I spent the rest of the day drinking Diet Coke and watching Jerry Springer and then like four hours screaming my face off and trying to escape. Somehow Kenny tied me to the wall, to the door handles?

(**MARY:** *What?*)

No, no, he had to. He had to.

Edith Can Shoot Things and Hit Them
by A. Rey Pamatmat

CHARACTERS: EDITH, a Filipino American (12 years old)

PLACE: A schoolyard

CIRCUMSTANCE: Edith's mother is dead and her father leaves her and her brother, Kenny, without adult supervision. Edith shoots and wounds her soon-to-be stepmother, who shows up unannounced late one night. Edith's father ships her off to boarding school.

(*She's dressed to leave and talking to the frog.*)

EDITH: Okay, Fergie. This is probably our biggest mission ever, and it's not that I think you can't handle it . . . but we have to execute every stage with utmost precision, or it's over before it even starts. It's just me and you now. You're all I have. You. A stuffed frog. From my mom. My mommy. Let's review the mission parameters. To blow this joint, what we have to do is—I mean, what you have to do. I don't know what you have to do. What I have to do is . . . stop talking to a stupid stuffed frog who never really did anything. Maybe, Fergie, it's time for me to go it alone. I don't think Mom really gave you to me anymore, and that when I talk to you I'm talking to her. I'm not talking to anyone. Because Kenny is a liar. He lies, and it's not funny anymore. He tells stories, like that Mom got us all Christmas presents before she died. And that Dad asks about me when he calls. And that he's going to come and get me. Because Kenny's not going to come and get me. The only person who can take care of me is me. I've got to do this all by myself, like I have to do everything. No Kenny, no Mom, and no you. I'm going solo. I don't need you, frog.

(EDITH *puts the frog on the ground and turns away. Ten seconds.* EDITH *turns back to the frog, snatches her up, and holds her at arm's length.*)

It's just . . . I. I'm alone now, Fergie. And I had to. It was a test. Because what we're doing is dangerous and important and probably illegal. So I had to know I could trust you. Because it's hard to know who to trust now that we're all alone. Because this . . . this is the test. *The* test. Kenny can't come, because I have to prove to him that I'm a grown-up. That it's time to grow my wings and fly away. Fergie, we have to get rid of any parts of us that are still little girls. No more useless, weak, little girls. I'm going to take care of everyone. You. Kenny. Even Benji. But first we have to make sure that he's taken care of. Permanently. Make sure he can never leave us in a place like this again. Never, ever again. So I had to be sure that we were in this together no matter what.

(**EDITH** *takes some matches out of her pocket, strikes one, and watches it burn.*)

Here we go.

End Days
by Deborah Zoe Laufer

CHARACTER: SYLVIA, Rachel's mother (40s)

PLACE: Their suburban home; late September 2003

CIRCUMSTANCE: After 9/11 the Steins fled NYC, Sylvia has renounced Judaism and converted to an Evangelical Christian. She has a new, close relationship with Jesus.

SYLVIA: I'm terrified for you, Rachel. You're going to be left behind. When the Rapture comes . . .

(RACHEL: *Then I'll stay behind! I'll take frogs and leeches and blood in the streets over all your holier than thou crap.*)

That's it! Go to your room!

(RACHEL: *I have school.*)

You're not going to school today. Get upstairs.

(RACHEL: *Jesus wants me to be a truant now?*)

Listen, you. Do not talk to me like that. I'm your mother. If I decide to homeschool you . . .

(RACHEL: *Homeschool me?*)

. . . then you don't go to public school any more.

(RACHEL: *You're never home!*)

(*Overlapping.*) If I send you to religious school, you go to religious school. If I send you to reform school, you go to reform school.

(JESUS *tries to calm* SYLVIA *down. She shrugs him off and he quickly walks offstage.*)

(RACHEL: (*Over* SYLVIA.) *Reform school? You're nuts. You've totally lost your mind.*)

You're a minor. You do what I say. And you are going to church Sunday morning. If I have to drag you by the hair I'll do it.

(RACHEL: *Gee, that doesn't sound very Christian.*)

(*Completely frustrated and furious.*) Look! Look, you people! I am trying to do something here. I am trying to save this family! I have found something . . . I have finally found something that has given me hope and joy and peace. I'm happy. Since Jesus came into my life, I am finally happy! And you people are not going to ruin this for me. You hear? Rachel? Arthur? You're both coming with me on Sunday and you are going to listen to the Good Word, and you are going to open your hearts and let Jesus save you!

Equivocation
by Bill Cain

CHARACTER: JUDITH, Shakespeare's daughter (19)

PLACE: a stage

JUDITH: (*Mostly to herself.*) Plays have beginnings and endings. That's two lies right there. And people listen. When does that ever happen? And they care what happens—even if it's not happening to them.

(*To the audience.*)

How could there be anything true about a play?

(JUDITH *surveys the audience. Then speaks to them.* JUDITH *doesn't judge things. She simply notices them. Here are some of the things she notices.*)

I don't like theater. . . . And I don't like soliloquies.

(*She sits with the irony of that. Then—amused—*)

So it's odd that I'm the one who has them.

(*Judith crosses out a soliloquy. Then rises and approaches the audience.*)

Soliloquies. People you've never met telling you things you'd rather not know. . . . Because nobody ever tells anybody anything good in a soliloquy, do they?

(JUDITH *is in no hurry. She's just thinking. With us.*)

It's always somebody who just killed his father telling you he's on his way to sleep with his mother. If anybody did that in real life—

(*Picking up stray pages.*)

But people do it in plays as if it was the most natural—because—in plays—everybody's got—a secret story.

(*Nonsense; then back to pages.*)

And he always gives soliloquies to the wrong people. As if you needed to know one more thing about Hamlet. . . . He should give them to minor characters—people's daughters, for instance.

(*A moment.*)

But that wouldn't work, would it?

(*A moment.*)

According to him, a daughter's job is to love and be silent. So—there'd be nothing to say. Besides—

(*A moment, at a cost.*) Who would listen?

(*Silence as* JUDITH *says nothing.*)

Pilgrims Musa and Sheri in the New World
by Yussef El Guindi

CHARACTERS: SHERI, a single American waitress

PLACE: Musa's apartment; night

CIRCUMSTANCE: Sheri has been invited up to the apartment of Musa, her cab-driver.

EDITOR'S NOTE: This monologue was compiled from a number of Sheri's speeches. Intermittent dialogue with Musa has been omitted.

SHERI: You know—somehow—the mess I'm trying to avoid usually finds its way back into my life in the shape of a guy. Like almost always, actually. It's been weirdly predictable. So that—whatever guy I find somehow ends up like—embodying the very things I don't want to deal with. A sort of karmic synchronicity I call it. Like if I've been particularly bad about paying my bills, I'll find a guy who doesn't know how to open up. Give of himself. Or else the guy will end up throwing in my face everything I feel bad about because I've usually told him my life story in the first five minutes of meeting him. This has led to some terrific fights. Where the police have been called in.

On two occasions I only knew the guys for like forty-eight hours, but somehow managed to crunch six months worth of going out with someone into that short period. But, you know, I think this is why guys are drawn to me, because I'm that accessible. (**MUSA** *starts to speak, but is interrupted.*) Except when I say accessible, I don't mean easy. Just to put you in the picture, I'm surprisingly on the good girl side of things. Though God knows, I don't hold my liquor well, I mean—(*A laugh, half under her breath.*)—in about ten minutes I'm going to be a cinch to bang. But just so you know, I'm not the kind of girl who drinks scotch at a stranger's apartment at two a.m., and all that suggests. I guess that's what I'm trying to say.

I mean, let's be honest, it's not like this won't probably lead to sex. I just don't want you to think I'm sleazy. Because you do seem like a nice guy and I'd prefer you didn't think I was "that kind of girl" at the very beginning. Wait. I just had a horrible thought. You—you do want to have sex with me, don't you? (*MUSA stares at her.*) I'm not like presuming something.

I'm assuming you find me—you know, attractive. Or did you really just want to talk? My God, how embarrassing if you really did just want a drink and I've been imagining an attraction that wasn't there. (*Musa starts to reply but she cuts him off.*)

But then why would you have picked me up? Oh my God: you're a taxi driver, of course you picked me up. But why would you have invited me to your place? Oh my God, do you or do you not want to go to bed with me?

There is no right or wrong answer. I won't think you're a pig if you say "yes." (**MUSA** *doesn't know how to answer.*) Let me say "yes" for you, and if that's wrong, just say so, otherwise we'll carry on like I never brought this up.

Splinters
by Emily Schwend

CHARACTER: SAM, (17)

PLACE: In Sam's car in the parking lot of a SuperTarget

CIRCUMSTANCE: Sam's younger sister had recently been found dead after missing for a year.

SAM: Because it was empty, Conner. Like, it was the middle of the day on a Tuesday and the parking lot was, like . . . totally deserted. The only cars were parked way the fuck over there, like, where they make the cashiers and managers and those fucking greeters park. Like, there was no one here. And I parked there, right there, where that blue Volvo is. By the chain of shopping carts, like, so close to the entrance. You know? And it was literally, like, one minute I went to go smoke. I made her hold on to the bag with her new shoes in it—Keds, which she hates—and I buckled her into the front seat even though she's technically, you know, supposed to be in the backseat, for, like, safety or whatever. But I wanted to keep her happy, you know, like a bribe or something so I could slip out for a cigarette. And for one second I thought, maybe I won't. Maybe I'll just get in the car and go home because we were about to hit traffic from the elementary school kids getting out of school, and hell, if I wanted to get stuck behind a school bus, and, like, I thought about it, Conner, and then I was just like, fuck it. One cigarette. So I lied to her—I told her I'd forgotten to pay so I could sneak in a cigarette before getting into older sister babysitting house arrest for the night. And I snuck around the side, right there, where the Coke machines are all lined up. And I left her. Here in the parking lot while I smoked a Parliament. Two of them. Actually. And then . . .

(*A beat.*)

(CONNER: *You didn't know.*)

What if l just hadn't smoked that second one? Or if I hadn't let her sit in the front seat where anyone could see her just waiting to be, like, offered up, like bait. Or if I just . . . fucking drove home like—

Time Stands Still
by Donald Margulies

CHARACTER: **Sarah**, a photojournalist who covers wars and global strife (late 30s–early 40s)

PLACE: James and Sarah's loft in NYC

CIRCUMSTANCE: Sarah was severely hurt by a roadside bomb in Iraq.

Sarah: Today . . . I'm shooting these women. The inmates. With the babies they'd had in prison.

(**James:** *Yeah . . .*)

And some of these women were seriously bad. I mean, homicide; drug dealing, trying to kill their grandmother for her ATM card, that kind of thing. . . . Anyway, I'm shooting . . . sort of getting in the zone and this one woman . . . big . . . heavily tattooed with Hell's Angels kind of skulls with fire shooting out of the eye sockets, comes up to me, gets right in my face . . . and looks at me with such . . . contempt . . . (*Brutish voice.*) "What you want to take my picture for? Huh?" And all of a sudden, I was back in Mosul.

(**James:** *Was I with you?*)

You were off doing a story in the south; it was when I was there for the AP.

(**James:** *What happened that day? I don't remember.*)

(**Sarah:** *That's because I never told you. I never told anybody.*)

(**James:** *Tell me now. [She shakes her head. Gently.] Come on. Tell me. [Pause.]*)

I was sitting in a café with the Reuters guys . . . and a car bomb went off, like a block or two away, in this market. And I just ran, took off. Without even thinking. (*A beat.*) The carnage was . . . ridiculous. Exploded produce. Body parts. Eggplants. Women keening. They were digging in the rubble for their children. I started shooting. And suddenly this woman burst out from the smoke . . . covered in blood . . . her skin was raw and red and charred, and her hair was singed—she got so close I could smell it—and her clothes, her top had melted into her, and she was screaming at me. Screaming! (*Shouts.*) "Go way, go way! No picture, no picture!" And she started pushing me, pushing my camera with her hand on the lens . . .

(**JAMES:** *What did you do?*)

Nothing. I kept on shooting. Then, somehow, I got the hell out of there. I stopped to catch my breath . . . and check out my cameras . . . (*Pause.*) There was blood on my lens. (*Moved.*) Her blood was smeared on my lens. (*She breaks down.*) I feel so ashamed . . .

(**JAMES:** *No! Why?*)

It was wrong. . . . What I did was so wrong . . . (**JAMES:** *It wasn't wrong.*)

It was indecent.

(**JAMES:** *You were doing your job.*)

They didn't want me there! They did not want me taking pictures! They lost children in that mess! To them it was a sacred place. But there I was, like a, like some kind of ghoul with a camera shooting away. No wonder they wanted to kill me; I would've wanted to kill me, too.

Play Sources and Acknowledgments

Grateful acknowledgment is made for permission to reprint excerpts from the following:

Annapurna by Sharr White. Copyright © 2013 by Sharr White. Used by permission of Sharr White. All inquiries should be addressed to Jonathan Lomma, William Morris Endeavor Entertainment, 1325 Avenue of the Americas, New York, NY 10019 (#212-903-1552 / jdl@wmeentertainment.com).

Becky's New Car by Steven Dietz. Copyright © 2010 by Steven John Dietz. Used by permission of Steven Dietz. All inquiries should be addressed to Dramatists Play Service, Inc., 440 Park Avenue South, New York, NY 10016.

Compulsion by Rinne Groff. Copyright © 2012 by Rinne Groff. Used by permission of Rinne Groff. All inquiries should be addressed to Chris Till, Creative Artists Agency, 162 Fifth Avenue, 6th Floor, New York, NY 10010.

The Crowd You're in With by Rebecca Gilman. Copyright © 2009. Published by Northwestern University Press in 2009. Used by permission of Northwestern University Press.

Dead Man's Cell Phone by Sarah Ruhl. Copyright © 2008 by Sarah Ruhl. Published by Theatre Communications Group. Used by permission of Theatre Communications Group.

Detroit by Lisa D'Amour. Copyright © 2011 by Lisa D'Amour. Published by Faber and Faber, Inc. in 2011. Used by permission of Faber and Faber, Inc., an affiliate of Farrar, Straus and Giroux, LLC, in the US, Canada, and the open market throughout the rest of the world excluding the UK and British Commonwealth. Used by permission of Faber and Faber Ltd. throughout the UK and British Commonwealth.